THE EMERGENCE OF MULTIPARTY
COMPETITION IN MEXICAN POLITICS

To Armando, Carmen,
Elia, Jose Luis,
Brian and Itxel

The Emergence of Multiparty Competition in Mexican Politics

PATRICIA HUESCA-DORANTES

LONDON AND NEW YORK

First published 2003 by Ashgate Publishing

Reissued 2018 by Routledge
2 Park Square, Milton Park, Abingdon, Oxon OX14 4RN
711 Third Avenue, New York, NY 10017, USA

Routledge is an imprint of the Taylor & Francis Group, an informa business

Copyright © Patricia Huesca-Dorantes 2003

Patricia Huesca-Dorantes has asserted her moral right to be identified as the author of this work in accordance with the Copyright, Designs and Patents Act, 1988.

All rights reserved. No part of this book may be reprinted or reproduced or utilised in any form or by any electronic, mechanical, or other means, now known or hereafter invented, including photocopying and recording, or in any information storage or retrieval system, without permission in writing from the publishers.

Notice:
Product or corporate names may be trademarks or registered trademarks, and are used only for identification and explanation without intent to infringe.

Publisher's Note
The publisher has gone to great lengths to ensure the quality of this reprint but points out that some imperfections in the original copies may be apparent.

Disclaimer
The publisher has made every effort to trace copyright holders and welcomes correspondence from those they have been unable to contact.

A Library of Congress record exists under LC control number: 2002043976

ISBN 13: 978-1-138-71551-6 (hbk)
ISBN 13: 978-1-138-71550-9 (pbk)
ISBN 13: 978-1-315-19750-0 (ebk)

Contents

List of Figures		*vi*
List of Tables		*ix*
Acknowledgements		*xi*
1	Introduction	1
2	Diffusion Processes	3
3	The Present Study	14
4	Shares of the Popular Vote	51
5	Change in Shares of the Popular Vote	103
6	Change in the Dissimilarity Index	126
7	Conclusions: The Emergence of Competitive Politics	142
Bibliography		*145*
Index		*147*

List of Figures

3.1 Vote shares. PAN presidential elections 1964-2000   16
3.2 Vote shares. PAN senatorial elections 1964-2000   17
3.3 Vote shares. PAN representative elections 1964-2000   18
3.4 Vote shares. PRI presidential elections 1964-2000   19
3.5 Vote shares. PRI senatorial elections 1964-2000   20
3.6 Vote shares. PRI representative elections 1964-2000   21
3.7 Vote shares. Other parties presidential elections 1964-2000   22
3.8 Vote shares. Other parties senatorial elections 1964-2000   23
3.9 Vote shares. Other parties representative elections 1964-2000   24
3.10 Dissimilarity index. PAN presidential elections 1964-2000   25
3.11 Dissimilarity index. PAN senatorial elections 1964-2000   26
3.12 Dissimilarity index. PAN representative elections 1964-2000   27
3.13 Dissimilarity index. Other parties presidential elections 1964-2000   28
3.14 Dissimilarity index. Other parties senatorial elections 1964-2000   29
3.15 Dissimilarity index. Other parties representative elections 1964-2000   30
3.16 G_i^* test for vote shares. PAN presidential elections 1964-2000   32
3.17 G_i^* test for vote shares. PAN senatorial elections 1964-2000   33
3.18 G_i^* test for vote shares. PAN representative elections 1964-2000   34
3.19 G_i^* test for vote shares. PRI presidential elections 1964-2000   35
3.20 G_i^* test for vote shares. PRI senatorial elections 1964-2000   36
3.21 G_i^* test for vote shares. PRI representative elections 1964-2000   37
3.22 G_i^* test for vote shares. Other parties presidential elections 1964-2000   38
3.23 G_i^* test for vote shares. Other parties senatorial elections 1964-2000   39
3.24 G_i^* test for vote shares. Other parties representative elections 1964-2000   40

3.25	G_i^* test for dissimilarity index. PAN presidential elections 1964-2000	41
3.26	G_i^* test for dissimilarity index. PAN senatorial elections 1964-2000	42
3.27	G_i^* test for dissimilarity index. PAN representative elections 1964-2000	43
3.28	G_i^* test for dissimilarity index. Other parties presidential elections 1964-2000	44
3.29	G_i^* test for dissimilarity index. Other parties senatorial elections 1964-2000	45
3.30	G_i^* test for dissimilarity index. Other parties representative elections 1964-2000	46
4.1	G_i^* test for residuals. PAN vote share presidential election 1964	55
4.2	G_i^* test for residuals. PAN vote share presidential election 2000	59
4.3	G_i^* test for residuals. PAN vote share senatorial election 1964	62
4.4	G_i^* test for residuals. PAN vote share senatorial election 2000	64
4.5	G_i^* test for residuals. PAN vote share representative election 1964	66
4.6	G_i^* test for residuals. PAN vote share representative election 2000	70
4.7	G_i^* test for residuals. PRI vote share presidential election 1964	72
4.8	G_i^* test for residuals. PRI vote share presidential election 2000	74
4.9	G_i^* test for residuals. PRI vote share senatorial election 1964	77
4.10	G_i^* test for residuals. PRI vote share senatorial election 2000	79
4.11	G_i^* test for residuals. PRI vote share representative election 1964	82
4.12	G_i^* test for residuals. PRI vote share representative election 2000	85
4.13	G_i^* test for residuals. Other parties vote share presidential election 1964	88
4.14	G_i^* test for residuals. Other parties vote share presidential election 2000	90
4.15	G_i^* test for residuals. Other parties vote share senatorial election 1964	93
4.16	G_i^* test for residuals. Other parties vote share senatorial election 2000	95

4.17	G_i^* test for residuals. Other parties vote share representative election 1964	97
4.18	G_i^* test for residuals. Other parties vote share representative election 2000	100
5.1	G_i^* test for residuals. Change in vote share for PAN presidential elections 1964–2000	105
5.2	G_i^* test for residuals. Change in vote share for PAN senatorial elections 1964–2000	107
5.3	G_i^* test for residuals. Change in vote share for PAN representative elections 1964–2000	110
5.4	G_i^* test for residuals. Change in vote share for PRI presidential elections 1964–2000	112
5.5	G_i^* test for residuals. Change in vote share for PRI senatorial elections 1964–2000	115
5.6	G_i^* test for residuals. Change in vote share for PRI representative elections 1964–2000	117
5.7	G_i^* test for residuals. Change in vote share for other parties presidential elections 1964–2000	120
5.8	G_i^* test for residuals. Change in vote share for other parties senatorial elections 1964–2000	122
5.9	G_i^* test for residuals. Change in vote share for other parties representative elections 1964–2000	124
6.1	G_i^* test for residuals. Change in dissimilarity index for PAN presidential elections 1964–2000	128
6.2	G_i^* test for residuals. Change in dissimilarity index for PAN senatorial elections 1964–2000	131
6.3	G_i^* test for residuals. Change in dissimilarity index for PAN representative elections 1964–2000	134
6.4	G_i^* test for residuals. Change in dissimilarity index for other parties presidential elections 1964–2000	137
6.5	G_i^* test for residuals. Change in dissimilarity index for other parties senatorial elections 1964–2000	139
6.6	G_i^* test for residuals. Change in dissimilarity index for other parties representative elections 1964–2000	141

List of Tables

3.1	Physical regionalization: categorical variables	50
4.1	Coefficients in initial vote share models: presidential election for PAN, 1964	54
4.2	Coefficients in ending vote share models: presidential election for PAN, 2000	58
4.3	Coefficients in initial vote share models: senatorial election for PAN, 1964	61
4.4	Coefficients in ending vote share models: senatorial election for PAN, 2000	63
4.5	Coefficients in initial vote share models: representative election for PAN, 1964	65
4.6	Coefficients in ending vote share models: representative election for PAN, 2000	69
4.7	Coefficients in initial vote share models: presidential election for PRI, 1964	71
4.8	Coefficients in ending vote share models: presidential election for PRI, 2000	73
4.9	Coefficients in initial vote share models: senatorial election for PRI, 1964	76
4.10	Coefficients in ending vote share models: senatorial election for PRI, 2000	78
4.11	Coefficients in initial vote share models: representative election for PRI, 1964	81
4.12	Coefficients in ending vote share models: representative election for PRI, 2000	84
4.13	Coefficients in initial vote share models: presidential election for other parties, 1964	87
4.14	Coefficients in ending vote share models: presidential election for other parties, 2000	89
4.15	Coefficients in initial vote share models: senatorial election for other parties, 1964	92
4.16	Coefficients in ending vote share models: senatorial election for other parties, 2000	94
4.17	Coefficients in initial vote share models: representative election for other parties, 1964	96
4.18	Coefficients in ending vote share models: representative election for other parties, 2000	99

5.1	Coefficients for change in vote share models: presidential elections for PAN, 1964-2000	104
5.2	Coefficients for change in vote share models: senatorial elections for PAN, 1964-2000	106
5.3	Coefficients for change in vote share models: representative elections for PAN, 1964-2000	109
5.4	Coefficients for change in vote share models: presidential elections for PRI, 1964-2000	111
5.5	Coefficients for change in vote share models: senatorial elections for PRI, 1964-2000	114
5.6	Coefficients for change in vote share models: representative elections for PRI, 1964-2000	116
5.7	Coefficients for change in vote share models: presidential elections for other parties, 1964-2000	119
5.8	Coefficients for change in vote share models: senatorial elections for other parties, 1964-2000	121
5.9	Coefficients for change in vote share models: representative elections for other parties, 1964-2000	123
6.1	Coefficients for change in dissimilarity index models: presidential elections for PAN, 1964-2000	127
6.2	Coefficients for change in dissimilarity index models: senatorial elections for PAN, 1964-2000	130
6.3	Coefficients for change in dissimilarity index models: representative elections for PAN, 1964-2000	133
6.4	Coefficients for change in dissimilarity index models: presidential elections for other parties, 1964-2000	135
6.5	Coefficients for change in dissimilarity index models: senatorial elections for other parties, 1964-2000	138
6.6	Coefficients for change in dissimilarity index models: representative elections for other parties, 1964-2000	140

Acknowledgements

I would like to express my gratitude to my advisor Dr. Brian J. L. Berry for his guidance, assistance, encouragement and especially his patience, and for introducing me to this fascinating field of study. I also want to thank Sheila Amin Gutierrez de Piñeres, Jennifer Holmes and Euel Elliott, for their help and understanding throughout the whole process.

Appreciation is also extended to the Center for Spatially Integrated Social Sciences from the University of California at Santa Barbara, in particular to Dr. Arthur Getis and Dr. John Weeks for their enlightening and wonderful suggestions, and to the Instituto Tecnológico y de Estudios Superiores de Monterrey for gathering the data I needed to begin this project.

Special thanks to Dr. Lawrence Redlinger for his deep understanding and cooperation, and to my friend Dr. Rodolfo Hernández Guerrero from the Center for US-Mexico Studies at The University of Texas at Dallas, whose help in the critical moments was invaluable.

Finally, I am deeply indebted to my parents, sisters and brother, and especially to my husband Brian Martin, without their love and patience this dissertation would not have been possible.

Chapter 1

Introduction

Mexico's most recent presidential election marks the end of 71 years of one-party rule, after a slow process of emergence of democratic institutions and viable second-party candidates. Yet the process of democratization has been uneven, proceeding much more rapidly in some regions than in others.

The purpose of this study is to see whether diffusion processes have been at work, and if so to try to isolate the points of origin, to trace the lines and channels of movement, clarifying causes and the nature of the diffusion process.

The alternative hypothesis is that broad national processes of change have unfolded across an uneven socioeconomic map, and that Mexican politics remain marked by regionalism of other kinds.

There is an abundance of literature on diffusion processes, focusing on the "locational distribution of innovations, culture traits and other economic, social, political or physical issues" (Brown 1968). Studies of the diffusion of democracy have been undertaken at both global and regional levels, but no study has been located that explores how multiparty politics have emerged in a single country. Mexico offers a significant opportunity to undertake a country case study. Having such contrasting borders, the United States to the north and Guatemala and Belize to the south, different kinds of geography, levels of industrialization and development, I believe that such a study can involve all these variables, plus the socio-economic aspects of the population that display sharp regional differentiation.

The study not only deals with the spatial diffusion process; it also necessarily deals with the process of political development in Mexico, and the links between the two. In what follows, I begin by reviewing the literature on spatial diffusion and political development, outline my strategy for analyzing the Mexican case, proceed to an analysis of changing vote share by party and by level of political representation, and then offer an interpretation of the process of political change in Mexico.

This study contains seven chapters, including the present introduction. Chapter two discusses the diffusion process, introducing both spatial diffusion theories and political development theories and discussing how these two fields have been conjugated in research over the last couple of decades. An extension of this analysis is proposed for the Mexican context in chapter three. Chapter four is devoted to an analysis of the vote shares of three different party categories in Mexico at initial and ending conditions of a 36-year time span, isolating factors that might have contributed to spatial variations in the shares. Chapter five explores the factors contributing to variations in the rate of change in vote shares over the time span, and chapter six uses dissimilarity indices to reveal the processes contributing to the emergence of competitive multiparty politics. Finally, chapter seven draws together the analyses and offers a broad interpretation of the patterns and process that characterize Mexican political dynamics.

Chapter 2

Diffusion Processes

Spatial Diffusion Theories

The concept of spatial diffusion has been used in the geographical literature since the beginning of the last century. To have a better understanding of the use of the concept in this study it is necessary to know the meaning of the terms that are used. The use of the term 'spatial' puts space or territorial area in a position of importance. As Hägerstrand (1967:6) explained, "the term 'spatial' emphasizes the fact that a quantitative analysis of locational relationships is constantly pursued." This statement is in order to contrast the use of the term 'geographical,' related only to the use of a "given part of the earth's surface" so commonly pursued by more traditional geographers.

The term diffuse is defined as "to disperse or to be dispersed from a center; widely spread or scattered; to disseminate; to pour or spread out and disperse." Studies of spatial diffusion have been a major component of geographical research. Brown (1968) defines spatial diffusion as "the spread or dispersion of a phenomenon within a given area through time." Some authors refer to the process as expansion diffusion (Cliff et al. 1981).

The model of diffusion most commonly used is the innovation diffusion model. Three empirical regularities are embodied in this model (Haggett 1977:235). These are the neighborhood effect, the logistic curve (to explain the temporal built-up in the number of adopters) and the urban-centered hierarchical diffusion process. Each of these is described briefly below.

Neighborhood Effect

Hägerstrand developed a Monte Carlo model to simulate the recorded number of acceptors of some stimulus in agriculture (Haggett et al. 1977:234-5; Cliff et al. 1981:17). He assumed that the model was stochastic, and that the decision to accept the stimulus was based on the information transmitted orally face to face, between the people with the propensity to adopt and the 'carriers' of this stimulus. This way of transmitting information is known as the neighborhood effect, in which contagious spread depends on direct contact (Cliff et. al. 1981:21), in "face to face meetings between the potential adopter and carriers" (Haggett et al. 1977:235; Cliff et al. 1981:21).

This process is influenced by distance. Individuals who are closer will learn about the innovation more rapidly than individuals in remote areas. It is assumed in the model that the probability that a carrier meets and spreads the 'item' to a potential adopter is inversely proportional to the distance between them (Haggett et al. 1977:235).

Contagious diffusion is another name given to the neighborhood effect, which tends to occur from the source outwards in a 'centrifugal' fashion (Cliff et al. 1981:7). Relocation diffusion is a variant of this process. The difference, Cliff et al. explain, is that the items being diffused leave the areas where they originated as they move to new areas. Migratory movements are a good example of this diffusion process.

The Logistic Curve

Hägerstrand described the logistic curve as the temporal pattern of acceptance of diffusion and it is subsequent to the neighborhood effect. Adding the dimension 'time' into the diffusion process equation, it is possible to see that the number of adopters will grow following an S-shaped curve that accounts for the cumulative proportion at a given time. In the beginning, the adoption of the innovation is slow, followed by a rapid build-up, known as the take-off of the process, until it reaches a threshold in which saturation of the susceptible population is approached (Haggett, 1977:238; O' Loughlin et al. 1998:553).

A logistic model is normally able to capture the proportion of adopters at any given time. The equation for the logistic model is given by $p_t = \left(1 + e^{a-bt}\right)^{-1}$ where p_t is the proportion of adopters from the total population at time t; or by $y_t = k\left(1 + e^{a-bt}\right)^{-1}$ where y_t denotes the cumulative number of adopters in the total population at risk; a, b and k are parameters; and k is interpreted as the saturation level, the maximum number of adopters in the population.

The rate of change r is the first derivative of the previous model and is given by: $r_t = \frac{dp_t}{dt} = -bp_t(1-p_t)$. Since p_t is the proportion of the population that has actually adopted at time t, $(1-p_t)$ is the proportion that has not adopted yet, known as the population at risk. Therefore b represents the rate at which the proportion of adopters will meet the potential adopters.

Hierarchical Diffusion

The third empirical regularity cited by Haggett et al. (1977:240) is that of hierarchical diffusion. The spread in this modality of diffusion occurs through the urban hierarchy, proceeding from large centers to small towns. This kind of diffusion is observed for certain types of innovations, such as fashions. It is introduced to the main city or cities and from there it filters down through the hierarchy, and this is known as the diffusion down the central place hierarchy.

Innovation Diffusion Models

Berry (1972), Haggett et al. (1977), Cliff et al. (1981), as well as many other researchers, agree that most diffusion processes are a mixture of neighborhood effects and hierarchical diffusion. Berry (1972) argued that developmental role of growth centers "involves the simultaneous 'filtering' of the innovations that bring growth down the urban hierarchy and the 'spreading' of the benefits accruing from the resulting growth, both nationally from core to hinterland regions and within these regions from their metropolitan centers outward to the intermetropolitan periphery." Berry (1972:114) uses Pedersen's formula, based on the gravity principle of attraction, and applies it to calculate the information flow per unit of time between urban centers. The general formula to capture all the information flow interactions among n towns at any t time is

$$I_t^j = \sum_{t=1}^{n} K \cdot \frac{P_i P_j}{s_{ij}^x}$$ where s_{ij} is the distance between towns i and j, P_i and P_j are the sizes of the towns involved in the exchange. Therefore, the time for adoption of innovations will be in function of two factors. If the right-hand side of the information flow formula

$K'P_j \sum_{i=1}^{n} \frac{P_i}{S_{ij}^x}$ is rewritten, the component K'P$_j$ will be the position of

the center in the urban hierarchy and $\sum_{i=1}^{n} \frac{P_i}{S_{ij}^x}$ will be the 'force' applied on that center by centers that have already adopted that innovation. Population potential is the term given to the latter. There will be a minimum size of population to which innovation will not be able to penetrate. Adoption time will be a function of population size, distance and hierarchical position, with heavy weight being placed on the location of the center with respect to the location of the centers that have already adopted the innovation (Berry, 1972:114-5).

Diffusion barriers A number of barriers can affect interpersonal communication. First, social, cultural and language differences may impede receptivity to new ideas. Second, physical features can act as barriers to innovation waves. Mountain systems, rivers, deserts all in one way or another will have an impact on the simple possibility or the speed of communication. Any model of a diffusion process must also account for these factors.

Political Development Theories

There is no single model of what a democracy is or should be. Beginning with the Greeks, democracy was defined as a system based on direct citizen participation in government in which all qualified citizens are directly involved in collective decision-making. Democracy, as Plato wrote in The Republic "is a charming form of government, full of variety and disorder, and dispensing a sort of equality to equals and unequals alike." After the Greeks it then evolved to representative democracy, emerging from the British experience in terms of clashes between nobles and the King, and then between Parliament and the crown. This was followed by the liberal, representative democracy that was born in the French and American revolutions (Pye, 2000:22).

Pye (2000:21) states that

> "in the modern world the legitimacy of governments depends upon an acknowledgement of the superior virtues of democracy. There are though variations in practices of democracy. Because democracy is based on interactions among individuals in society, it has evolved."

Democracy is not static but rather a dynamic process leading to adapt to changing needs.

With the rise of political science, new theories about democracy took shape. Robert Dahl identified eight essential guarantees backed up by solid institutional protection in order to be identified and organized into policy programs. These guarantees reflect what Americans associate with liberal democracy. Summarized by Pye (2000: 23-24) they are:

- freedom to form and join organizations. These organizations need to be out of state control;
- freedom of expression, therefore freedom of speech is absolutely basic;
- right to vote without intimidation or inhibition;
- free and fair elections in which vote is secret and where people not belonging to the government are allowed to openly check the ballots;
- right of political leaders to compete for support, which prevents the state from limiting competitors;
- the existence of sources of information to enable the people to hear different views; the state cannot control mass media or the press;
- fair rules of eligibility institutionally guaranteed with no government screening of candidates for office;
- the process of policy-making must represent what the representatives of the people vote, not what the government wants.

There has to be strong legal support in order to implement these guarantees. Liberal democracy cannot operate without a system of rule by law. The respect for the law will set the base for the enforcement of political guarantees for liberal democracy.

Joseph Schumpeter defined the democratic method as "the institutional arrangement for arriving at political decisions in which individuals acquire the power to decide by means of a competitive struggle for the people's votes" (1975:269).

Another characteristic of democracy is the concept of civic culture. Citizens need to have certain attitudes and values such as a reasonable degree of knowledge about government and how the operation of the political system, tolerance for political views of others, and willingness to cooperate with the citizen fellows in order to achieve collective goals (Pye 2000:24). Civic culture excludes fanatical behavior towards government: it is not possible to maintain democratic institutions if this kind of behavior prevails.

Transition to Democratic Political Systems

Many theories about regime change and the achievement of liberal democracy have emerged since Aristotle's typology of political systems and their transition from one type to another. Classic theory assumed that in order to achieve democracy a strong middle class is required, therefore, economics determine the viability of democracy.

Contemporary theories about transitions fall into three main categories. The first category emphasizes the social, structural and economic conditions that favor democratic development (Pye, p. 25). Lipset argued that economic growth is a key factor for achievement and maintenance of democracy: "the more well-to-do a nation is the greater the chances it will sustain democracy" (1959: 75). To this he attaches the idea that there are social prerequisites for economic development, such as the level of urbanization, education and industrialization, each of which may help explain the level of democratization (Schatz 2000:1, 17-8). The second category is based on elite decision-making and "the purposeful acts of leadership groups." Pye states that change comes when autocratic rulers find out the cost of continued repression is greater than the risk of democracy (2000:27). The third category involves pluralism, in which organizations and their public actions influence the political process. Pye concludes "the key for democratic development is the existence of voluntary associations which can mobilize political power by articulating and aggregating the interest of major elements of society" or what is known as 'civil society.' A civil society allows democracy to operate; brings balance between state and society, that is, between government and the citizens (2000:26). Recent studies of transitions and regime transformations have combined these three approaches.

As described by Shin, the "transition stage of democratization is regarded as a period of great political uncertainty, one specially fraught with the risk of reversion" (1994:143). Because of such uncertainties, political developments have come in waves. The first wave emerged in the nineteenth century from the British experience, shaped by the French and American revolutions. Huntington dates this first wave from 1828-1926, and describes it as a long wave of democratization (Barro 1999). The second wave (1950s to 1960s) came after World War II and was marked by decolonization "and the extension of democratic forms of government into cultures and societies that, in most cases, had weak civil societies and no previous history of popular government or market economies" (Hollifield 2000:10). The third wave is considered "the greatest, in terms of the number of states as well as the number of people involved" (Shin 1994:150). It occurred between the 1970s and the 1990s and developed along three pathways, each of them following the liberal-democratic classical model of political development: The first path involved Southern Europe and some South American countries that were ruled by the military. The second path included authoritarian regimes ruled by a single dominant party, as in some Asian and South African countries. The third and final transition involved regimes dominated by a communist oligarchy, and included the former Soviet Union and East Central Europe (Hollifield 2000:10).

The case of Mexico Mexico seems to fit within the second path taken in the third wave of democratization, where authoritarian regimes with a single dominant party allowed the change towards democracy. Schatz, however, explains that there are important differences in the democratic transformation of non-Leninist single-party systems (2000:6). Mexico's authoritarian regime differed from those where the central role of the 'authoritarian state' is one of organizing social classes, especially the middle class and labor. Mexico has not repeated the western European democratization experience, in which a 'land-industry/rural-urban' social cleavage translated into a political conflict between "landowners and urban industrial entrepreneurs" (Schatz 2000:6). Mexico also has showed a 'delayed' transition to democracy. To be sure, there were two decades of political liberalization followed then by democratization, but it was not until the end of the 20th century that the transition to fully competitive and open electoral politics took place (Schatz 2000:3).

Countries with similar characteristics, such as non-Leninist single-party systems, had the same delayed transition to democracy. In chronological order, from the time the party was founded, Mexico appears as the oldest, in 1929. It was followed by Taiwan, 1949; Malaysia and Tunisia, 1957; Ivory Coast and Senegal, 1960; Kenya, 1963; Tanzania and Zambia, 1964; Singapore, 1965; Botswana, 1966 and Zimbabwe, 1979 (Ibid).

Lipset has studied the conditions under which the transition to democracy might be achieved, calling them 'prerequisites for democracy.' The level of industrialization that a country experiences; the proportion of the labor force in agriculture at less than 2 percent and literacy levels higher than 96 percent (Schatz

2000:18) are some of them. Mexico shows a delayed transition to democracy based on these 'prerequisites.' Some Mexican states appear to be 'democracy ready' within certain ranges of these prerequisites and at the same time they do not show the same readiness under other characteristics.

Literature on the Diffusion of Democracy

There have been two recent attempts to explore the diffusion of democracy. Both are on a cross-national basis, by O' Loughlin et al. (1998) and Gleditsch and Ward (2000). O' Loughlin et al. used an empirical measure of democracy based on structures of democracy and authority (p. 545), and attempted to extract the changes of the polities under study and at the same time to examine the nature of these changes while exploring spatial-temporal regularities and irregularities of the diffusion process. Maps and graphs helped to explain the democratic process around the world and at the regional level. Southern African and Latin American countries were used as case study to illustrate the rate and nature of democratic change for both regional and global contexts. Both regions experienced domestic as well as external influences that shaped the democratic process in time and space. On the basis of their study they attempted to predict possible change or reversal of trends in some of the new democracies.

To conduct their analysis they created a measure that combines four aspects of contemporary democracy, "constraints on the executive decision makers, the extent of competition among political forces, the regulation of political participation and the openness and recruitment into the decision making bodies" (p. 548). These assessments were derived from a theory of authority relations that resulted from the study of patterns of authority in social units that included national systems.

Their dataset, known as Polity III, was initially developed from a study of persistence and change of political systems (Jaggers and Gurr 1996). It uses 21 different levels of democracy, allowing consideration of various degrees of democracy and autocracy as well as changes in regime behavior. In contrast, the most commonly used dichotomous measures of democracy focus simply on outcomes, democratic versus non-democratic regimes (p. 548).

Two scales were constructed using Polity III, one labeled autocracy and the other institutional democracy. The difference between the two scales is the index used for the level of democracy (p. 548). O' Loughlin et al. state that, "by correlating independent economic and social characteristics with broad indicators of democracy, a general cross-sectional model is expected to predict where future democratizing trends are likely to be seen" (p. 548). Regionally clustered states are more likely to be affected by democratization than others due to internal conditions as well as 'the contagion effect.' Socio-economic indicators such as GDP per capita, levels of education, industrialization and urbanization to name few, are considered requisites for democracy. These internal characteristics have external impacts. For instance, neighboring states, "share a regional positive diffusion effect or a regional learning curve" (p. 550) and it is reflected through time and space. Specifically, they tested two hypotheses:

- Internal domestic circumstances drive the democratic transition, while external influences affect the consolidation of autocracy;
- The alternative hypothesis is that both, internal and external influences have impacts, but inertia overrides other considerations (pp. 560-561).

One problem in conducting their study was that they encountered changing political boundaries over the period studied. After identifying the periods where creation or dissolution of polities in the international political arena took place (from 1946-54, 1955-74, 1975-89, 1990, 1991-92 and 1993-94), contiguity matrices for each year from 1946 to 1994 were created, the changes in democracy and autocracy were computed, and the results mapped (p. 548). Spatial-temporal patterns showed reversals as well as waves of democratization (p. 555). The globe was then divided in zones characterized by the increasing democracy or increasing autocracy. Employing methods of exploratory spatial data analysis (ESDA), spatial statistics of global correlation known as Moran's I were obtained, with resulting values significant for all years. In the regions that clusters appeared, they calculated the local spatial statistic correlation index, known as G_i^* in order to extract local differences that did not showed up using Moran's I at the regional level. Results from these computations helped the authors understand the degree of democratic change, as well as to pinpoint the countries that had the strongest influence on the regional patterns. By adopting a spatial-diffusion framework, they were able to "emphasize the interconnections among temporal and spatial changes" (p. 545), making it possible to map political changes in a geographical context.

Inferential models linking GDP to democracy then were calibrated. The residuals were tested for spatial autocorrelation, providing positive results at the global level. At the local level the authors found high positive values in Latin America and high negative values in Western Africa. Even when controlling for the economic development variable, the model provided a strong indicator of the effects of geographical location on regime type (p. 557).

Gleditsch and Ward (2000) also demonstrated the importance of spatial clustering and its impact on both democratization and war (p. 1) as they reexamined the claims that "democracies are less likely to be involved in international wars; countries are less likely to be involved in international wars as they become more democratic; and countries with a high degree of volatility in their regime structures will face greater likelihood of war involvement" (p. 2).

Their analysis also drew on the dataset Polity III for regime characteristics and "implied system membership" (Jaggers and Gurr 1996), as well as for the overall democracy indicator, defined as "the democracy scale minus the autocracy scale" (Gleditsch and Ward 2000:5). For war involvement, the authors used the Correlation of War-International War database, known as COW-IW (Singer and Small 1994), revising it for statehood criteria and updating it for conflicts for the years after 1992 (Gleditsch and Ward 2000:6).

Using spatial data analysis techniques, exploratory and descriptive analysis of clusters of democracy and war in space was attempted. To obtain a measure of contiguity, they used the shortest distance between the closest physical locations among the units of analysis (p. 7). This matrix, known as the contiguity metric, is the one most frequently used in democracy diffusion studies, in contrast to the 'squared inter-centroid distance,' commonly used in geographical studies (O' Loughlin 1998:554). Bands of 50, 475 and 950 kilometers were used to obtain three different matrices in order to capture all possible land border relationships. When two different units were found to be contiguous, the number corresponding to them in the matrix was one, and zero otherwise. The rows of this matrix were then weighted by the number of units of analysis that are positive (with a '1' on them) and multiplied by the matrix of the indices of democracy. This resultant vector is known as the first-order spatial lag. The authors define this vector as "the weighted average of the democracy scores on those countries that are contiguous at a distance of 50 kilometers or less" or 475 or 950 kilometers in the other two cases (Gleditsch and Ward 2000:9).

An inferential model was formulated to clarify the linkage between democratization and war (p. 2). The polities were divided in established democracies and newly emergent democracies that experienced 'rocky' transitions. Estimated coefficients and variance-covariance matrices were derived for both sets of countries (Ibid.). A dichotomous variable was used as the dependent variable, measuring whether or not a country was involved in an "interstate or extra-systemic" war for the period from 1816 to 1996 (p. 12). Having a dichotomous dependent variable permitted the use of a generalized additive model based on the general logit form. The generalized additive model allowed non-linearities in the functional relationship (p. 18).

In a second model, the primary independent variable was the level of democracy D_i. From this variable the authors derived four more variables. They are (p. 13):

- the amount of change in democracy experienced by a country ΔD_i;
- the direction of this change in terms of zero, minus one and positive one, depending the type of change or no-change experienced by the country for the given years;
- the variance of democracy by decades in order to measure "the lumpiness of democratization," $\sigma^2 D_i$;
- two versions of the same measure, one for democracy ($G_i^* D_i$) and one for autocracy ($G_i W_i$). These incorporated into the model "the localized spatial context" utilizing the local measure of spatial correlation and the measure of democracy or autocracy, computed for the 50, 475 and 950 kilometers distance bands.

The statistic G_i^* is normally distributed, and indicates the extent to which similarly valued observations are clustered around a particular observation i. A positive value at a particular location indicates spatial clustering of high values; a negative value indicates a spatial grouping of low values. Two control variables, for power status of the country and for the time the country has been at peace during the period prior to the current year, were applied. Statistically significant values for both global spatial correlation and local clustering were found (p. 16). There was a strong and significant effect of spatial-temporal context on the likelihood of war (p. 20).

Chapter 3

The Present Study

Building on the literature reviewed, including the two recent investigations that explicitly explored the role of space and region, I devote this study to an analysis of increased democratization via emergence of multiparty politics in Mexico. I begin by describing the dependent variables that are used to capture the progress of party competition at the state level; next discuss the primary test for spatial autocorrelation of the dependent variables to determine whether a spatial diffusion process or a pattern of contiguous regionalization might be present; then outline the model used to evaluate concepts drawn from the theory of political development, detailing the spatial variables intended to enrich the model of political development by capturing geographic effects; and finally discuss the tests of the residuals from this enriched model designed to see whether the spatial effects have been captured or whether missing variables need to be identified and incorporated into an expanded model.

Dependent Variables

I used Mexican Federal Elections data, at the state level, for the period 1964 to 2000 for elections for President, Senators and Representatives. The Presidential and Senatorial election years are 1964, 1970, 1976, 1982, 1988, 1994 and 2000. The election years for Representatives are 1964, 1967, 1970, 1973, 1976, 1979, 1982, 1985, 1988, 1991, 1994, 1997 and 2000. The official source of these data is the Instituto Federal Electoral (Castellanos and Zertuche 1997). Three party categories will be used: PRI, PAN and "others." The last category is due to the creation and disappearance of political parties over the time period of the study. The PRI and PAN were active over the entire time span. For each level of representation, political change indices are created:

- share of votes by party for every election;
- percent change in vote shares;

- dissimilarity indices based on party segmentation.

The first two sets of indicators are straightforward. The dissimilarity index, widely used in segregation studies, measures evenness in the distribution of votes among the parties; it varies from zero at one. Modifying the description given by Massey and Denton (1989:374) it "represents the proportion of minority members that would have to change voting districts to achieve an even distribution." Evenness is the "differential distribution of voters across districts within a state" and it is maximized, that is, segregation is minimized, when all districts have "the same relative number of voters as the whole urban state" (Massey and Denton 1987:805).

The concept is parallel to the measure of concentration in population studies, from which "any measure of concentration seeks simply to make operational the notion of the degree of unevenness" (Duncan 1957:29). The dissimilarity index works more as a behavioral than mathematical relationship (Massey and Denton 1987:814).

As a measure of political change, the dissimilarity index can be applied to compute the evenness of voting results of minority parties contrasted to the majority party: greater evenness implies more competitive party politics. Comparing the political arena to the demographic arena then, the majority party can be seen as the majority segment of the population; in the same fashion, minority parties can mirror minority populations. Applied to the political arena, the dissimilarity index behaves as follows: If the percentage of minority voting rises, the dissimilarity index will decrease, and vice versa.

The formula of the dissimilarity index is: $D_i = 0.5 * \sum \left| \frac{x_i}{X} - \frac{y_i}{Y} \right|$ where x_i and y_i are the minority and majority populations, in a unit of area i, and the totals X and Y are the minority and majority totals of the population, respectively.

With this indicator in hand, GIS techniques can be used to map vote shares by party and by election. Figures 3.1 to 3.3 show the vote shares for PAN for presidential, senatorial and representative elections as the party grew into the primary challenge for to PRI. It was not until after the elections of 1982 that PAN was able to have a strong presence in the political arena. In the northern states Chihuahua and Coahuila, and in a southwestern state Jalisco, PAN obtained shares of more than 25 but still under 50 percent of all votes. The strong northern support diluted

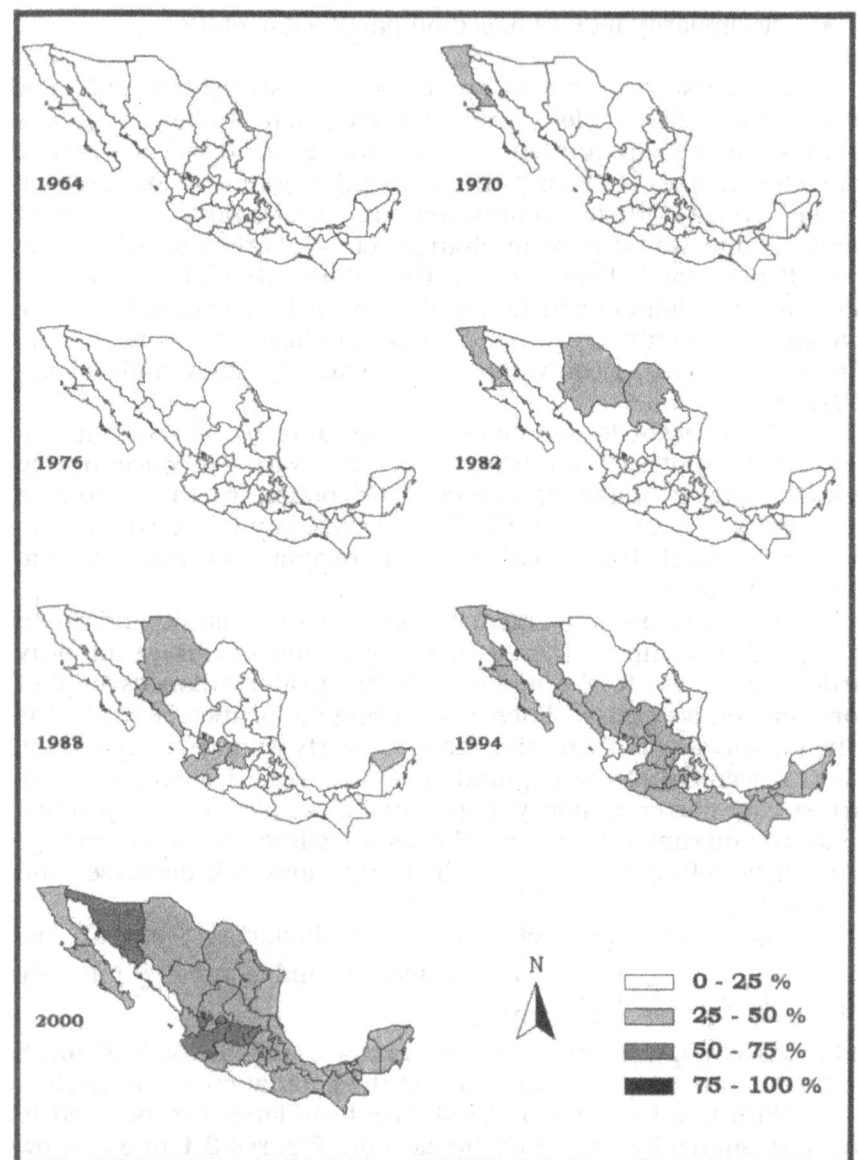

Figure 3.1 Vote shares. PAN presidential elections 1964-2000

somewhat over the 1988 election, in which the southern as well as central states increased their support. In 1976 PAN did not have a candidate for the presidential election due to internal struggle. By 2000 the support was in almost the whole territory, except for the southern most states in senatorial and representative elections. For presidential elections the support was over 50 percent of vote shares for PAN in five states and only two states cast less than 25 percent.

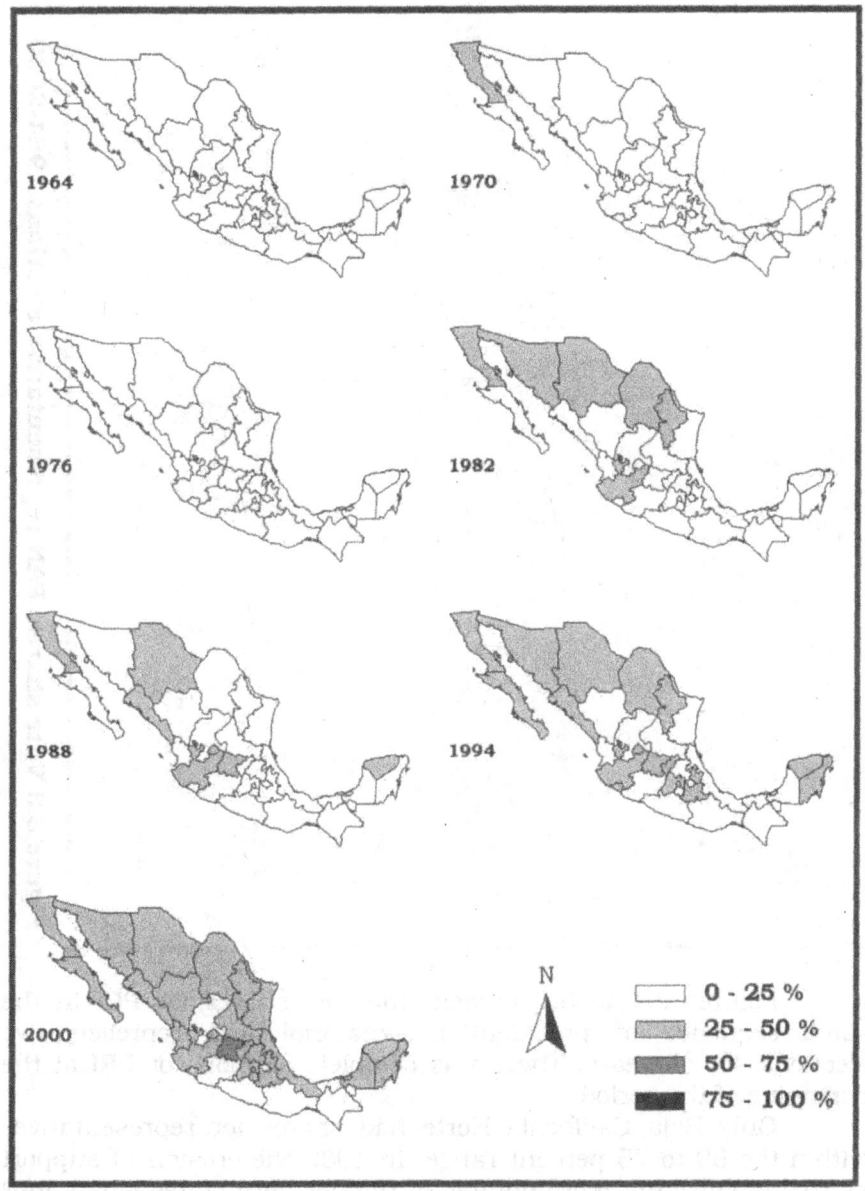

Figure 3.2 Vote shares. PAN senatorial elections 1964-2000

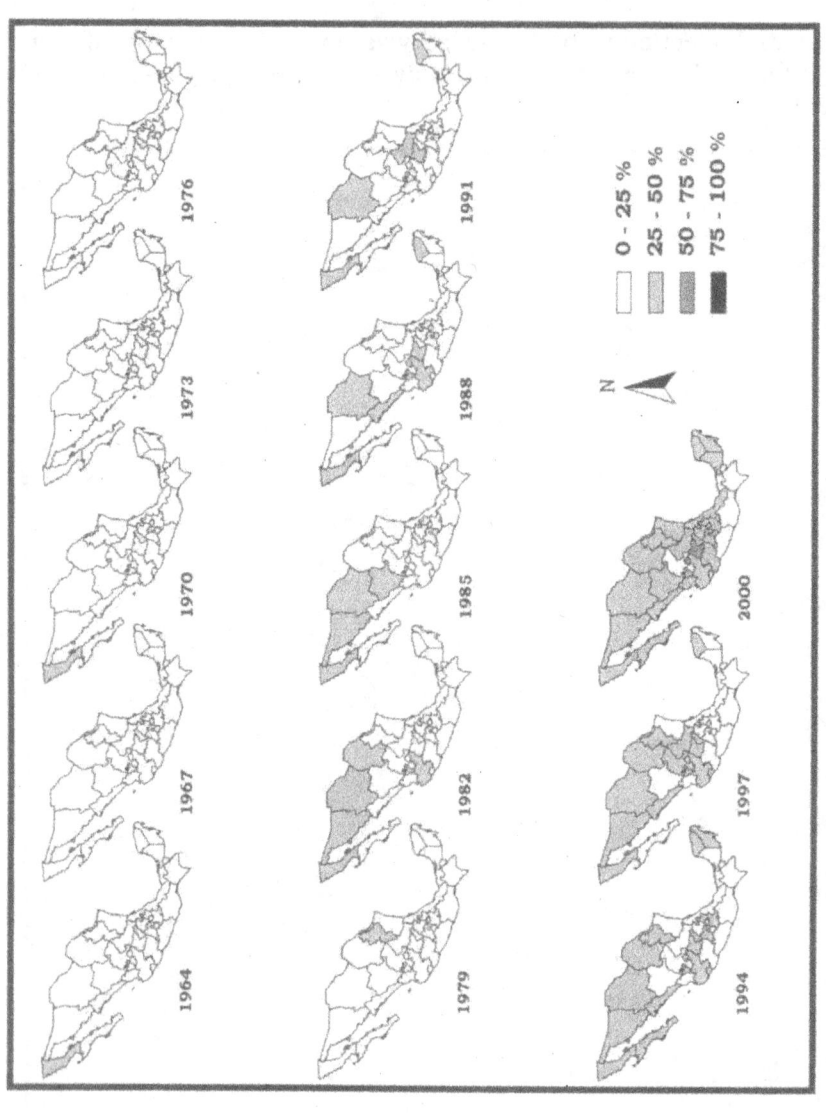

Figure 3.3 Vote shares. PAN representative elections 1964-2000

Figures 3.4 to 3.6 present the vote shares for PRI in the same sequence of presidential, senatorial and representative elections, for all years. There was complete support for PRI at the beginning of the period.

Only Baja California Norte had shares for representatives within the 50 to 75 percent range. In 1982 the erosion of support started to show up, more notably in the northern states where PAN was increasing its support. By 1988, only Chiapas retained vote shares higher than 75 percent and Michoacan that same year dropped its support to less than 25 percent of the shares cast to PRI.

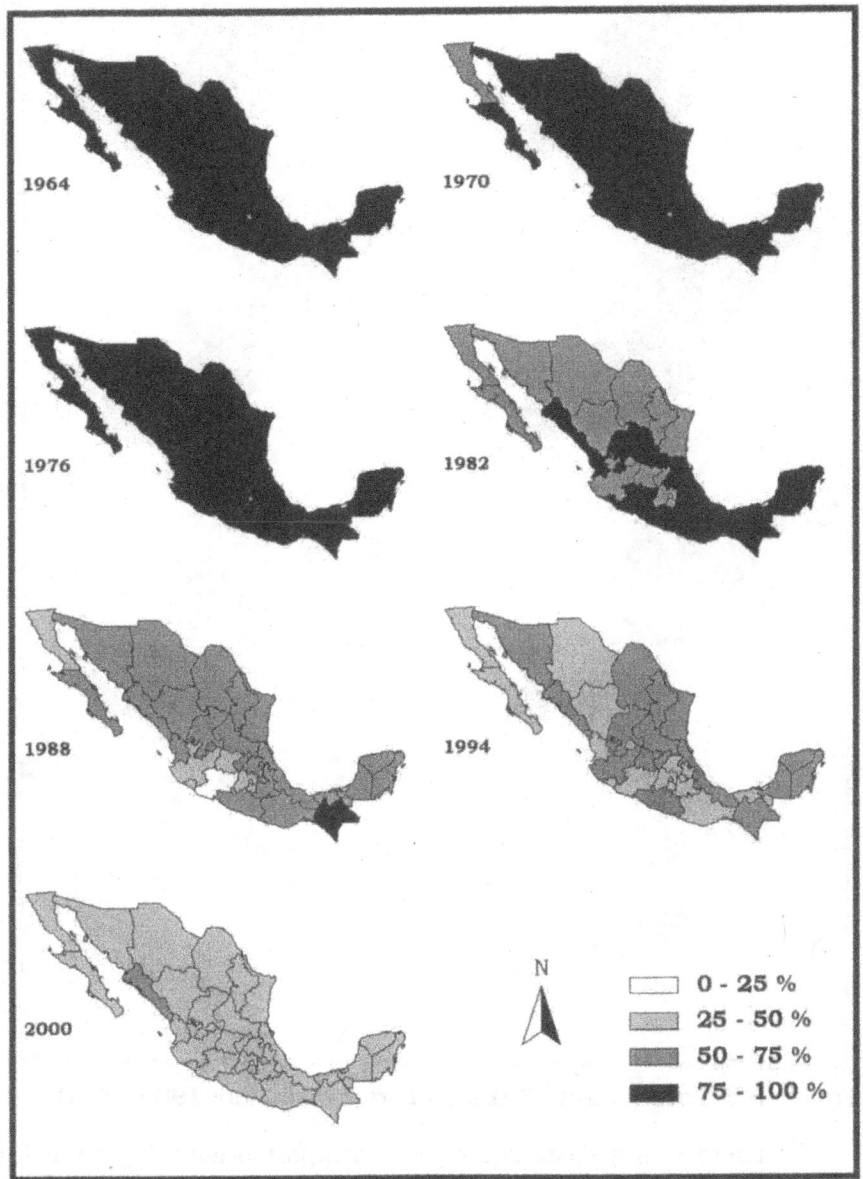

Figure 3.4 Vote shares. PRI presidential elections 1964-2000

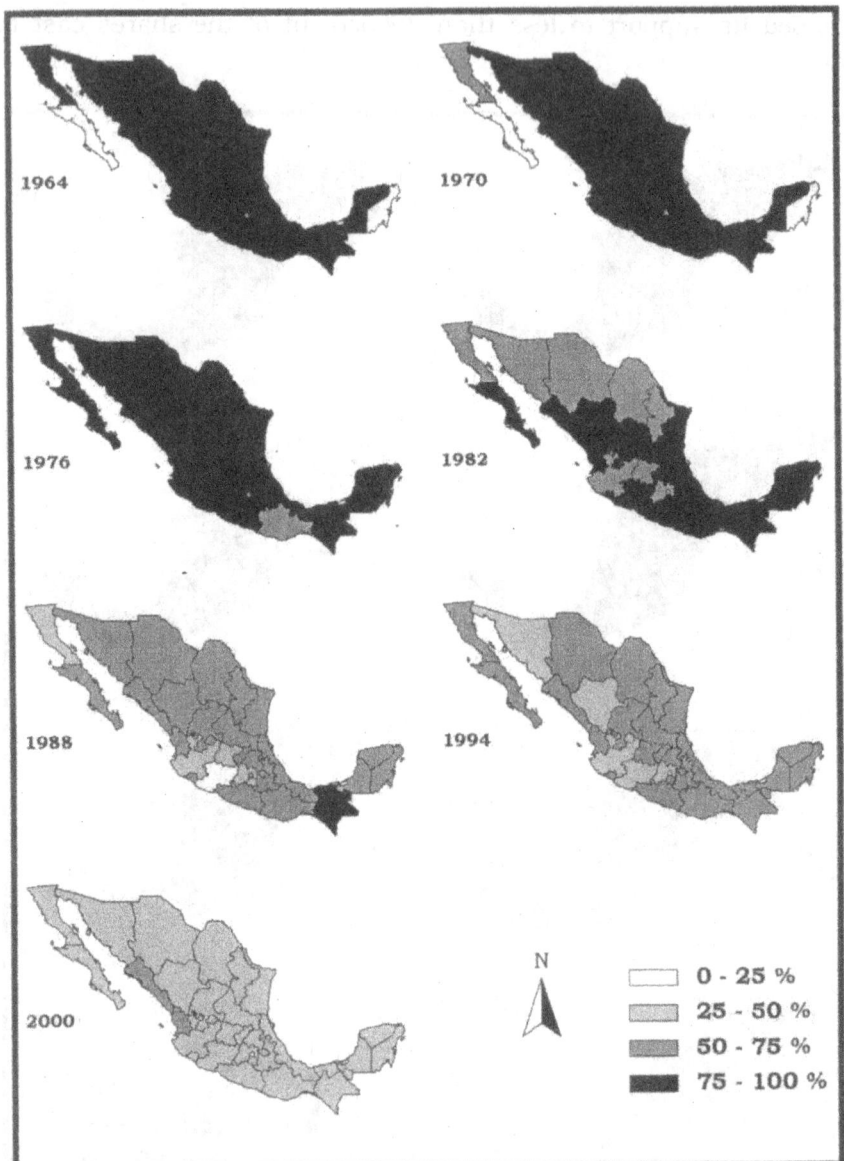

Figure 3.5 Vote shares. PRI senatorial elections 1964-2000

There was a clear decrease of support originating from the north and proceeding to the south, with the main breakout on 1982 for presidential and senatorial elections and in 1973 for

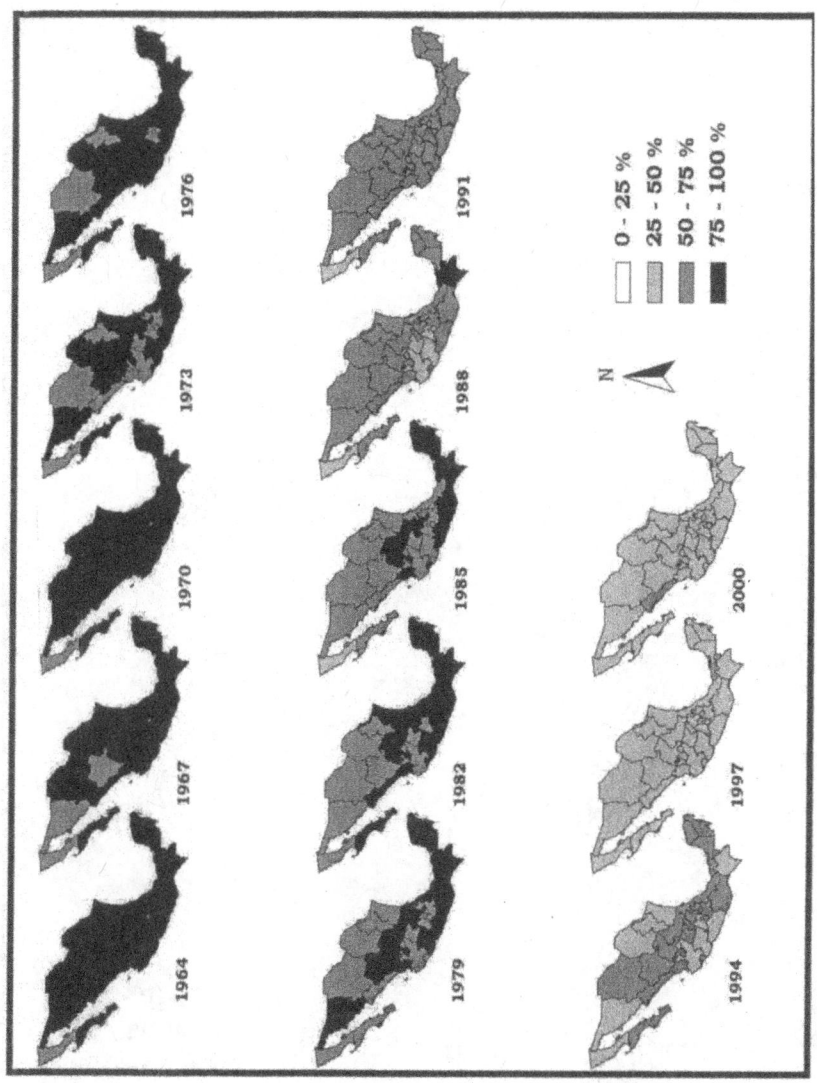

Figure 3.6 Vote shares. PRI representative elections 1964-2000

representative elections. By the end of the time span, only Sinaloa for all levels of representation and Nayarit for senatorial elections, cast shares greater than 50 percent for PRI. The Federal District cast less than 25 percent in this election.

Figures 3.7 to 3.9 show the vote shares for the other parties, again for presidential, senatorial and representative elections, for all years. It was not until 1988 that parties other than PAN or PRI emerged as political contenders in the Mexican elections. A strong

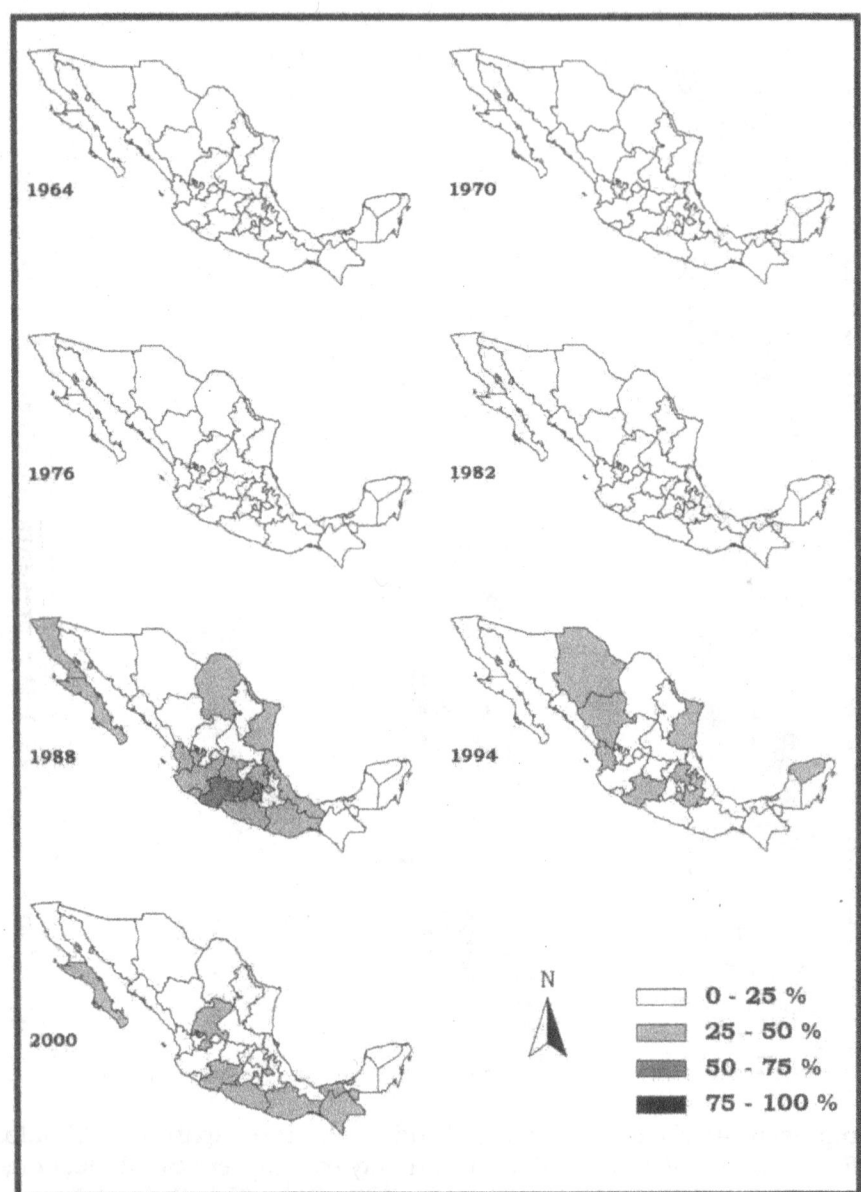

Figure 3.7 Vote shares. Other parties presidential elections 1964-2000

cluster was present in around the southern states, specifically in Michoacan and Morelos and along the Gulf of Mexico.

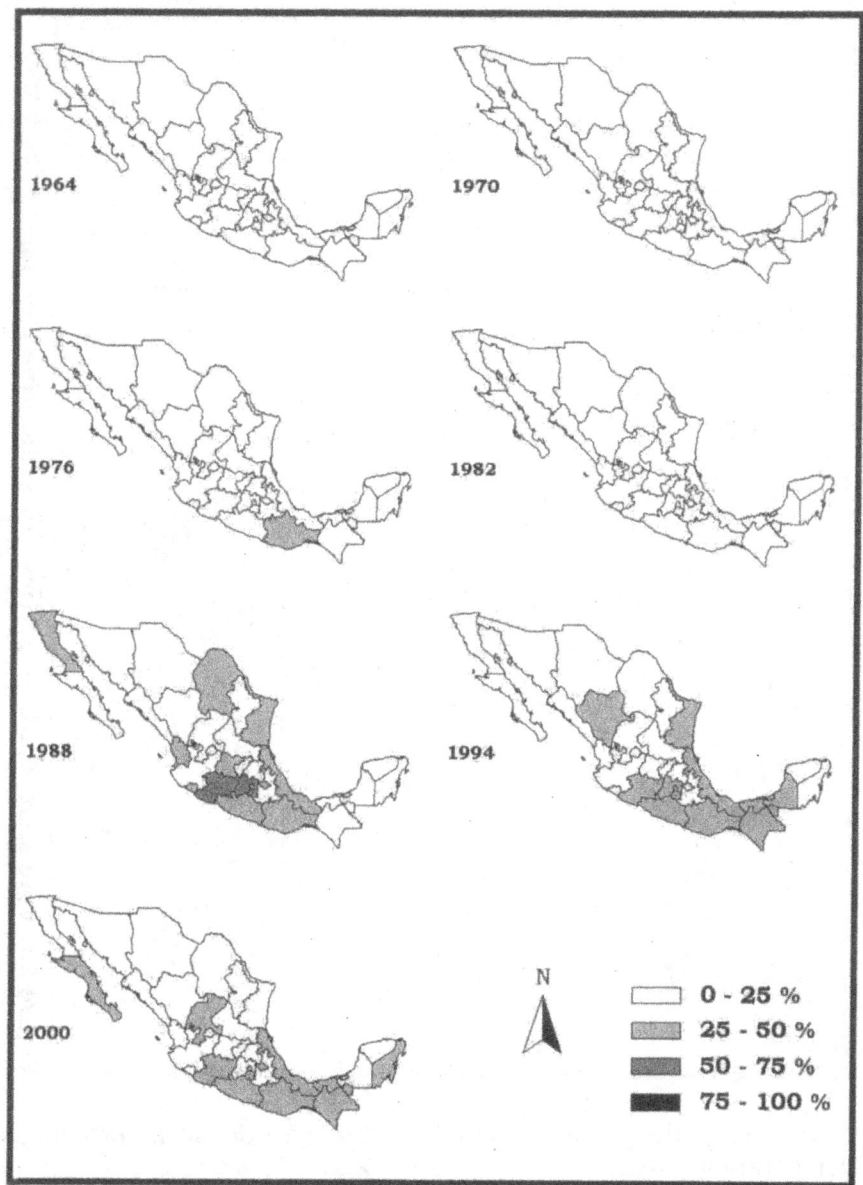

Figure 3.8 Vote shares. Other parties senatorial elections 1964-2000

By the end of the period, the strongest support for other parties was concentrated in the most southerly states, Guerrero, Oaxaca, Chiapas, Tabasco and in Baja California Sur. The Federal

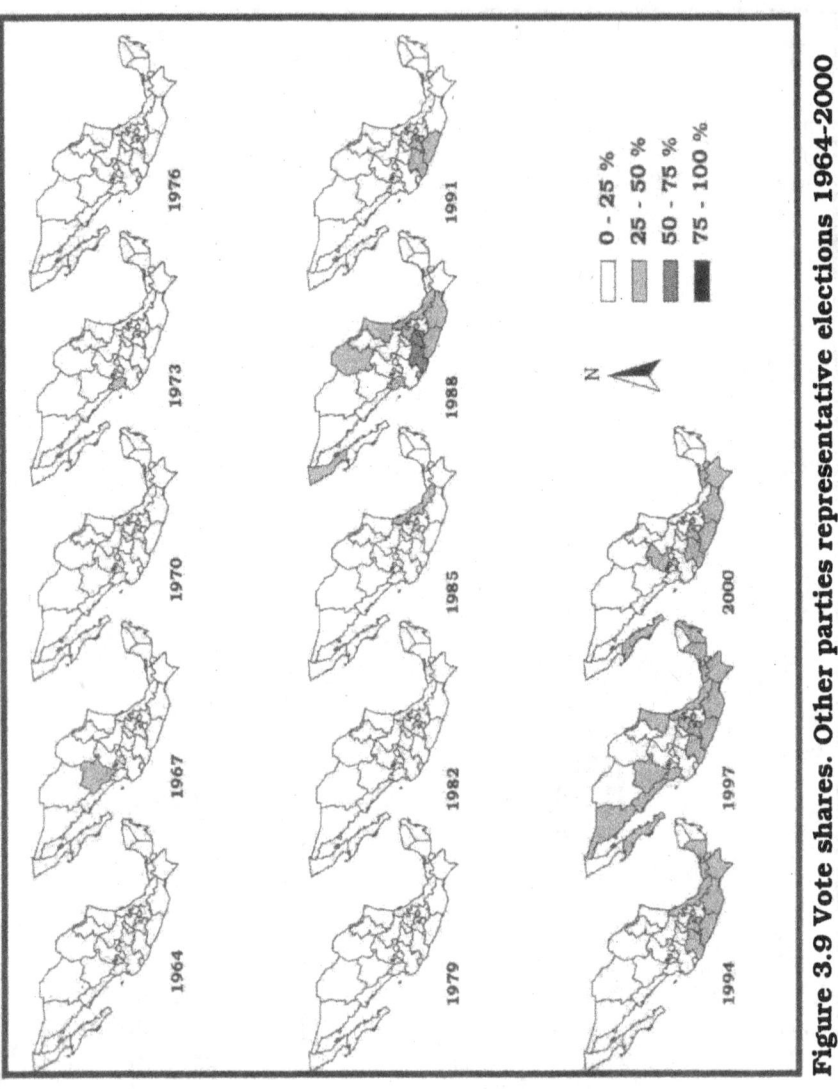

Figure 3.9 Vote shares. Other parties representative elections 1964-2000

District cast the highest shares for the Partido de la Revolucion Democratica, PRD.

Figures 3.10 to 3.12 present the dissimilarity indices for PAN in presidential, senatorial and representative elections, for all years. The greatest dissimilarity index initially was in the Federal District but it had diluted by the end of time span. Lower dissimilarity indexes were found in northern states, indicating more

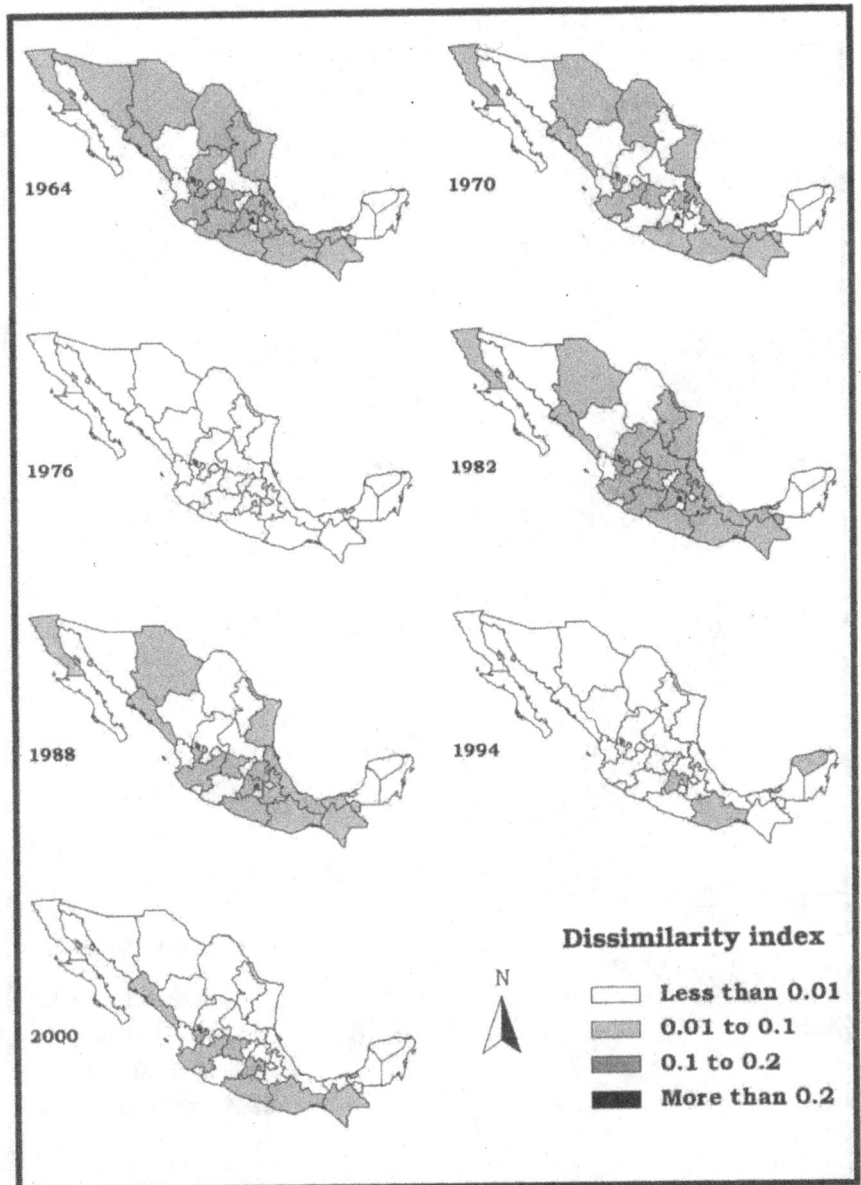

Figure 3.10 Dissimilarity index. PAN presidential elections 1964-2000

competitive politics. In the 1982 elections, a belt of low dissimilarity indices emerged from Coahuila to Nayarit with low dissimilarity values extending on to both sides of the belt.

26 *The Emergence of Multiparty Competition in Mexican Politics*

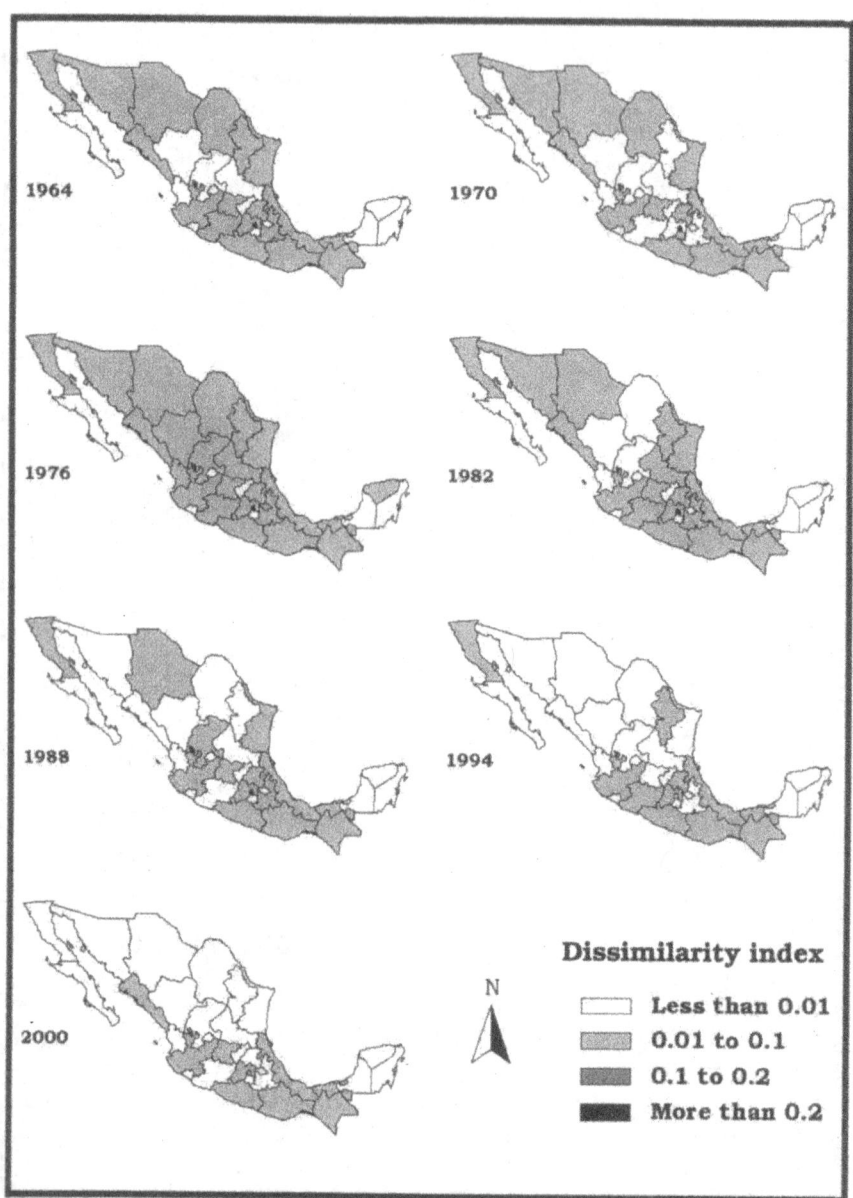

Figure 3.11 Dissimilarity index. PAN senatorial elections 1964-2000

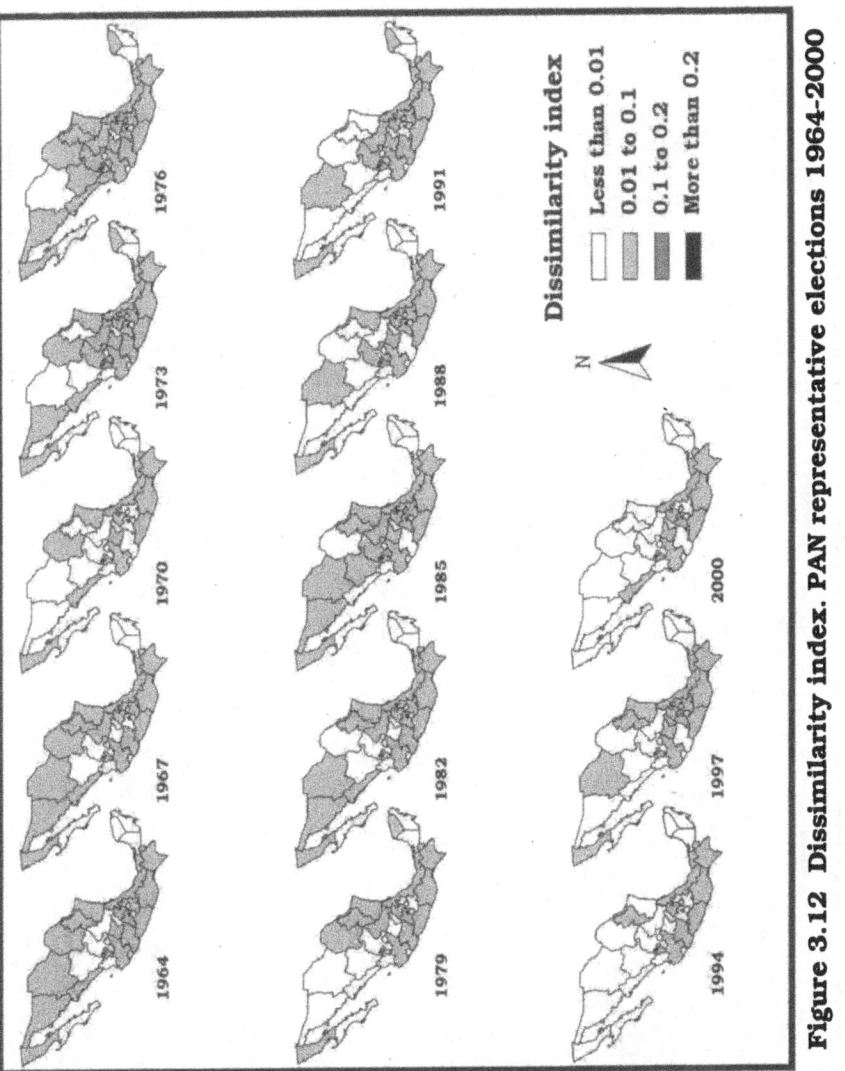

Figure 3.12 Dissimilarity index. PAN representative elections 1964-2000

Figures 3.13 to 3.15 show the dissimilarity indices for other parties, again for presidential, senatorial and representative elections for all years. The Federal District presents high initial values that diluted to 1994 but resurfaced in the 2000 elections, consistent with the changing fortunes of the PRD. The states with lowest dissimilarity indices were in the south of Mexico, and included as well the south of the Yucatan peninsula.

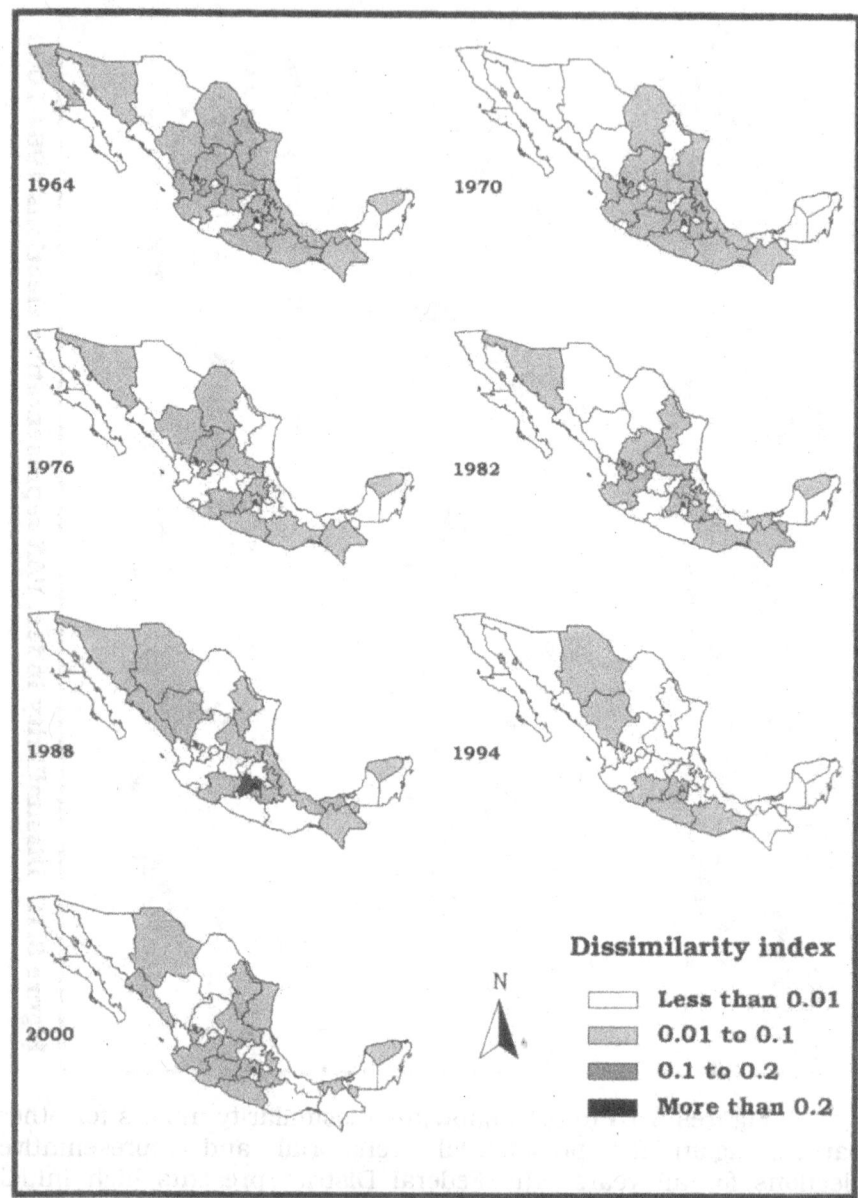

Figure 3.13 Dissimilarity index. Other parties presidential elections 1964-2000

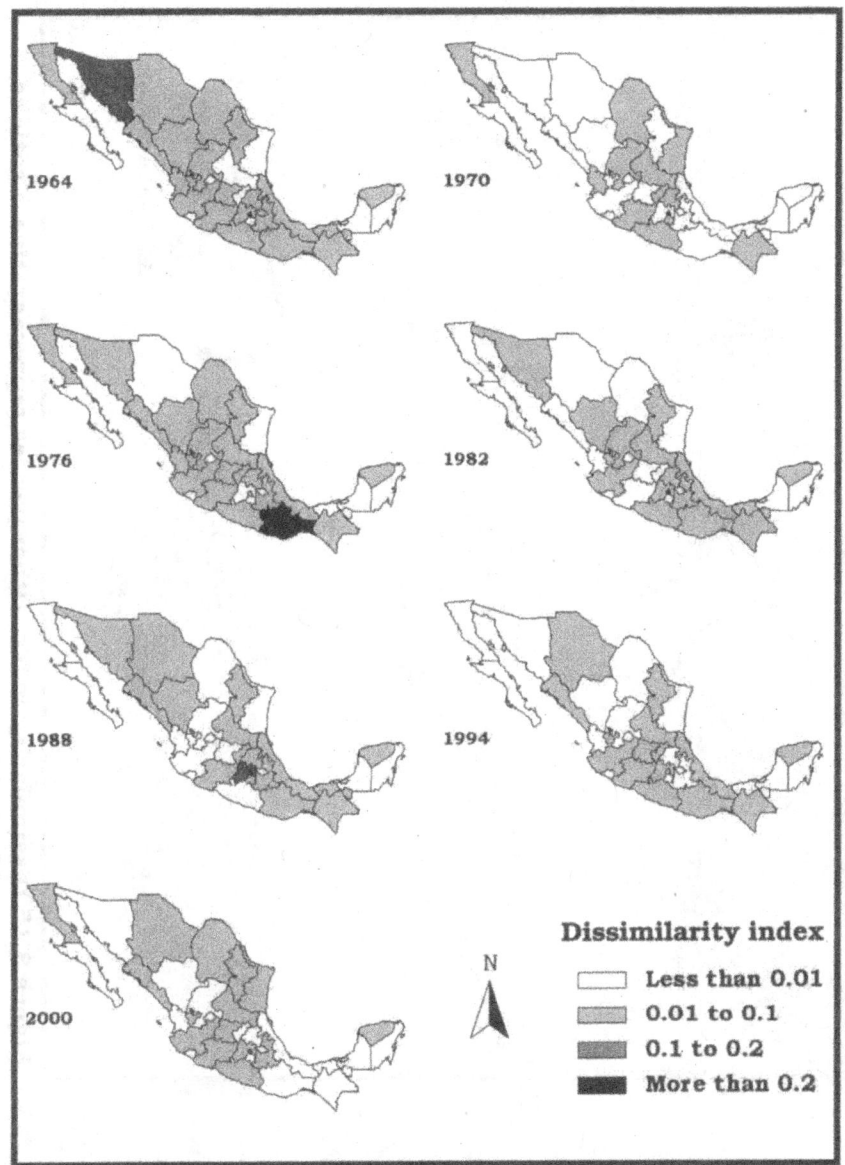

Figure 3.14 Dissimilarity index. Other parties senatorial elections 1964-2000

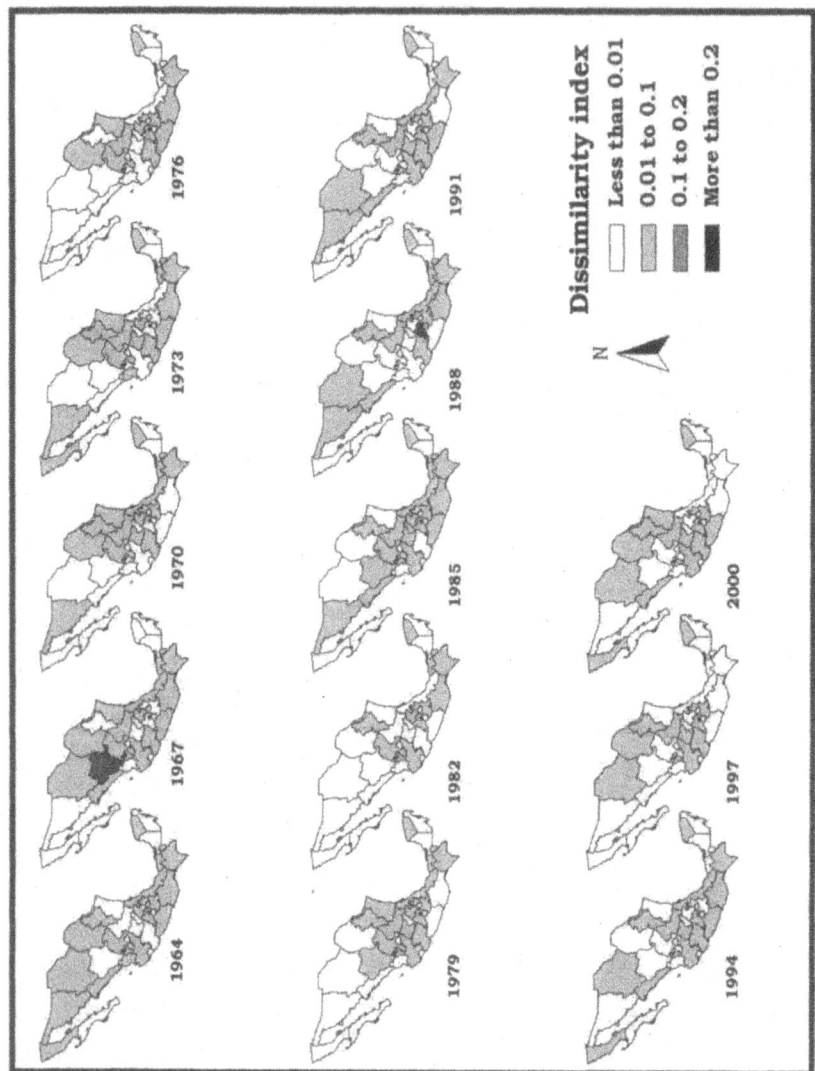

Figure 3.15 Dissimilarity index. Other parties representative elections 1964-2000

Testing for Spatial Autocorrelation

I computed the Ord-Getis' G_i^* statistics (Getis and Ord, 1992; Ord and Getis, 1995) for each of the dependent variables to determine whether spatial autocorrelation is present, indicating either the operation of a spatial diffusion process or strong regional bases of party support.

The Ord-Getis G_i^* measures local spatial association. It only works if there are no rearrangements, disappearances or emergences of units of analysis (O' Loughlin 1998:554). The measure is used to determine "to what extent each observation is clustered or resembles those around it" (Gleditsch and Ward 2000:14). It is given by:

$$G_i^* = \frac{\sum_j s_{ij} y_j - \sum_i (s_{ij} + s_o) \bar{y}}{\hat{\sigma}_y \sqrt{n \sum_j s_{ij}^2 - \sum_i s_{ij}^2 / (n-1)}}$$

and detects which entities have the strongest influence on neighbors in the area or region. In order to compute these spatial statistics, a matrix delineating all possible linkages among the units of analysis needs to be developed (Gleditsch and Ward 2000:8; O' Loughlin et al. 1998: 554). To this end, a contiguity matrix for the Mexican states was prepared.

After applying the G_i^* spatial autocorrelation was present in different degrees for all dependent variables, more obvious in the vote share variables and less so for the dissimilarity indices where clustering was mainly concentrated in central Mexico. Figures 3.16 to 3.18 present the G_i^* test statistics implemented on the dependent variable "vote shares for PAN." In 1976 PAN did not have a presidential candidate. Northern states show clusters of highly significant values prior to 1988. These vanish and are replaced by a cluster centering on Vicente Fox's home state of Guanajuato in 2000. Beginning in the 1980s clusters of low significant values emerged especially in the south, in Tabasco, Chiapas and Oaxaca.

Figures 3.19 to 3.21 show the G_i^* statistics for PRI. Because there were no contestants for PRI in the 1976 presidential elections the map shows little clustering of negative. The strong support for PRI along the southern Gulf states prevailed until the 1988 presidential and senatorial elections. For representative elections these clusters of support diluted in 1994 and 2000 elections but were sporadically present in the 1991 and 1997 elections. The northeast support (San Luis Potosi, Nuevo Leon and Tamaulipas) for PRI in the 1994 presidential elections shifted to the northwest in the 2000 elections. Sinaloa, Nayarit, Durango and Chihuahua retained support for PRI for all levels of representation. Clusters of low values were present in Cuauhtemoc Cardenas' home state, Michoacan.

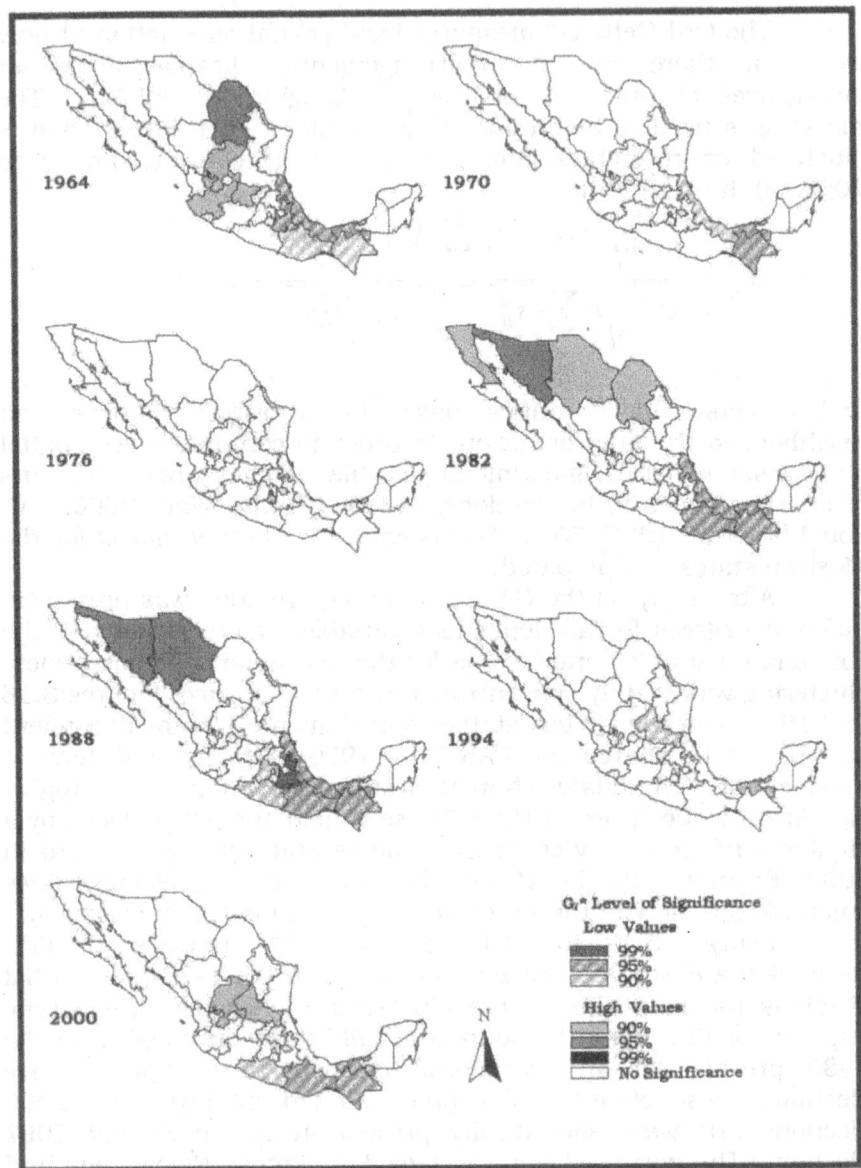

Figure 3.16 G_i^* test for vote shares. PAN presidential elections 1964-2000

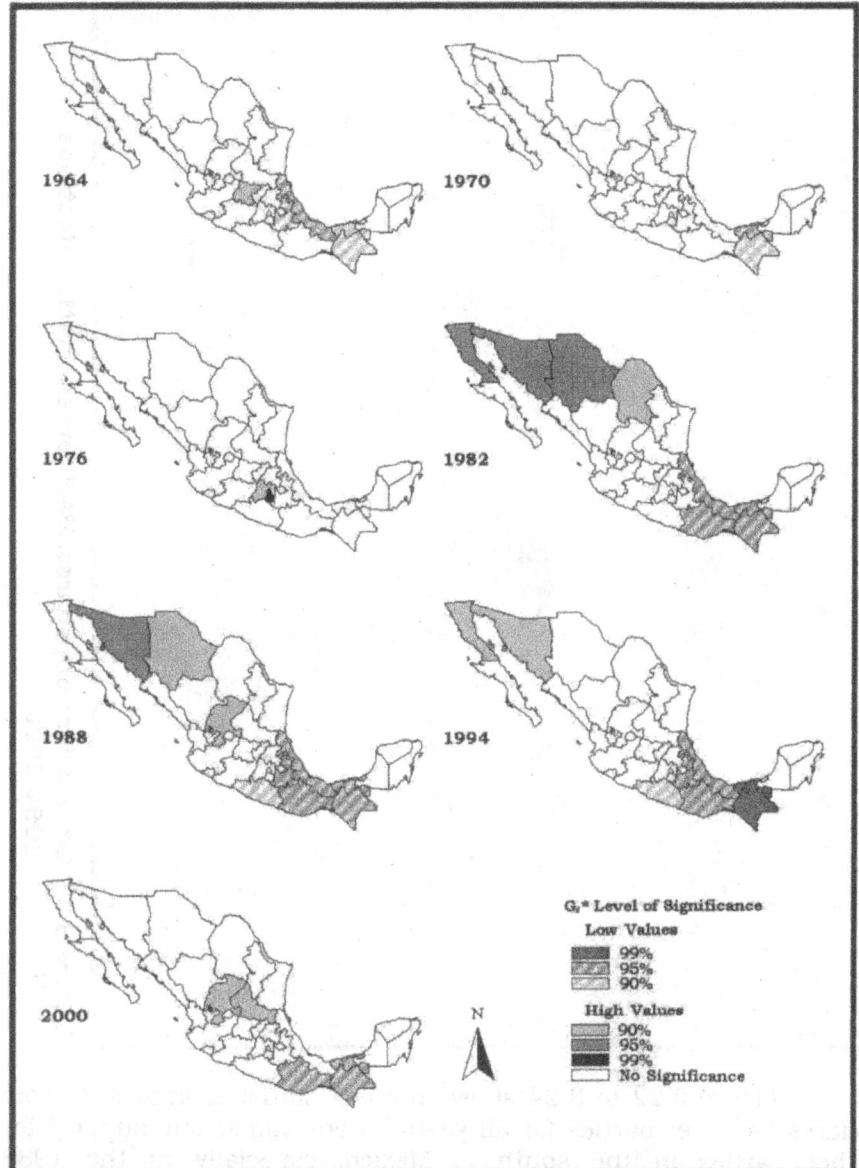

Figure 3.17 G_i^* **test for vote shares. PAN senatorial elections 1964-2000**

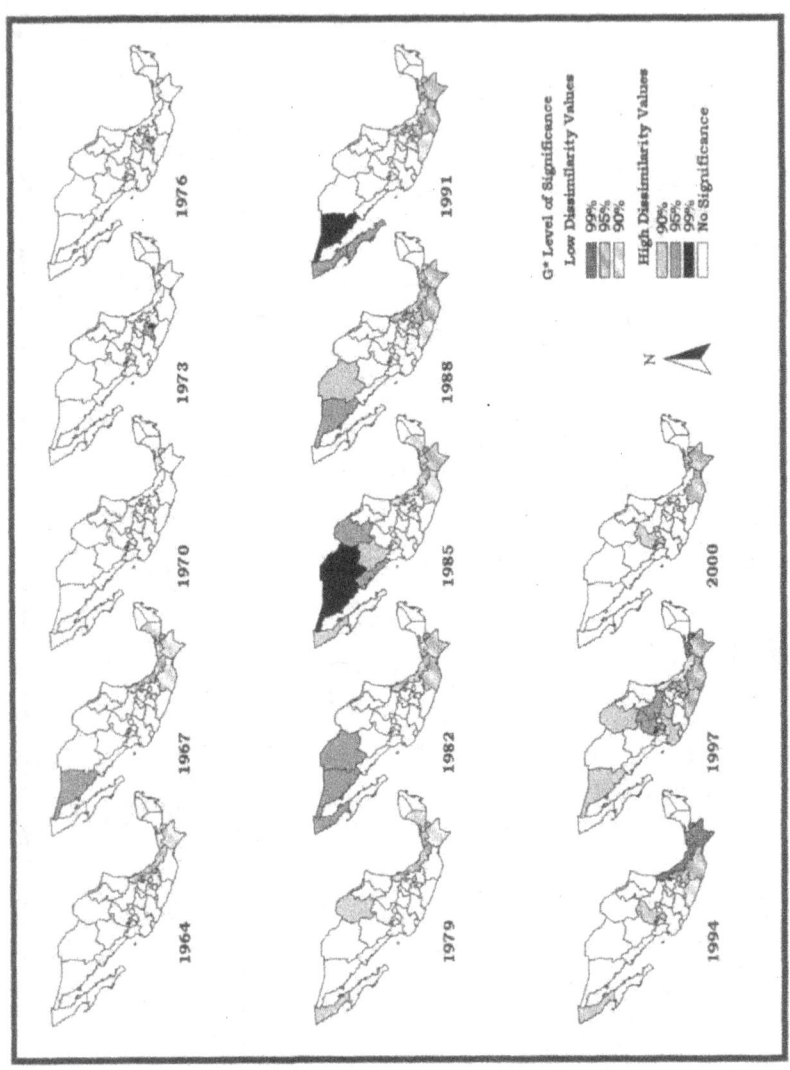

Figure 3.18 G_i^* test for vote shares. PAN representative elections 1964-2000

Figure 3.22 to 3.24 shows the test statistics applied to vote shares for other parties for all years. There was strong support for other parties in the south of Mexico, especially in the 1988 elections. Guerrero, Tabasco and Chiapas had predominant highly significant values. The northern states evidenced low support for other parties over the time span.

G_i^* statistics were also computed for the final set of dependent variables, the dissimilarity indices. The results are mapped for PAN in figures 3.25 to 3.27.

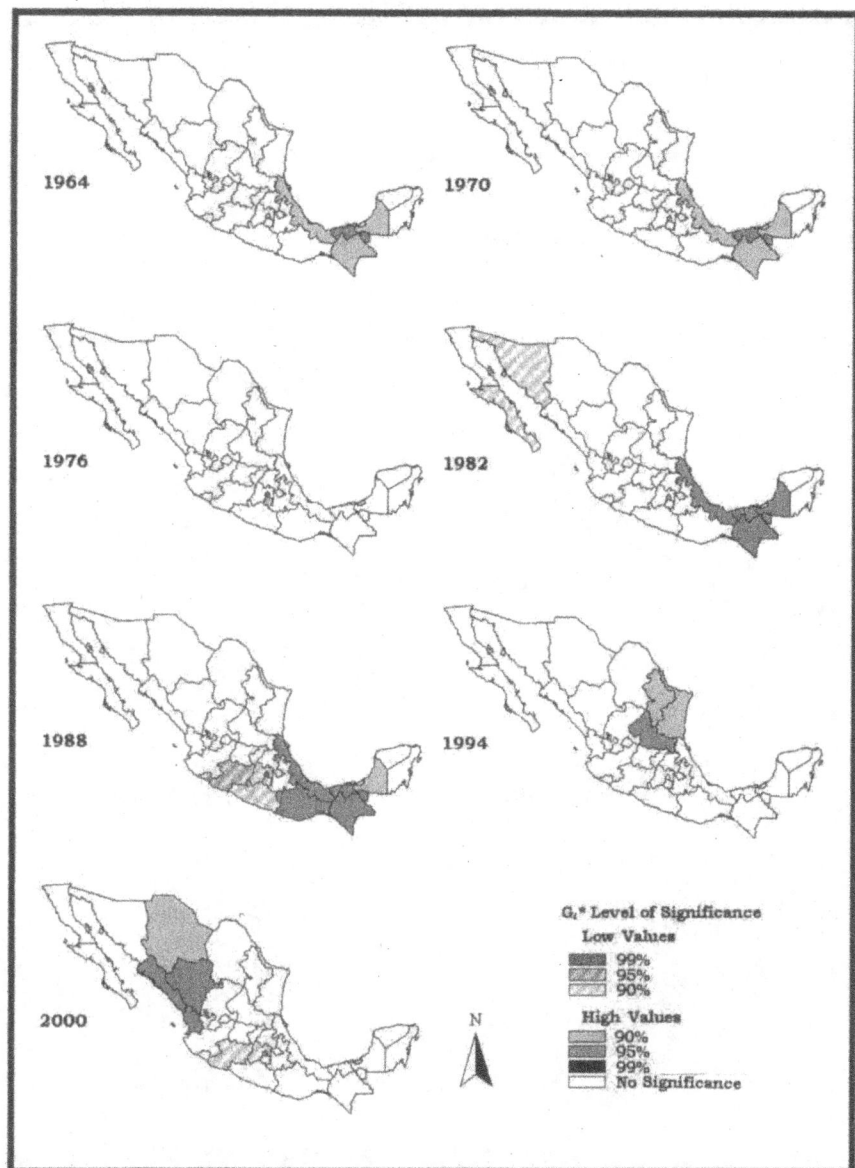

Figure 3.19 G_i^* test for vote shares. PRI presidential elections 1964-2000

The southern states remained dominated by PRI. The competitive states were in the north and the center. Figures 3.28 to 3.30 show the G_i^* test statistics.

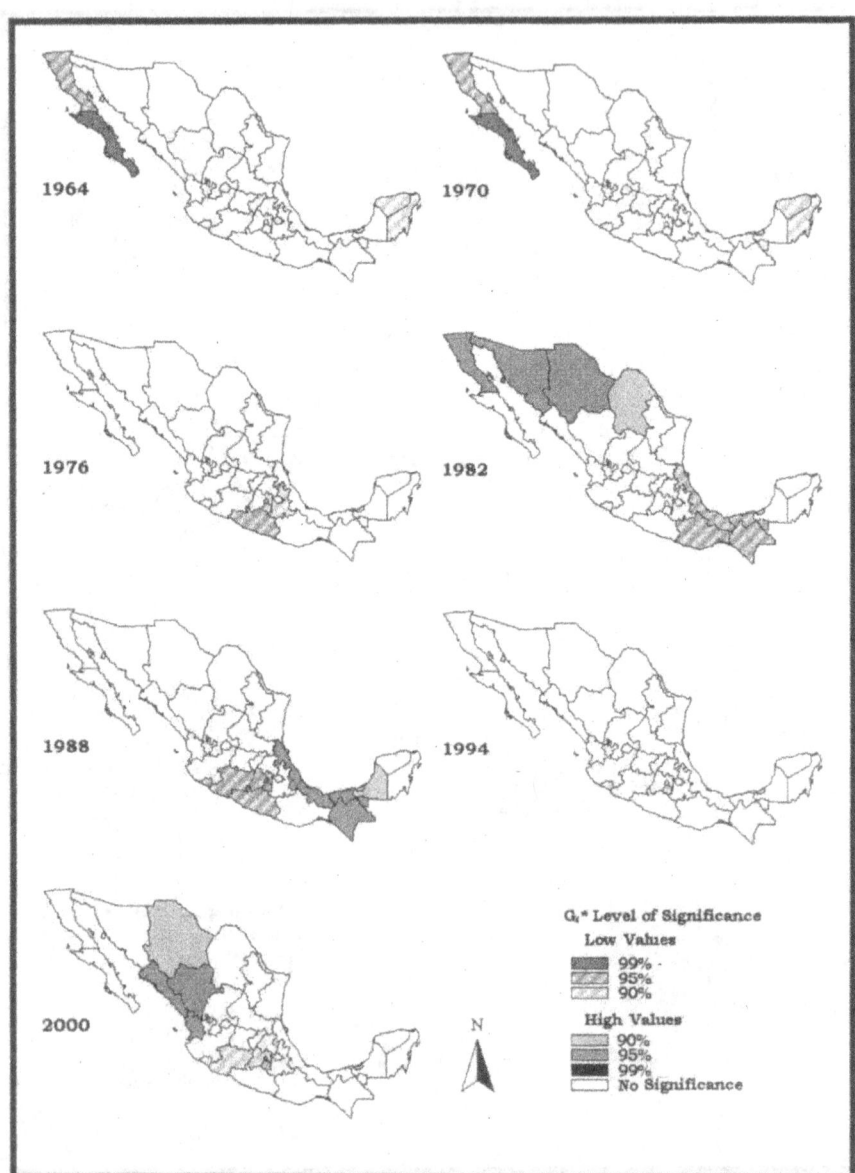

Figure 3.20 G_i^* **test for vote shares. PRI senatorial elections 1964-2000**

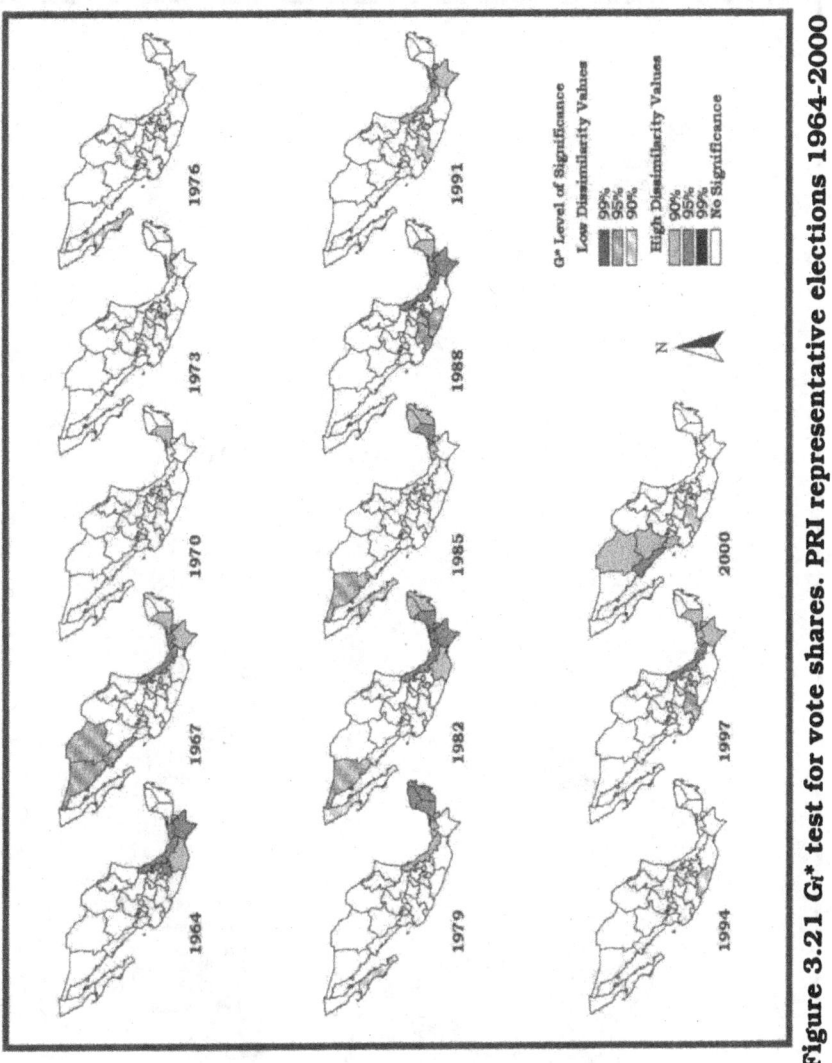

Figure 3.21 G$_i^*$ test for vote shares. PRI representative elections 1964-2000

The Federal District and the states that surround it are the only clusters of highly significant values, reflecting PRD dominance.

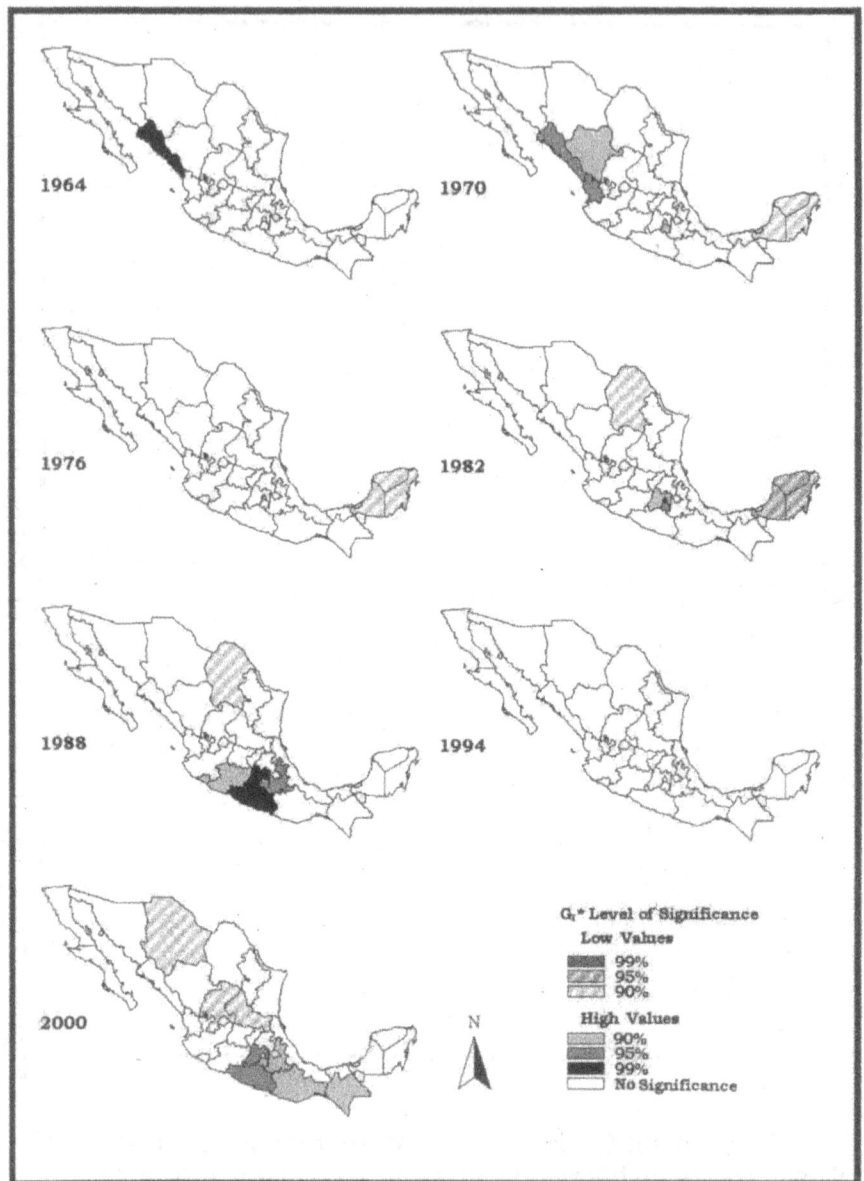

Figure 3.22 G_i^* test for vote shares. Other parties presidential elections 1964-2000

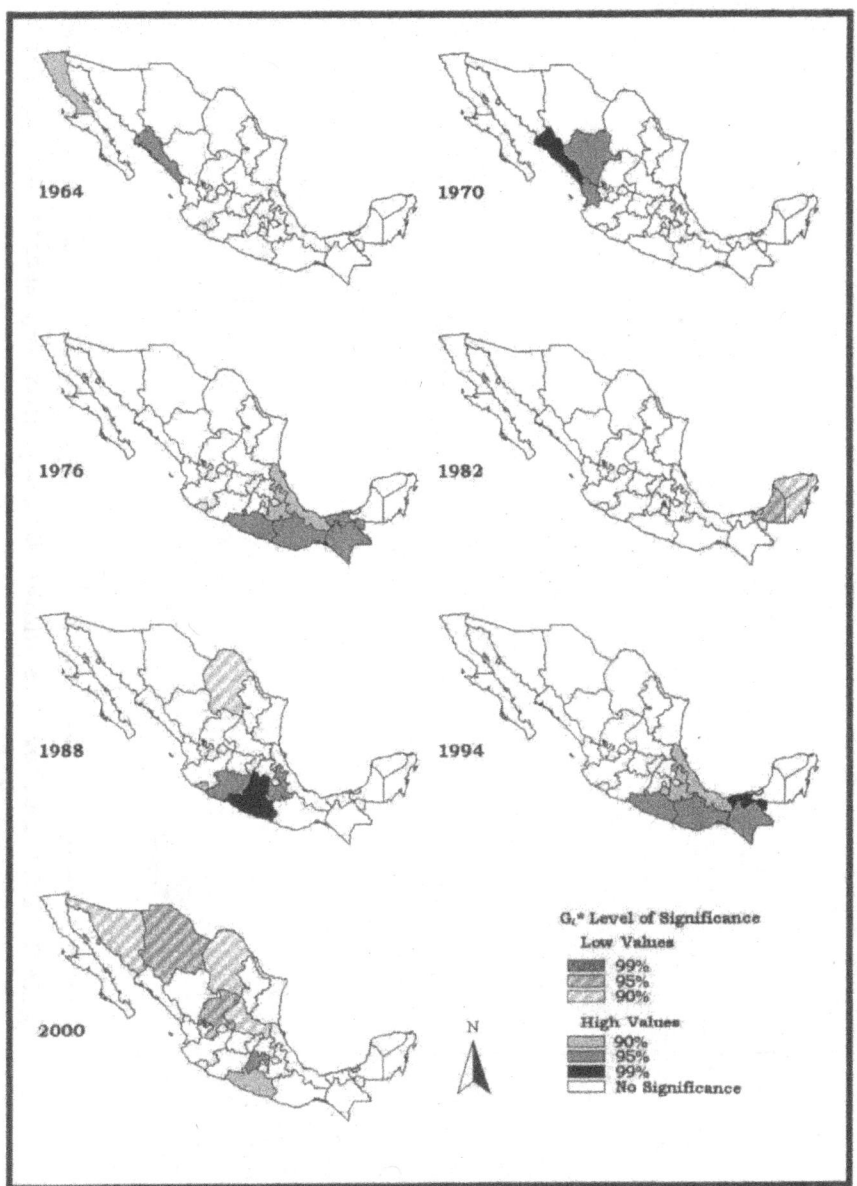

Figure 3.23 G_i^* test for vote shares. Other parties senatorial elections 1964-2000

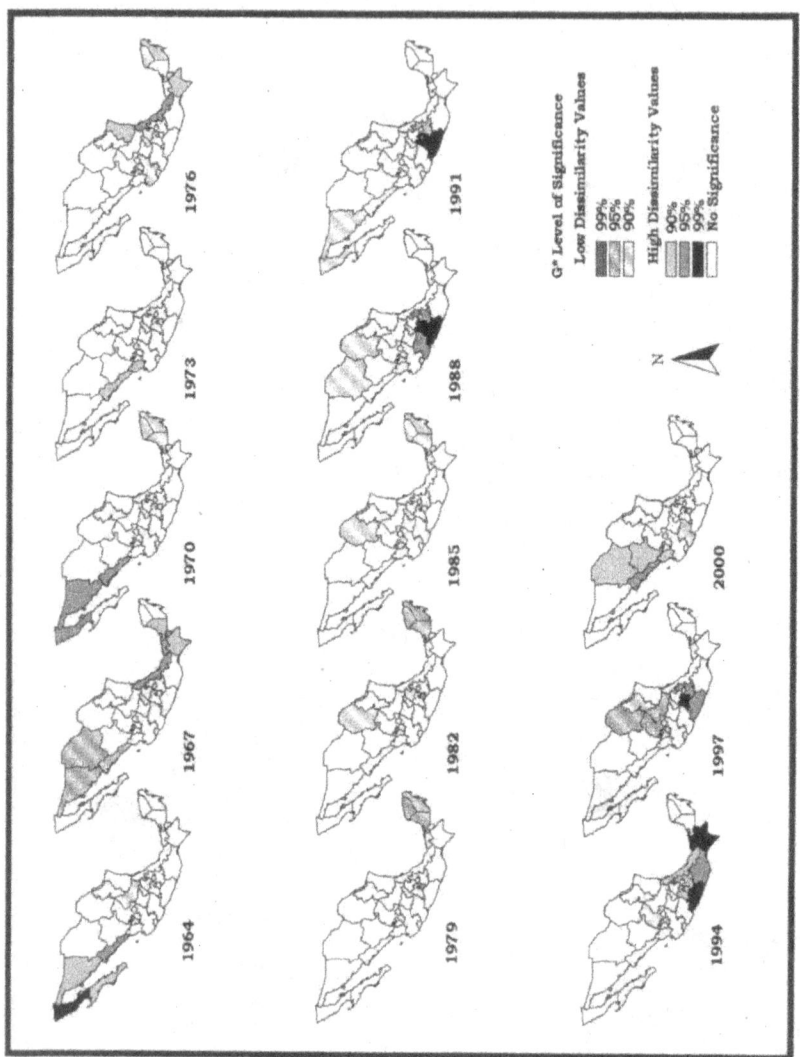

Figure 3.24 G_i^* test for vote shares. Other parties representative elections 1964-2000

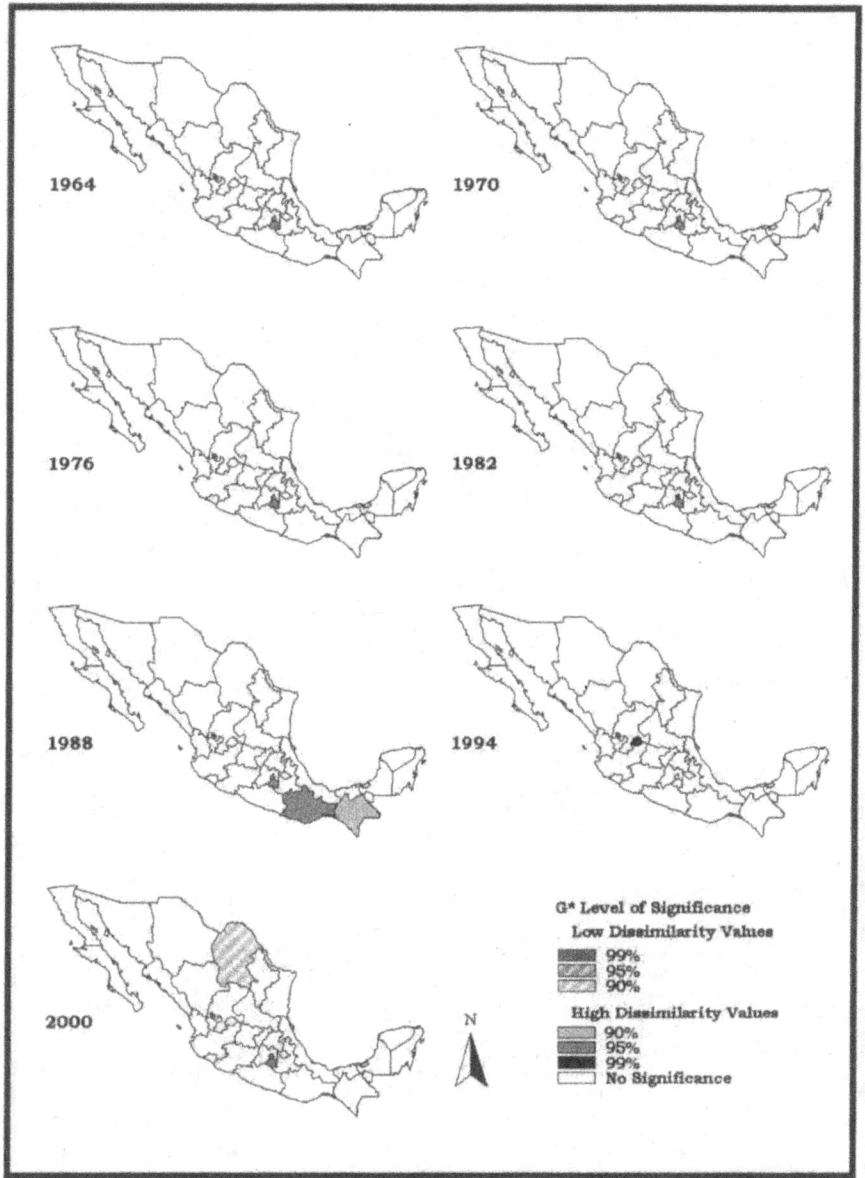

Figure 3.25 G_t^* test for dissimilarity index. PAN presidential elections 1964-2000

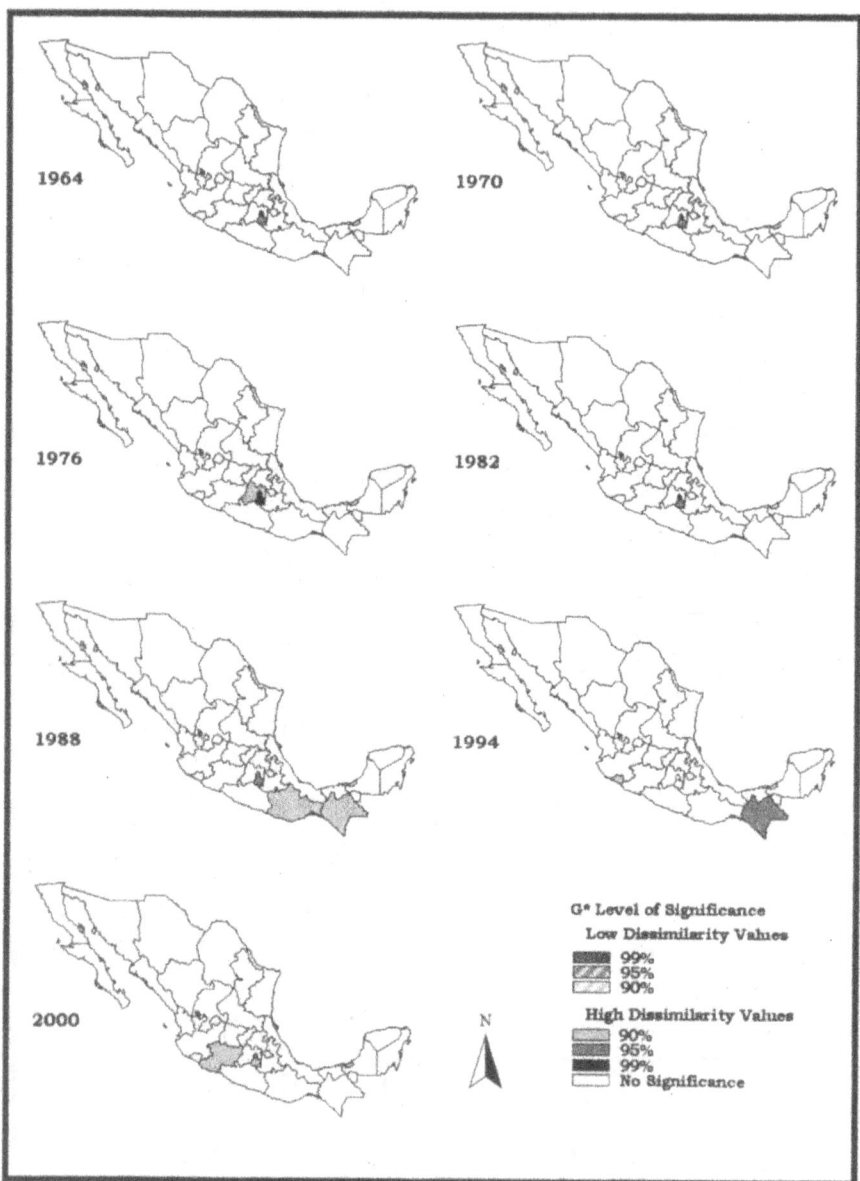

Figure 3.26 G_i^* test for dissimilarity index. PAN senatorial elections 1964-2000

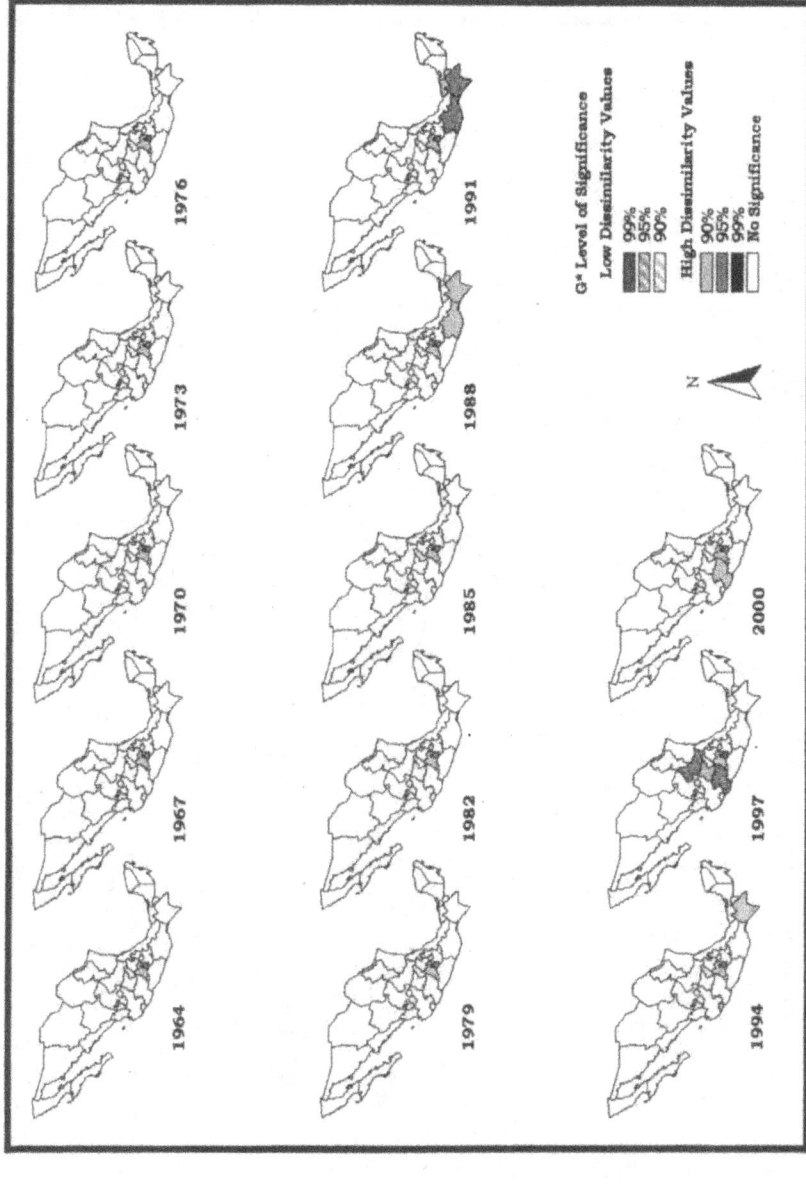

Figure 3.27 G_i^* test for dissimilarity index. PAN representative elections 1964-2000

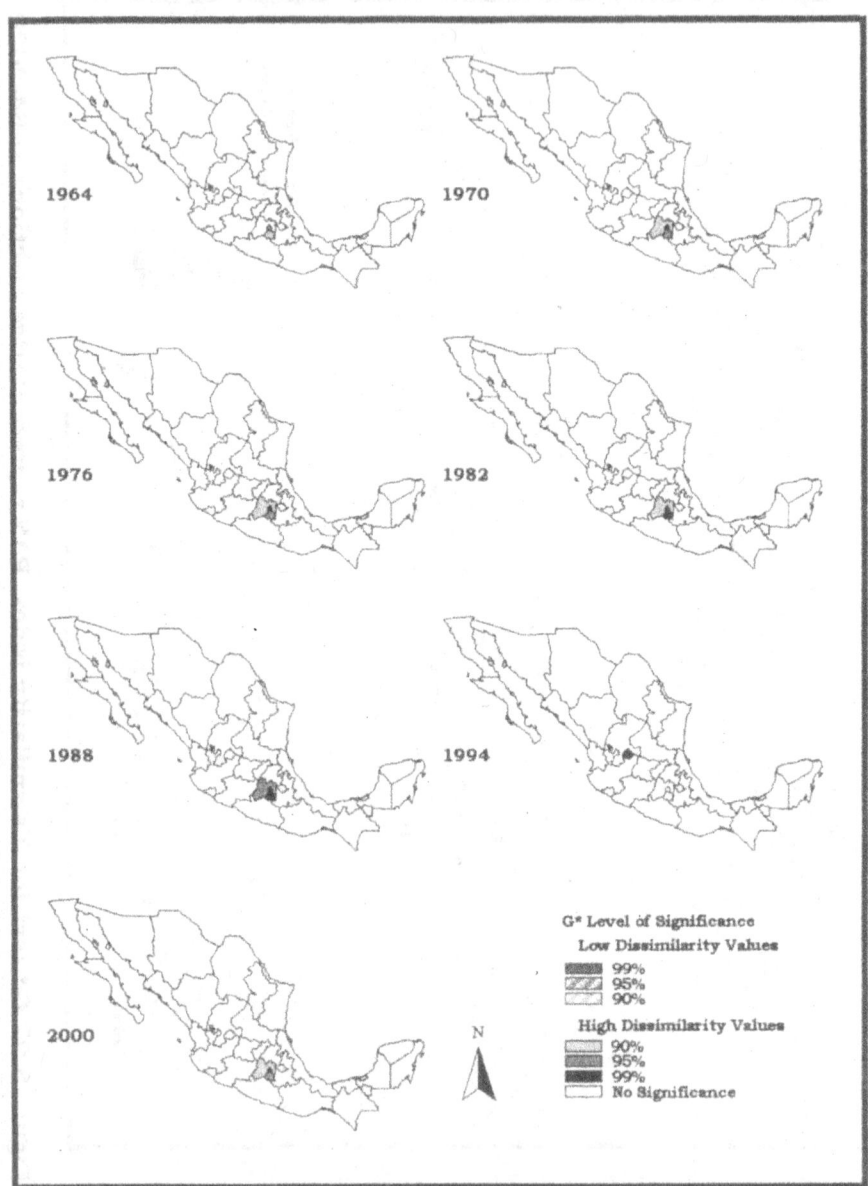

Figure 3.28 G_i^* test for dissimilarity index. Other parties presidential elections 1964-2000

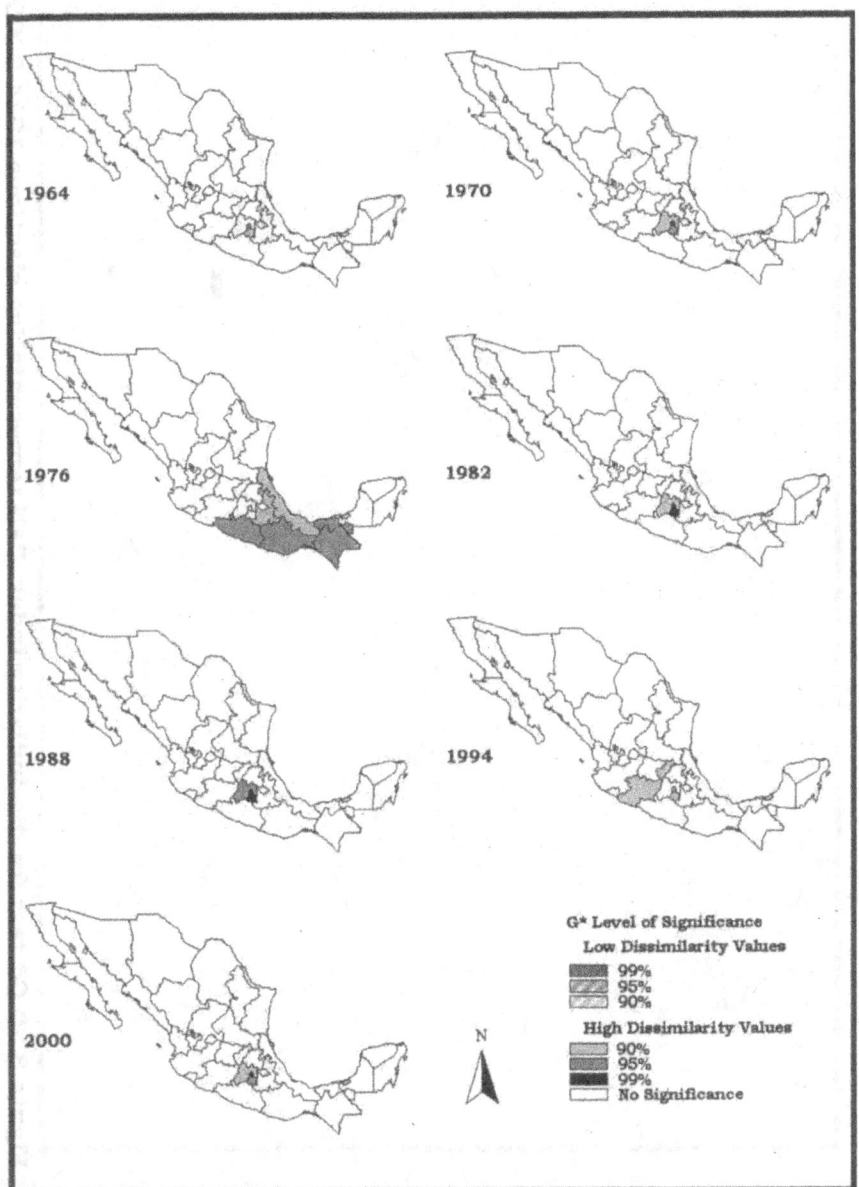

Figure 3.29 G_i^* test for dissimilarity index. Other parties senatorial elections 1964-2000

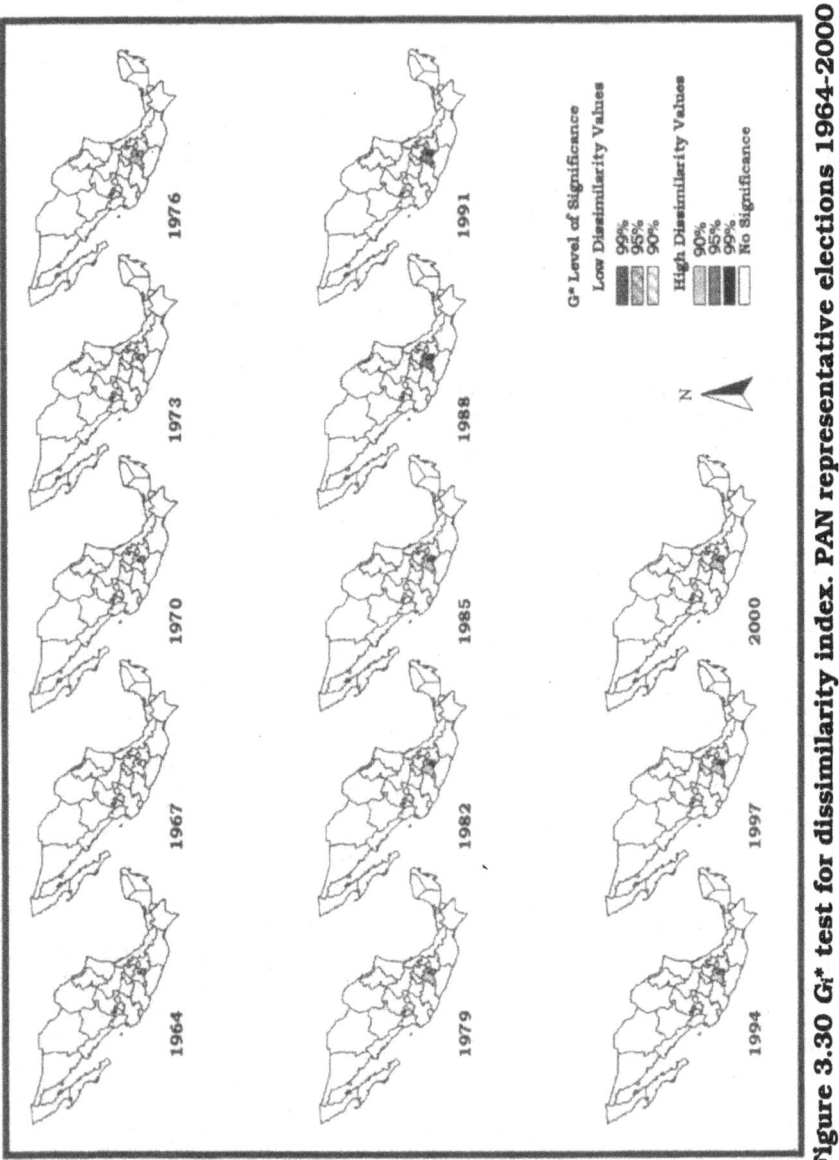

Figure 3.30 G_i^* test for dissimilarity index. PAN representative elections 1964-2000

Modeling Strategy

The previous results revealed significant spatial autocorrelation in the dependent variables. Does it arise from the influence of social and economic variables that are normally thought to influence behavior, which may themselves be spatially patterned, or is it the result either of a process of spatial diffusion of competitive politics or the influence of strong regional bases of party support? To answer these questions I proceed sequentially.

From the literature of political development I postulate that the dependent variables are a function of:

i. literacy levels in initial and ending conditions and the changes between them (EDU);
ii. economic development, measured by gross state product for initial and ending conditions, and for the changes between them (GSP);
iii. urbanization, i. e. in the proportion of urban population for initial and ending conditions and the changes between them (URB).

The model I explore (called "Socio Econ" in the tables and "base 1" in the maps) takes the general form:

$POL_{ijk} = f(GSP_i, URB_i, EDU_i)$, where the dependent variable

POL_{ijk} is either:

- SHR_{ijk} = vote shares for PAN, PRI and other parties, for all levels of representation, where k is either initial or ending conditions;
- $\Delta SHR_{ij\Delta k}$ = change in votes shares between initial and ending conditions for PRI, PAN and other parties; or
- $\Delta DISS_{ij\Delta k}$ = change in dissimilarity indices between initial and ending conditions for PRI, PAN and other parties.

The particular formulae are:

$SHR_{ijk} = f(GSP_{ik}, URB_{ik}, EDU_{ik})$,

$\Delta SHR_{ij\Delta k} = f(\Delta GSP_{i\Delta k}, \Delta URB_{i\Delta k}, \Delta EDU_{i\Delta k})$, and

$\Delta DISS_{ij\Delta k} = f(\Delta GSP_{i\Delta k}, \Delta URB_{i\Delta k}, \Delta EDU_{i\Delta k})$ for each i state, at j = level of representation.

G_i^* statistics computed for the residuals from these regressions reveal that spatial autocorrelation remains; i.e. it is not controlled by the socioeconomic variables. Thus, spatial autocorrelation may be there because a spatial diffusion process has worked to spread democratization from key states of origin to the rest of the country, or because there is strong regionalization of political beliefs and party power bases in Mexico.

Variables that might capture spatial diffusion were suggested by Berry (1972) viz.:

- hierarchical level of major city (HL), because "diffusion should spread outwards from core to periphery, from rich and more highly urbanized regions to those that are poor and less urbanized" (Berry et al. 2000);
- population potential (POPOT) to capture core-periphery differences;
- relative location (RELOC) which captures the information flow interactions among states, similar to the gravity principle of attraction.

Adding these variables to the basic socio-economic formulation, I construct a set of socio-spatial models, referred in the tables as Socio-spatial and called 'base 2' in the maps:

$SHR_{ijk} = f(GSP_{ik}, URB_{ik}, EDU_{ik}, HL_{ik}, POPOT_{ik}, RELOC_{ik})$,

$\Delta SHR_{ij\Delta k} = f(\Delta GSP_{i\Delta k}, \Delta URB_{i\Delta k}, \Delta EDU_{i\Delta k}, HL_{i\Delta k}, POPOT_{i\Delta k}, RELOC_{i\Delta k})$,

$\Delta DISS_{ij\Delta k} = f(\Delta GSP_{i\Delta k}, \Delta URB_{i\Delta k}, \Delta EDU_{i\Delta k}, HL_{i\Delta k}, POPOT_{i\Delta k}, RELOC_{i\Delta k})$

The principal types of regionalization that have been discussed in Mexico are:

- Cultural: in the proportion of dialectically monolingual population by state (INDLANG);
- Economic: in the form of industrialized north, depressed south, where states with oil extraction industry might differ from states with non-extractive industries (dummy variable OIL equals 1 if is a state with oil extractive industry, 0 otherwise);
- Physical:
  - political borders with USA, Guatemala, Belize (dummy variable BORDER equals 1 if the states has political borders, 0 otherwise);
  - division of the territory by cardinal point characteristics (dummy variable CARDINAL equals 1 if states belong to Central, North, South, West Central states, 0 for East Central states);

- littoral states (dummy variable LITTORAL equals 1 if states are along the Pacific or Atlantic coast, 0 otherwise);
- 13 physical-geographical regions (dummy variable REGIONS equals 1 if states are included within regions I through XII, 0 if they belong to region XIII).

Table 3.1 describes the physical variables in more detail. Adding these variables to the socio-economic models leads to the following socio-regional models, called in the tables Socio-Border (named 'Border 1' in the maps), Socio-Cardinal ('Cardinal 1'), Socio Littoral ('Littoral 1') and Socio-Regions ('Regions 1').

The formulae are:

$$SHR_{ijk} = f\ (GSP_{ik},\ URB_{ik},\ EDU_{ik},\ INDLANG_{ik},\ D_iOIL,\ D_iBORDER,\ D_iCARDINAL,\ D_iLITTORAL,\ D_iREGIONS),$$

$$\Delta SHR_{ij\Delta k} = f\ (\Delta GSP_{i\Delta k},\ \Delta URB_{i\Delta k},\ \Delta EDU_{i\Delta k},\ INDLANG_{i\Delta k},\ D_iOIL,\ D_iBORDER,\ D_iCARDINAL,\ D_iLITTORAL,\ D_iREGIONS),\ \text{and}$$

$$\Delta DISS_{ij\Delta k} = f\ (\Delta GSP_{i\Delta k},\ \Delta URB_{i\Delta k},\ \Delta EDU_{i\Delta k},\ INDLANG_{i\Delta k},\ D_iOIL,\ D_iBORDER,\ D_iCARDINAL,\ D_iLITTORAL,\ D_iREGIONS).$$

In order to avoid excessive overlapping of states, the dummy variables border, cardinal, littoral and regions are mutually exclusive in the regressions.

A final set of models contains both spatial and regional variables and follows the same exclusion rule as in the socio-spatial models. These "overall" models are called in the tables Border Overall ('Border 2' in the maps), Cardinal Overall ('Cardinal 2'), Littoral Overall ('Littoral 2') and Regions Overall ('Regions 2'). The formulae are:

$$SHR_{ijk} = f\ (GSP_{ik},\ URB_{ik},\ EDU_{ik},\ HL_{ik},\ POPOT_{ik},\ RELOC_{ik},\ INDLANG_{ik},\ D_iOIL,\ D_iBORDER,\ D_iCARDINAL,\ D_iLITTORAL,\ D_iREGIONS),$$

$$\Delta SHR_{ij\Delta k} = f\ (\Delta GSP_{i\Delta k},\ \Delta URB_{i\Delta k},\ \Delta EDU_{i\Delta k},\ HL_{\Delta k},\ POPOT_{i\Delta k},\ RELOC_{i\Delta k},\ INDLANG_{i\Delta k},\ D_iOIL,\ D_iBORDER,\ D_iCARDINAL,\ D_iLITTORAL,\ D_iREGIONS),\ \text{and}$$

$$\Delta DISS_{ij\Delta k} = f\ (\Delta GSP_{i\Delta k},\ \Delta URB_{i\Delta k},\ \Delta EDU_{i\Delta k},\ HL_{\Delta k},\ POPOT_{i\Delta k},\ RELOC_{i\Delta k},\ INDLANG_{i\Delta k},\ D_iOIL,\ D_iBORDER,\ D_iCARDINAL,\ D_iLITTORAL,\ D_iREGIONS).$$

Ord-Getis G_i^* statistics are computed for residuals from each of the spatially enriched models of democratization. When the addition of spatial or regional controls removes residual spatial autocorrelations, clues are provided about the circumstances under which competitive party politics has emerged in Mexico.

Table 3.1 Physical regionalization: categorical variables

BORDER VARIABLES (0,1)
    a) States along Northern political border (US).
    b) States along Southern political border.

CARDINAL ORIENTATION (0,1)
    a) Northern states.
    b) Southern states.
    c) Central states.
    d) Central western states.

LITTORAL VARIABLES (0,1)
    a) Atlantic.
    b) Pacific.

REGION DUMMIES (0,1)
    I   Baja California peninsula.
    II   Central Plateau.
    III   Great plains of North America.
    IV   North Gulf plains.
    V   Northern Sierras and plains.
    VI   Southern Gulf coast.
    VII   Occidental Sierra Madre.
    VIII   Oriental Sierra Madre.
    IX   Southern Sierra Madre.
    X   Sierras of Chiapas and Guatemala.
    XI   Sonoran plains.
    XII   Yucatán peninsula.
    XIII   Neo-Volcanic system (omitted region, base case).

Chapter 4

Shares of the Popular Vote

This chapter focuses upon vote shares for PAN, PRI and other parties in 1964 ("initial conditions") and in 2000 ("ending conditions") in presidential, senatorial and representative elections. The purpose is to isolate the factors that may have contributed to spatial variations in vote shares, to determine whether there may be spatial autocorrelations, and to gain some understanding of the radical shifts in voting patterns and party support that have unfolded in the 1964–2000 time span.

Modeling

Ten models were formulated to capture the effects of different sets of variables on PAN, PRI and other parties' vote shares:

Two "Base" Models

The first base model regresses vote share on three socio-economic variables and the second on these three variables plus the three key spatial variables suggested by diffusion theory:

- socio-economic: $f\,(GSP_{tk}, URB_{tk}, EDU_{tk})$
- socio-spatial: $f\,(GSP_{tk}, URB_{tk}, EDU_{tk}, HL_{tk}, POPOT_{tk}, RELOC_{tk})$.

Eight Models

These eight models enhance the base models with two variables that capture regional differences in the dialectically monolingual indigenous population and in oil wealth, together with sets of dummy variables designed to capture the presence of local or regional pockets of party support. These are:

Border models These two models have the form:

- socio-border: $f(\ GSP_{tk},\ URB_{tk},\ EDU_{tk},\ INDLANG_{tk},\ D_tOIL,\ D_iBORDER)$

- border overall: $f(\Delta GSP_{i\Delta k},\ \Delta URB_{i\Delta k},\ \Delta EDU_{i\Delta k},\ HL_{\Delta k},\ POPOT_{i\Delta k},\ RELOC_{i\Delta k},\ INDLANG_{i\Delta k},\ D_tOIL,\ D_iBORDER)$.

Cardinal models These two models test for cardinal regionalization:

- socio-cardinal: $f(GSP_{tk},\ URB_{tk},\ EDU_{tk},\ INDLANG_{tk},\ D_tOIL,\ D_tCARDINAL)$

- cardinal overall: $f\ (\Delta GSP_{i\Delta k},\ \Delta URB_{i\Delta k},\ \Delta EDU_{i\Delta k},\ INDLANG_{i\Delta k},\ D_tOIL,\ D_tCARDINAL)$.

Littoral models Two models testing whether or not littoral location matters:

- socio-littoral: $f(\Delta GSP_{i\Delta k},\ \Delta URB_{i\Delta k},\ \Delta EDU_{i\Delta k},\ INDLANG_{i\Delta k},\ D_tOIL,\ D_iLITTORAL)$

- littoral overall: $f\ (\Delta GSP_{i\Delta k},\ \Delta URB_{i\Delta k},\ \Delta EDU_{i\Delta k},\ HL_{\Delta k},\ POPOT_{i\Delta k},\ RELOC_{i\Delta k},\ INDLANG_{i\Delta k},\ D_tOIL,\ D_iLITTORAL)$.

Regionalization models Finally, two models which control region-specific variance:

- socio-regions: $f(\Delta GSP_{i\Delta k},\ \Delta URB_{i\Delta k},\ \Delta EDU_{i\Delta k},\ INDLANG_{i\Delta k},\ D_tOIL,\ D_iREGIONS)$

- regions overall: $f(\Delta GSP_{i\Delta k},\ \Delta URB_{i\Delta k},\ \Delta EDU_{i\Delta k},\ HL_{\Delta k},\ POPOT_{i\Delta k},\ RELOC_{i\Delta k},\ INDLANG_{i\Delta k},\ D_tOIL,\ D_iREGIONS)$.

The purpose in estimating the successive spatial and regional models was, of course, to determine whether or not diffusion processes have been at work and whether or not specific regional factors are present. The residuals for these ten models were tested with G_i^* statistics in order to determine whether spatial and/or regional variables had removed spatial autocorrelation and therefore the spatial elements of the process.

There are many analyses. The presentation begins with the Partido Accion Nacional, PAN, and with initial condition vote shares in presidential elections, which are then compared with ending conditions. The comparison is repeated for the PAN vote in senatorial and representative elections. The discussion then turns to the Partido Revolucionario Institucional, PRI, where the sequence of analyses is repeated, followed by the same sequence for the other parties.

Partido Accion Nacional, PAN

Chihuahua and Baja California Norte were the two states were the PAN cast the most votes in the initial 1964 conditions, for all three levels of representation, while Tabasco was the state that had the lowest vote shares for the three levels of representation. In the 2000 presidential election, Guerrero and Tabasco delivered the lowest vote shares for PAN in all elections while Guanajuato (Vicente Fox's home state), Aguascalientes and Jalisco gave PAN the highest shares for all levels of representation.

Initial Conditions, PAN Presidential Elections

The states of Sonora, Jalisco, Queretaro, Aguascalientes and Guanajuato all cast more than 50 percent of their votes for PAN's presidential candidate, while Guerrero was the only state with less than 20 percent of the votes cast for PAN.

No variables were significant in the 1964 base models for PAN's presidential vote. However, the urbanization and indigenous language variables became significant once regional controls were introduced. PAN's vote share was greater both in the more highly urbanized states and in those with the greater percent of monolingual indigenous population. Table 4.1 shows the coefficients and the levels of significance for the ten models.

The significance of the variable "north" with a negative sign reflects the fact that PAN had less votes in the U.S. border states in 1964. Likewise, the vote share was low in the littoral states while states along regions II and V had significant higher vote shares than those states in the neo-volcanic system. The final pair of region-specific models reveals that while broader spatial patterns were present, region-specific variance did exist as well in 1964.

Test for spatial autocorrelation   Residuals from each of the regressions were tested using the G_i^* statistic in order to determine whether the variables in the models captured the spatial behavior of the dependent variable. Figure 4.1 shows these residuals for all ten

Table 4.1 Coefficients in initial vote share models: presidential election for PAN, 1964

Independent Variables	BASE MODEL		BORDER		CARDINAL		LITTORAL		REGIONS	
	Socio Econ	Socio Spatial	Socio Border	Border Overall	Socio Cardinal	Cardinal Overall	Socio Littoral	Littoral Overall	Socio Regions	Regions Overall
Literacy	0.022	0.554	0.368	0.964	1.734	1.820	-0.084	-0.876	-1.875	0.249
Gross State Product	1.980	0.857	1.883	0.167	1.501	0.603	1.595	1.555	2.663	1.426
Urbanization	1.617	1.266	2.053ᵃ	2.457ᵇ	1.967ᵃ	2.529ᵇ	2.138ᵇ	2.212ᵇ	2.116ᵇ	0.921
Hierarchical		-0.752		-0.614		-3.509		-2.765		-1.534
Population Potential		0.018		0.027		-0.008		-0.005		0.022
Relative Location		-0.022		-0.045		-0.025		-0.016		-0.032
Indigenous Language			1.589ᵇ	1.686ᶜ	2.384ᶜ	2.375ᶜ	1.555ᵇ	1.413ᵃ	0.652	0.138
Oil State			-0.003	0.006	-0.006	0.009	-0.019	-0.028	-0.044	-0.039
BORDER										
North			-0.025	-0.075ᵃ						
South			-0.046	-0.054						
CARDINAL										
North					-0.062	-0.160ᶜ				
South					-0.038	-0.102ᶜ				
Central					-0.042	-0.086ᵇ				
West Central					0.052	0.024				
LITTORAL										
Atlantic							-0.046	-0.068ᵇ		
Pacific							-0.040	-0.070ᵇ		
REGIONS										
Region I									0.045	0.027
Region II									0.101ᵇ	0.106ᵃ
Region III									0.086	0.054
Region IV									-0.020	-0.055
Region V									0.155ᵇ	0.098
Region VI									-0.002	-0.030
Region VII									0.018	-0.017
Region VIII									-0.012	-0.001
Region IX									-0.024	0.013
Region X									-0.048	-0.027
Region XI									-0.067	-0.128
Region XII									-0.001	0.004
Constant	0.005	0.294	-0.065	0.510	-0.155	0.352	-0.018	0.384	0.097	0.493
R-Squared	0.313	0.369	0.472	0.566	0.592	0.742	0.515	0.614	0.741	0.804

ᵃ Significant at 0.1 level, ᵇ at 0.05 level, ᶜ at 0.01 level.

models. There is statistically significant clustering in the two base models, parts of which are removed by the addition of successive spatial and regional variables. This leads to the following view of initial support conditions for PAN:

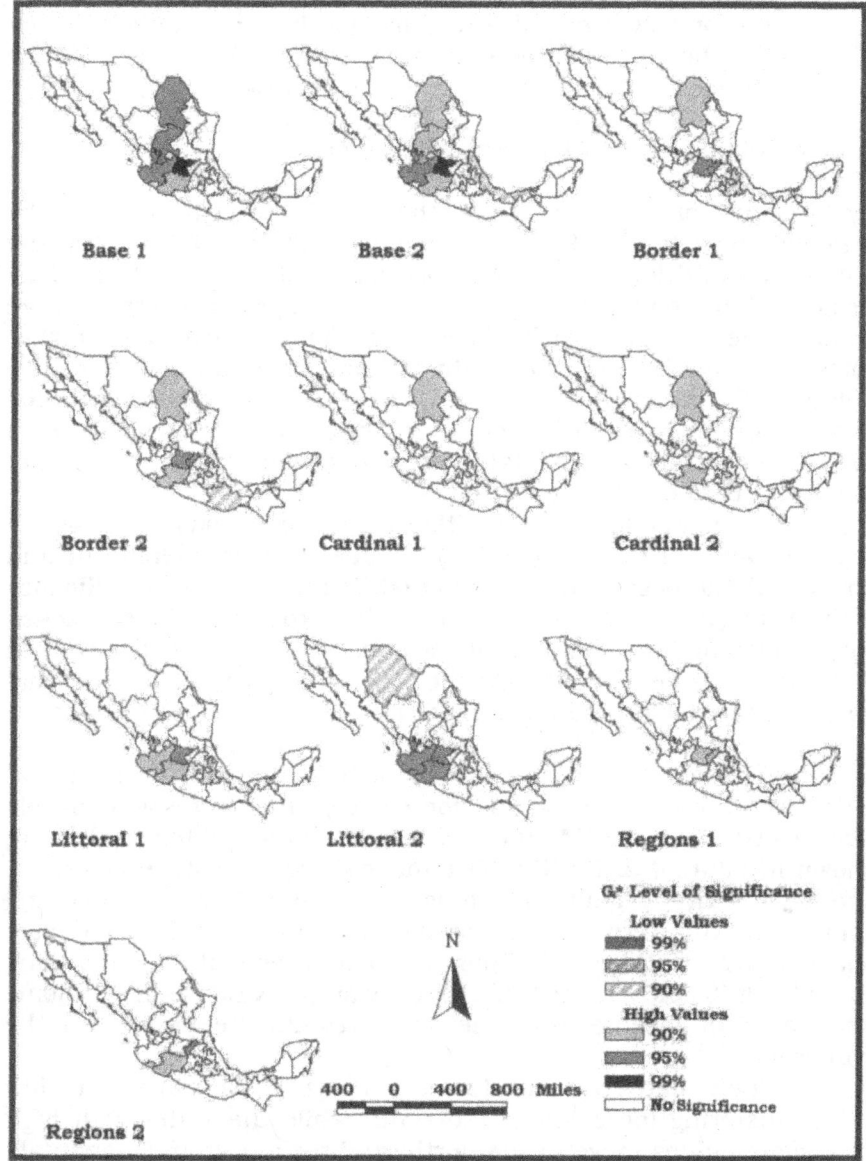

Figure 4.1 G_i^* test for residuals. PAN vote share presidential election 1964

- greater vote shares where the level of urbanization and the monolingual indigenous population are greater;
- no evidence of the prior operation of any process of spatial diffusion;

- but some evidence of regionalization in party support: a belt of higher vote shares extending from Coahuila through the interior states to Michoacan in the southwest.

Ending Conditions, PAN Presidential Elections

By the end of the time span the conditions surrounding the presidential vote for PAN had changed. Table 4.2 shows the coefficients and levels of significance for the ten tier 2000 models. Urbanization remained significant. Once spatial controls were applied, the oil state variable became significant: there were higher votes for the PAN in those states that have an oil extractive industry. Cardinal regionalization is still present in this year; the negative sign indicates that votes were lower in every cardinal region than the central eastern states. Region-specific variance was not present at the end of the process.

The main change from initial to final conditions is the switch of significance of the indigenous language variable. Significant and positive at the beginning of the period, it turns to non-significance with a negative sign at the end. Oil extractive states lacked significance at the beginning of the process but not at the end, at least within some models. At the end of the period, both spatial patterning variables and region-specific variance were significant.

Test for spatial autocorrelation What of end-state spatial autocorrelation? The residuals for each of the regression models were tested using the G_i^* statistic. The results for all ten models are shown in figure 4.2. For the base models only one state, Guerrero, shows negative significant values, meaning that a clustering comprising Guerrero and the states surrounding it had low vote share values for PAN, while Guanajuato (and the states surrounding it) had significantly higher vote share values, evidence of the home state base of Vicente Fox. The same results are present in the border models.

When states are divided into cardinal categories the low value clustering increases in the south while the states with high vote share values move in the northern direction, from Guanajuato to Zacatecas. The littoral models are almost a reflection of the cardinal 1 model, with the addition of Jalisco to the states with significant high vote share values. In the two final models, the clustering effect is removed by the addition of the region-specific variables.

We thus are left with the following key conclusions concerning ending conditions for PAN:

- greater vote shares where the level of urbanization is greater;
- no evidence of other spatial processes that might have resulted from diffusion;
- continuing evidence of regionalization of party support: high vote shares in central-western states alongside low support for the party in the central-southern states.

The strong support from the northern states during the initial conditions practically disappeared at the end of the period, as did support by the indigenous population. The clustering of significantly low G_i^* values shifted from the Atlantic to the Pacific in this time frame, while central-western states remained strong supporters of PAN.

Initial Conditions, PAN Senatorial Elections

In the senatorial election of 1964, Baja California Sur and Quintana Roo did not vote for PAN while Tabasco and Tamaulipas had shares close to zero. As in the presidential election, only four states cast more than 20 percent of their vote for PAN: Guanajuato (20.2 percent), Chihuahua (22.7 percent), Baja California Norte (24.9 percent) and the Federal District (29.3 percent). In the 2000 senatorial election, Guerrero had the lowest share for PAN (14.1 percent) while Guanajuato give PAN the highest of all, 57.4 percent, followed close by Jalisco, with 49.5 percent.

The ten models already introduced were applied to the senatorial elections for PAN. Table 4.3 shows the coefficients and the levels of significance of these. The urbanization variable was significant and positive in all the models. When the spatially and regionally enriched models were estimated, literacy emerged as significant but with negative value, implying with this that greater votes were cast in states with lower monolingual proportion of the indigenous population. The spatial variable "relative location" became significant as well. It indicates that PAN's vote shares are inversely proportional to relative location (i.e. interaction flow among states). Higher shares were present in states with lower monolingual indigenous populations and in the littoral states, in the central plateau and in the northern sierras' states.

Test for spatial autocorrelation The significant G_i^* statistics in each of the regression models are shown in figure 4.3. There is a strong

Table 4.2 Coefficients in ending vote share models: presidential election for PAN, 2000

Independent Variables	BASE MODEL		BORDER		CARDINAL		LITTORAL		REGIONS	
	Socio Econ	Socio Spatial	Socio Border	Border Overall	Socio Cardinal	Cardinal Overall	Socio Littoral	Littoral Overall	Socio Regions	Regions Overall
Literacy	-1.872	-0.616	-1.264	-0.053	-3.637	-5.678	-4.007	-10.610	-9.295	-6.459
Gross State Product	-1.157	-4.461	-2.904	-5.262	-4.456	-7.492	-3.350	-2.858	-0.445	-5.015
Urbanization	3.666[a]	0.351	4.282[a]	4.486[a]	5.193[b]	8.698[c]	4.319[b]	4.972[b]	5.335	4.368
Hierarchical		-0.167		-4.294		-5.256		1.712		2.737
Population Potential		-0.029		-0.012		-0.111		-0.103		-0.064
Relative Location		0.027		-0.003		-0.039		0.067		0.066
Indigenous Language			-1.128	-1.586	-0.706	0.499	-1.783	-3.852	-5.157	-6.158
Oil State			0.067	0.068	0.078[a]	0.132[c]	0.055	0.041	0.027	0.016
BORDER										
North			-0.029	-0.086						
South			-0.005	-0.006						
CARDINAL										
North					-0.065	-0.331[c]				
South					-0.065	-0.233[c]				
Central					-0.013	-0.145[a]				
West Central					-0.029	-0.110				
LITTORAL										
Atlantic							-0.044	-0.101		
Pacific							-0.032	-0.092		
REGIONS										
Region I									0.028	0.057
Region II									0.135	0.143
Region III									0.022	0.029
Region IV									0.024	0.028
Region V									0.128	0.150
Region VI									-0.009	-0.002
Region VII									0.039	0.049
Region VIII									0.074	0.087
Region IX									-0.021	0.018
Region X									0.244	0.298
Region XI									0.106	0.108
Region XII									0.034	0.073
Constant	0.319	-0.131	0.212	0.314	-0.388	0.388	0.483	0.298	0.852	-0.328
R-Squared	0.191	0.211	0.287	0.324	0.334	0.551	0.309	0.386	0.545	0.565

[a] Significant at 0.1 level, [b] at 0.05 level, [c] at 0.01 level.

pattern of statistically significant values in the base models, when spatial and specific-region controls are added to the models, the clustering dilutes, indicating that the controls captured the principal elements. Michoacan, Queretaro and Colima remained as a strong cluster throughout the models while low value clusters

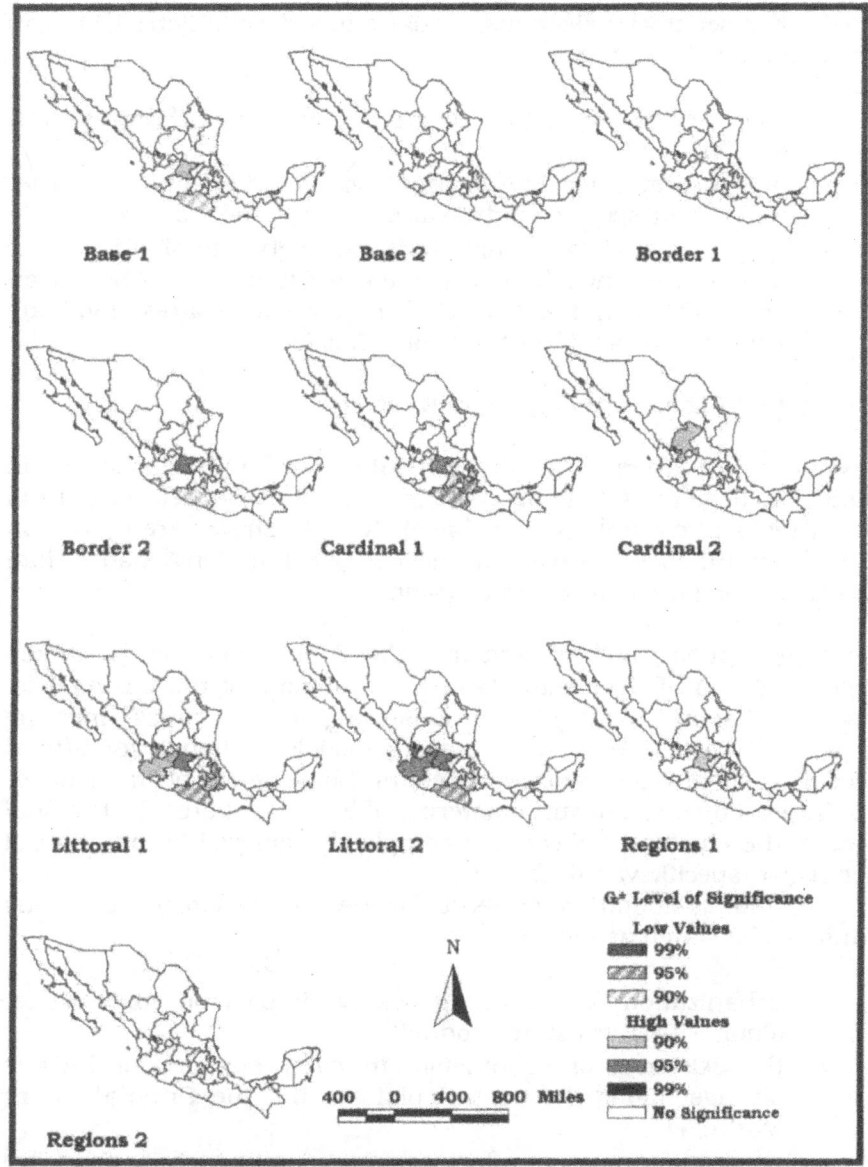

Figure 4.2 G_i^* test for residuals. PAN vote share presidential election 2000

were only sporadic in southern states such as Puebla and Oaxaca. Veracruz and Tabasco were significant for low values, for the base models.

For senatorial elections, initial support conditions thus can be summarized as follows:

- vote shares are higher where the level of urbanization is greater;
- presence of other spatial processes is revealed when border and region-specific controls are added to the models;
- regionalization is strong: there are high vote shares in the belt that extends from Coahuila in the north to Michoacan and Jalisco in the south west; low vote shares dominate states to the south of the Gulf of Mexico.

Ending Conditions, PAN Senatorial Elections

Level of urbanization is significant in all models in 2000 as shown in table 4.4. Regional effects are strong. In the final model, once a full set of regional controls is introduced the vote shares are greater in states along the central plateau and the Oriental Sierra Madre than in states along the neo-volcanic system.

Test for spatial autocorrelation There is a strongly marked regionalization of the residuals of the first nine of the ten models. Figure 4.4 shows the significant clustering of high values emerging in Central Mexico for nine of the ten models, although for littoral models a slightly differentiation occurs. Some states of the central-south presented significant clustering of low vote shares. In the final model, the clustering effect was completely removed by addition of the region-specific variables.

Ending condition support for PAN in senatorial elections thus can be stated as follows:

- urbanization had a strong positive impact on vote shares, along with gross state product;
- the existence of regionalism in party support for PAN is stronger along the central plateau and the Oriental Sierra Madre;
- no spatial processes affecting variations in party support are apparent.

The initially strong support for PAN in a belt from the northern to the southwestern states changed to a tight cluster in the center of Mexico, specially in Guanajuato and the clustering of high values in Coahuila disappeared.

Table 4.3 Coefficients in initial vote share models: senatorial election for PAN, 1964

Independent Variables	BASE MODEL Socio Econ	Socio Spatial	BORDER Socio Border	Border Overall	CARDINAL Socio Cardinal	Cardinal Overall	LITTORAL Socio Littoral	Littoral Overall	REGIONS Socio Regions	Regions Overall
Literacy	-1.068	-0.773	-0.928	-0.603	-0.300	-0.424	-1.053	-2.229	-3.454ᵃ	-1.605
Gross State Product	2.354	1.368	2.430	1.107	2.277	1.615	1.888	2.105	2.876	1.961
Urbanization	2.691ᵇ	2.483ᵇ	2.865ᵇ	3.471ᶜ	2.907ᵇ	3.639ᶜ	3.044ᶜ	3.337ᶜ	3.473ᵃ	2.549ᵃ
Hierarchical		-0.631		-0.191		-3.148		-2.721		-1.357
Population Potential		0.020		0.027		-0.005		-0.004		0.018
Relative Location		-0.029		-0.050ᵃ		-0.031		-0.023		-0.036
Indigenous Language			1.178	1.261	1.768ᵇ	1.812ᵇ	1.069	0.913	0.303	-0.080
Oil State			-0.005	0.010	-0.008	0.011	-0.013	-0.021	-0.044	-0.032
BORDER										
North			-0.008	-0.063						
South			-0.047	-0.069						
CARDINAL										
North					-0.031	-0.133ᵇ				
South					-0.039	-0.109ᵇ				
Central					-0.021	-0.065				
West Central					0.041	0.016				
LITTORAL										
Atlantic							-0.059ᵃ	-0.091ᶜ		
Pacific							-0.030	-0.071ᵇ		
REGIONS										
Region I									0.073	0.027
Region II									0.097ᵇ	0.089
Region III									0.100	0.056
Region IV									-0.038	-0.086
Region V									0.195ᶜ	0.114
Region VI									0.013	-0.029
Region VII									0.039	-0.010
Region VIII									0.005	0.006
Region IX									-0.018	0.001
Region X									-0.035	-0.041
Region XI									-0.052	-0.132
Region XII									-0.010	-0.031
Constant	0.024	0.426	-0.011	0.655ᵃ	-0.060	0.549ᵃ	0.010	0.547ᵃ	0.137	0.613
R-Squared	0.427	0.484	0.525	0.615	0.583	0.730	0.573	0.689	0.799	0.871

ᵃ Significant at 0.1 level, ᵇ at 0.05 level, ᶜ at 0.01 level.

Initial Conditions, PAN Representative Elections

Baja California Sur, Quintana Roo and Tabasco cast no votes for PAN representatives in the 1964 election, while Guanajuato (21.2

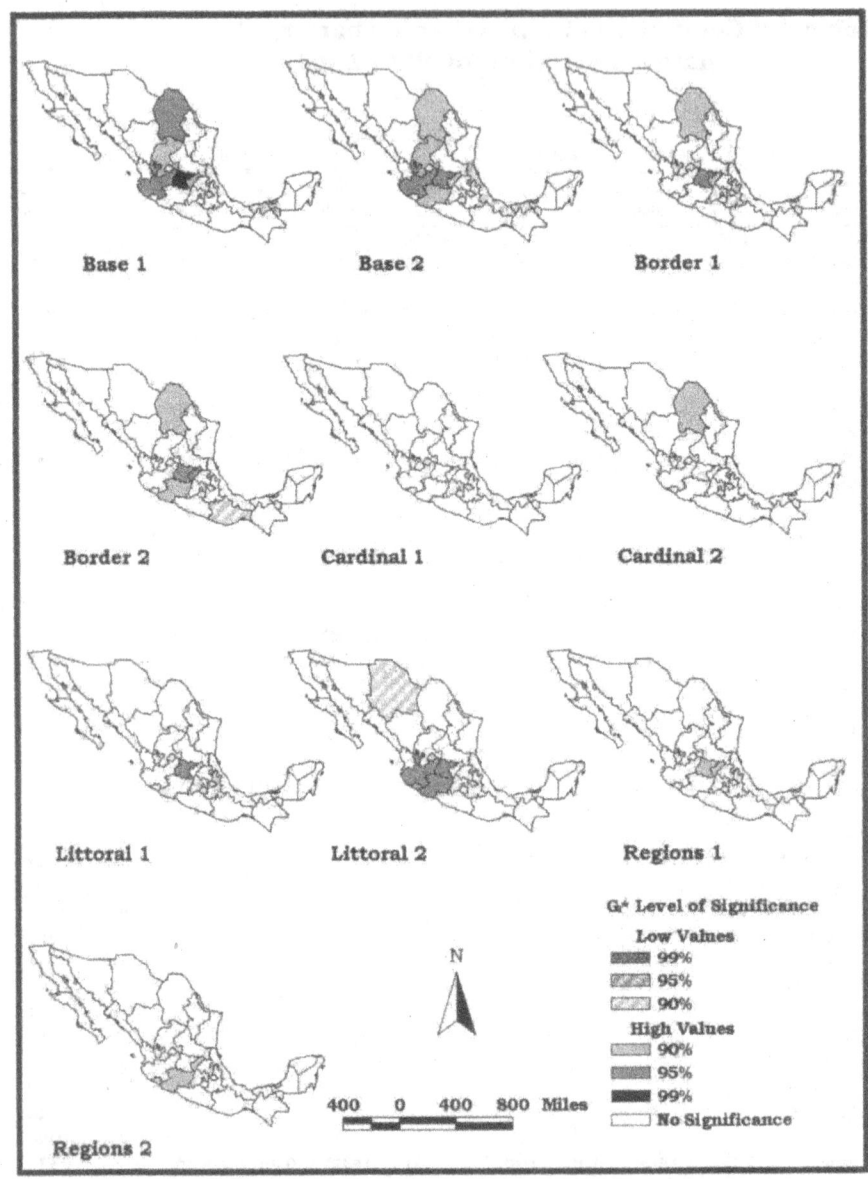

Figure 4.3 G_i^* test for residuals. PAN vote share senatorial election 1964

percent), Chihuahua (22.3 percent), Baja California Norte (25.4 percent) and the Federal District (29.4 percent) were the four states with shares over 20 percent. In the 2000 representative elections, the two states with less than 20 percent of the votes cast for PAN

Table 4.4 Coefficients in ending vote share models: senatorial election for PAN, 2000

Independent Variables	BASE MODEL Socio Econ	Socio Spatial	BORDER Socio Border	Border Overall	CARDINAL Socio Cardinal	Cardinal Overall	LITTORAL Socio Littoral	Littoral Overall	REGIONS Socio Regions	Regions Overall
Literacy	1.026	5.082	1.277	4.031	-1.550	-1.107	-0.801	-6.365	-16.135	-7.494
Gross State Product	-2.082	-11.097	-3.610	-10.268	-4.333	13.564^a	-5.206	-9.325	-1.946	-9.008
Urbanization	4.143^b	3.183	4.137^a	4.058	5.182^b	7.547^c	5.156^b	5.017^c	9.742^c	7.189^a
Hierarchical		-3.112		-2.274		-5.210		-2.556		-4.108
Population Potential		-0.029		-0.055		-0.121		-0.107		-0.048
Relative Location		0.032		0.043		0.066		0.068		0.038
Indigenous Language			0.087	-0.372	1.073	0.868	0.259	-2.612	-2.112	-4.427
Oil State			0.062	0.524	0.064	0.088	0.042	0.003	0.042	0.033
BORDER										
North			0.109	-0.048						
South			0.098^a	-0.081						
CARDINAL										
North					-0.024	-0.252^b				
South					0.094	-0.209^c				
Central					-0.003	-0.106				
West Central					0.003	-0.097				
LITTORAL										
Atlantic							0.083^a	-0.134^b		
Pacific							-0.066	-0.135^c		
REGIONS										
Region I									0.042	0.018
Region II									0.182^b	0.166^a
Region III									0.025	-0.036
Region IV									0.016	-0.044
Region V									0.155	0.104
Region VI									0.029	-0.012
Region VII									0.140	0.122
Region VIII									0.179^b	0.180^b
Region IX									-0.035	0.032
Region X									0.002	0.083
Region XI									0.121	0.041
Region XII									-0.011	0.040
Constant	-0.024	-0.706	-0.058	-0.774	0.134	-0.491	0.096	-0.017^a	1.055	0.093
R-Squared	0.339	0.475	0.472	0.532	0.476	0.658	0.488	0.655	0.684	0.772

^{a} Significant at 0.1 level, ^{b} at 0.05 level, ^{c} at 0.01 level.

where Guerrero (13.2 percent) and Tabasco (18.7 percent) whereas Aguascalientes and Guanajuato cast more than 50 percent of their vote to PAN, followed closely by Queretaro and Jalisco.

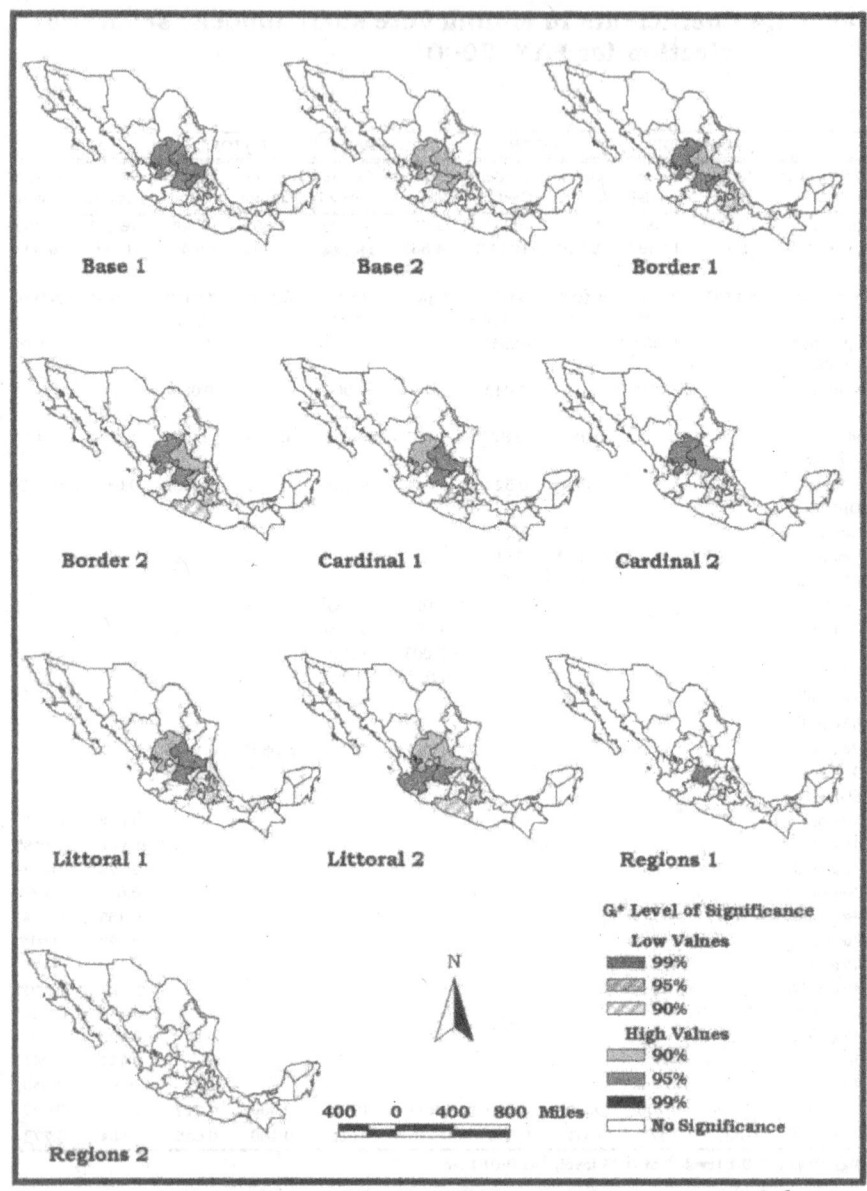

Figure 4.4 G_i^* test for residuals. PAN vote share senatorial election 2000

As in the preceding analyses, the ten models were applied and their coefficient values obtained, as table 4.5 shows. The urbanization variable remains significant and positive in all models.

Table 4.5 Coefficients in initial vote share models: representative election for PAN, 1964

Independent Variables	BASE MODEL Socio Econ	Socio Spatial	BORDER Socio Border	Border Overall	CARDINAL Socio Cardinal	Cardinal Overall	LITTORAL Socio Littoral	Littoral Overall	REGIONS Socio Regions	Regions Overall
Literacy	-1.032	-0.618	-0.844	-0.391	-0.124	-0.081	-0.999	-1.904	-3.383[b]	-1.189
Gross State Product	2.209	1.106	2.334	0.784	2.203	1.293	1.862	1.778	2.761	1.583
Urbanization	2.800[c]	2.483[b]	2.958[b]	3.497[c]	2.990[b]	3.632[c]	3.164[c]	3.300[c]	3.566[c]	2.384[b]
Hierarchical		-1.008		-0.590		-3.418		-2.800		-1.702
Population Potential		0.019		0.027		-0.005		-0.002		0.021
Relative Location		-0.028		-0.049[a]		-0.030		-0.022		-0.037
Indigenous Language		1.245	1.334[a]	1.890[b]	1.906[c]	1.182	1.034	0.341	-0.165
Oil State		-0.002	0.011	-0.005	0.012	-0.010	-0.019	-0.042	-0.032
BORDER										
North			-0.008	-0.064						
South			-0.048	-0.064						
CARDINAL										
North					-0.031	-0.134[b]				
South					-0.037	-0.104[c]				
Central					-0.022	-0.066[a]				
West Central					0.046	0.019				
LITTORAL										
Atlantic							-0.051[a]	-0.076[a]		
Pacific							-0.027	-0.062[b]		
REGIONS										
Region I									0.072	0.036
Region II									0.096[b]	0.097[b]
Region III									0.085	0.043
Region IV									-0.009	-0.055
Region V									0.185[b]	0.109
Region VI									0.012	-0.027
Region VII									0.038	-0.008
Region VIII									-0.001	0.006
Region IX									-0.016	0.015
Region X									-0.037	-0.028
Region XI									-0.056	-0.134
Region XII									-0.010	-0.019
Constant	0.019	0.404	-0.022	0.628[a]	-0.079	0.514[a]	-0.003	0.504[a]	0.129	0.604
R-Squared	0.454	0.521	0.557	0.652	0.619	0.768	0.584	0.694	0.791	0.852

[a] Significant at 0.1 level, [b] at 0.05 level, [c] at 0.01 level.

With the introduction of spatial and region-specific controls, the indigenous language variable became significant and positive with a stronger value in the overall cardinal model. The littoral states had low vote shares. The Central Plateau as well as the northern Sierras and plains cast high votes for PAN representatives.

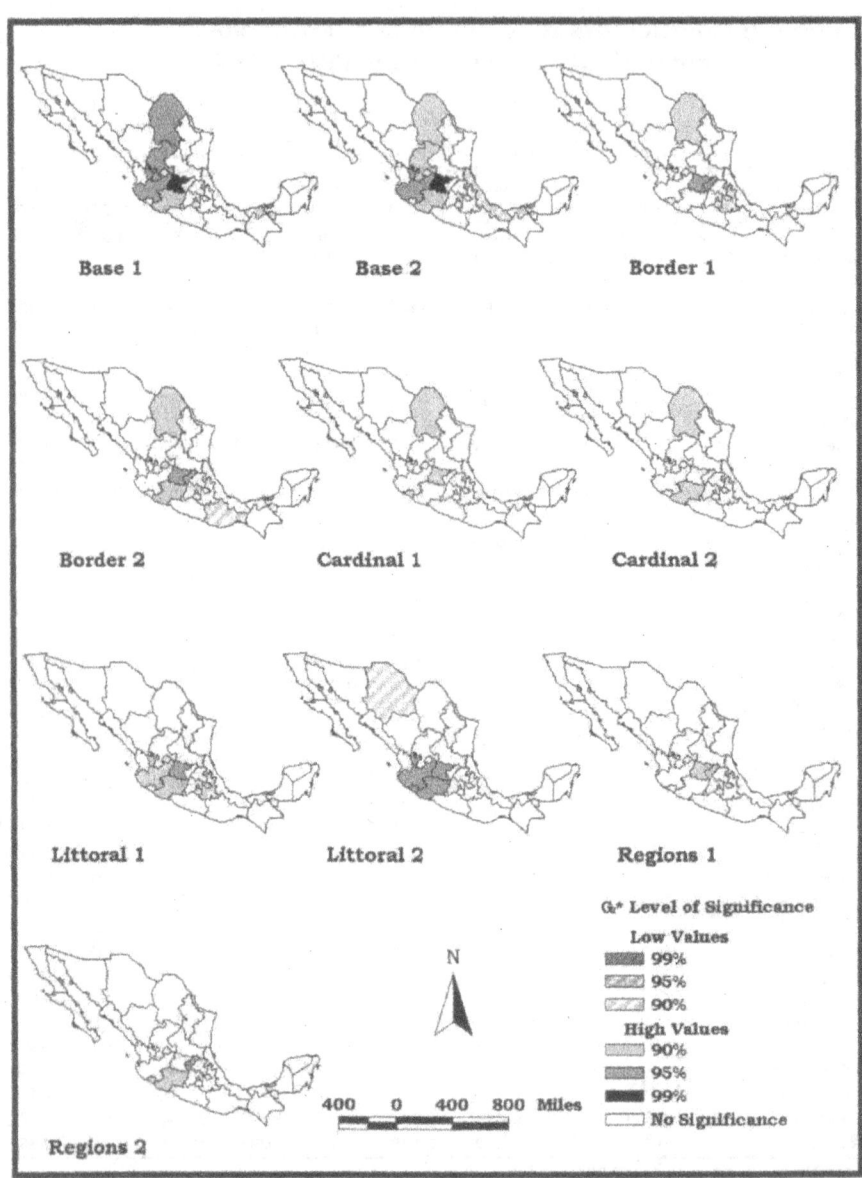

Figure 4.5 G_i^* **test for residuals. PAN vote share representative election 1964**

Test for spatial autocorrelation Strong clustering prevails through the north-southwest line of states in the base models. Figure 4.5 shows the G_i^* test of the residuals for the ten models. When spatial and region-specific controls were applied, the clustering diluted but did not disappear. Central-western states retained clusters of significant high values, Guanajuato and Queretaro are significant for most of the models. Veracruz, Puebla, Tabasco and Oaxaca in the south, had clusters of significant low values in different models.

Initial support for PAN in representative elections therefore, came as follows:

- greater vote shares where the level of urbanization and the indigenous monolingual populations were greater;
- lower vote shares in those states with higher relative location as well as those states with specific-regionalization features.
- spatial diffusion processes already appear to be operating.

Ending Conditions, PAN Representative Elections

Coefficients for the ten models and their levels of significance for ending conditions in representative elections are presented in table 4.6. Level of urbanization remains strongly significant in all models. Literacy shifts to significant and positive for the base socio-spatial model, and the same behavior is evidenced by the oil extractive states. On the other hand, the variable "gross state product" becomes significant with a negative sign, meaning that those states with the lowest gross state products cast the highest shares for PAN. Low vote shares are present in states along the Atlantic coast, specifically in those states that are situated in regions II and VIII.

Test for spatial autocorrelation Test statistics for residuals from the regressions are mapped in figure 4.6. Spatial autocorrelation was present in central Mexico, specifically in Jalisco and Zacatecas, for this period, but when region-specific controls are introduced the clustering diffuses.

Thus, for representative elections, urbanization remained significant. There is no evidence of spatial diffusion processes, in the other hand the influence of variables such as literacy is evident. The oil extractive states emerged as PAN supporters.

Summary: Vote Shares for PAN

Pulling together the previous analyses, there was limited early support for PAN in states where urbanization was greater, such as Coahuila and Nuevo Leon, and where there were higher proportions of monolingual indigenous population, such as Chihuahua and Zacatecas. In contrast, there was low PAN support in littoral states such as Oaxaca and in areas with high population potential, such as Puebla. By the end of the period, strong indigenous population support had vanished, but there now was a strong support in the oil extractive states. PAN's support also was concentrated in zones of greater urbanization outside the more populous core of the country, as well as in areas with higher literacy. Operation of spatial diffusion processes is counter-indicated, but there was a strong base of PAN support centering on Vicente Fox's home state Guanajuato.

Partido Revolucionario Institucional, PRI

In 1964 there was complete electoral domination by this party. The lowest vote share for PRI was cast in the Federal District, while Tabasco and Chiapas had the highest vote shares at all levels of representation. In the 2000 elections the Federal District and Guanajuato, centers from the Cardenas challenge from the left and Fox challenge from the right, had the lowest vote shares for PRI while Sinaloa and Nayarit had the highest, again, for all levels of representation.

Initial Conditions, PRI Presidential Elections

Tabasco, Chiapas and Hidalgo cast the highest votes for PRI in the presidential election of 1964, with over 98 percent. The Federal District with 72 percent and Guanajuato with 78 percent cast the lowest. By the end of the period, the Federal District and Guanajuato decreased their PRI vote shares to 24 and 28 percent respectively, while Sinaloa and its neighbor Nayarit cast the highest, with 49 and 64 respectively.

Table 4.7 shows the coefficients and the levels of significance for the ten models, as in the preceding section. No variables were significant in the 1964 presidential election base models, although both the urbanization and indigenous language variables became significant and negative once regional controls were introduced. PRI's vote share was greater in less urbanized states, in those with the smallest percent of monolingual indigenous population, in states with smaller gross state products and in states with higher relative location values. States along the central plateau and in the northern sierras and plains cast lower vote shares for PRI than those states along the neo-volcanic system. Evidence of spatial processes emerged when controlling for regions.

Table 4.6 Coefficients in ending vote share models: representative election for PAN, 1964

Independent Variables	BASE MODEL Socio Econ	Socio Spatial	BORDER Socio Border	Border Overall	CARDINAL Socio Cardinal	Cardinal Overall	LITTORAL Socio Littoral	Littoral Overall	REGIONS Socio Regions	Regions Overall
Literacy	0.259	3.586ᶜ	0.496	2.856	-0.218	0.259	-2.066	-7.752	-13.549	-7.437
Gross State Product	-2.920	-11.257ᵃ	-4.578	-10.938	-6.007	-13.792ᵇ	-5.821	-9.365	-3.079	-8.879
Urbanization	4.676ᵇ	3.927ᵃ	4.909ᵃ	4.828ᵇ	5.928ᵇ	8.390ᶜ	5.608ᶜ	5.697ᶜ	9.401ᶜ	7.564ᶜ
Hierarchical		-0.152		-0.762		-6.246		0.281		-2.121
Population Potential		-0.053		-0.066		-0.101		-0.127		-0.071
Relative Location		0.055		0.055		0.046		0.089		0.053
Indigenous Language			-0.511	-0.947	0.854	0.976	-0.353	-2.963	-2.567	-4.470
Oil State			0.064	0.055	0.072ᵃ	0.100ᵇ	0.041	0.010	0.045	0.042
BORDER										
North			-0.005	-0.055						
South			-0.067	-0.052						
CARDINAL										
North					-0.055	-0.287ᵇ				
South					-0.072	-0.191ᵇ				
Central					-0.009	-0.114				
West Central					0.001	-0.091				
LITTORAL										
Atlantic							-0.067	-0.119ᵇ		
Pacific							-0.069ᵃ	0.133ᶜ		
REGIONS										
Region I									0.009	-0.044
Region II									0.165ᵃ	0.143
Region III									0.020	-0.041
Region IV									-0.010	-0.074
Region V									0.125	0.055
Region VI									0.029	-0.023
Region VII									0.114	0.081
Region VIII									0.156ᵇ	0.148ᵃ
Region IX									-0.023	0.009
Region X									0.028	0.064
Region XI									0.090	-0.004
Region XII									0.012	0.023
Constant	0.012	-1.009	-0.033	-0.913	-0.031	-0.357	0.186	-0.289	0.864	-0.120
R-Squared	0.384	0.475	0.479	0.530	0.508	0.680	0.528	0.656	0.683	0.756

ᵃ Significant at 0.1 level, ᵇ at 0.05 level, ᶜ at 0.01 level.

Test for spatial autocorrelation Strong clustering of low values prevails from the Coahuila in the north to the central-western states, through Zacatecas, Jalisco and Guanajuato ending in Michoacan, for the base models. After introducing spatial and region-specific controls, the clusters decreased in size and

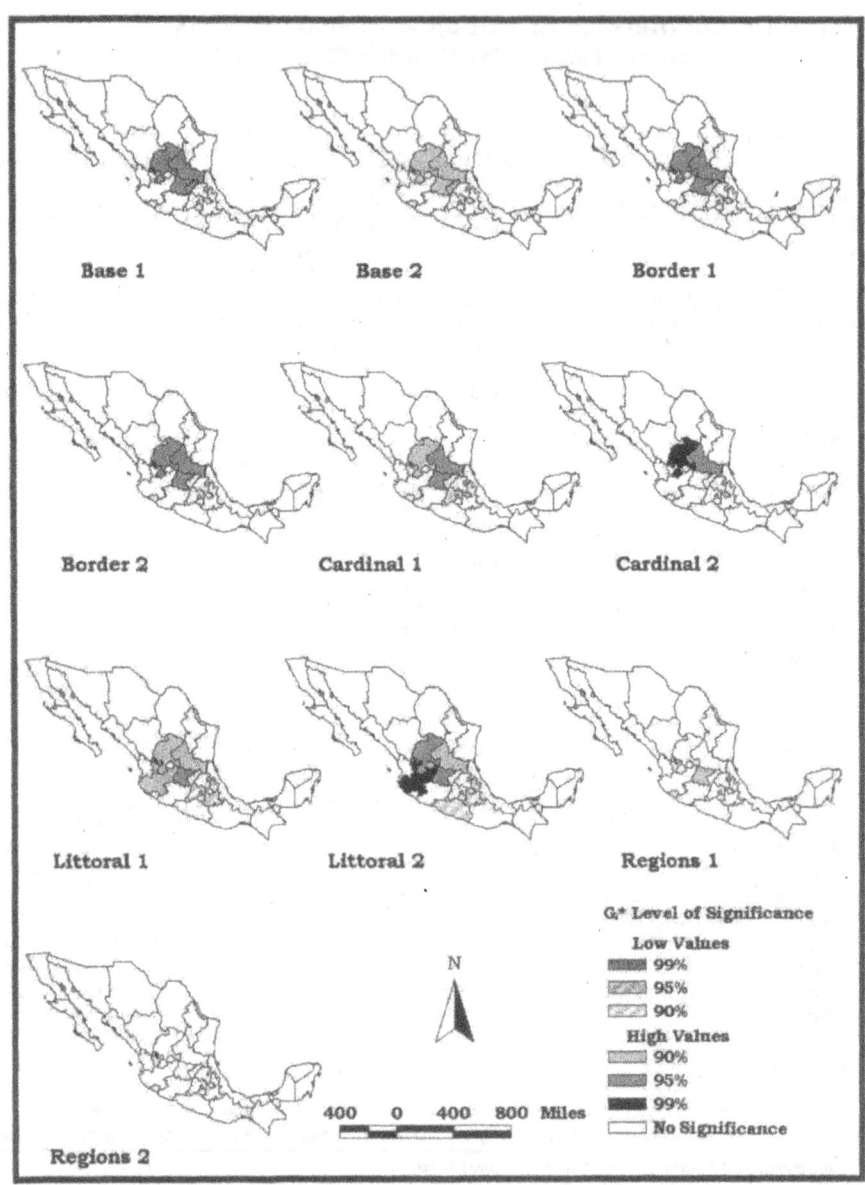

Figure 4.6 G_i^* test for residuals. PAN vote share representative election 1964

significance. Figure 4.7 shows the G_i^* test of the residuals for the ten models. States along the Atlantic coast had a cluster of significant positive values.

Table 4.7 Coefficients in initial vote share models: presidential election for PRI, 1964

Independent Variables	BASE MODEL		BORDER		CARDINAL		LITTORAL		REGIONS	
	Socio Econ	Socio Spatial	Socio Border	Border Overall	Socio Cardinal	Cardinal Overall	Socio Littoral	Littoral Overall	Socio Regions	Regions Overall
Literacy	-0.126	-0.716	-0.316	-0.965	-1.377	-1.518	-0.022	0.562	2.311	0.423
Gross State Product	-2.375	-1.008	-2.321	0.449	-2.092	-1.077	-1.924	-1.544	-2.909ª	-1.745
Urbanization	-1.593	-1.259	-1.873ª	-2.341ᵇ	-1.857ª	-2.404ᶜ	-2.041ᵇ	-2.072ᵇ	-2.309ᵇ	-1.244
Hierarchical		0.396		0.280		2.911		2.290		1.097
Population Potential		-0.025		-0.032		0.000		-0.003		-0.022
Relative Location		0.030		0.051ᵇ		0.033ª		0.024		0.029
Indigenous Language			-1.312ª	-1.428ᵇ	-2.081ᶜ	-2.106ᶜ	-1.254ª	-1.136	-0.574	-0.127
Oil State			0.008	-0.002	0.012	-0.003	0.020	0.029	0.049ª	0.045
BORDER										
North			0.016	0.070ª						
South			0.052	0.062						
CARDINAL										
North					0.047	0.139ᶜ				
South					0.040	0.099ᶜ				
Central					0.031	0.069				
West Central					-0.054	-0.030				
LITTORAL										
Atlantic							0.052ª	0.071ᵇ		
Pacific							0.032	0.059ᵇ		
REGIONS										
Region I									-0.043	-0.037
Region II									-0.103ᵇ	-0.110ª
Region III									-0.085	-0.062
Region IV									0.015	0.041
Region V									-0.159ᵇ	-0.117
Region VI									0.004	0.023
Region VII									-0.033	-0.006
Region VIII									0.020	0.008
Region IX									0.031	-0.005
Region X									0.056	0.032
Region XI									0.014	0.058
Region XII									0.008	-0.003
Constant	0.991ᶜ	0.604ª	1.036ᶜ	0.385	1.112ᶜ	0.516ᵇ	1.004ᶜ	0.527ª	0.870ᶜ	0.534
R-Squared	0.361	0.437	0.512	0.623	0.619	0.779	0.545	0.651	0.772	0.818

ª Significant at 0.1 level, ᵇ at 0.05 level, ᶜ at 0.01 level.

Once the regional controls were introduced, significant values spread further south from Veracruz and Tabasco to Chiapas. Clustering diluted, but did not disappear from Jalisco, Guanajuato or Queretaro, once the region-specific variables were introduced.

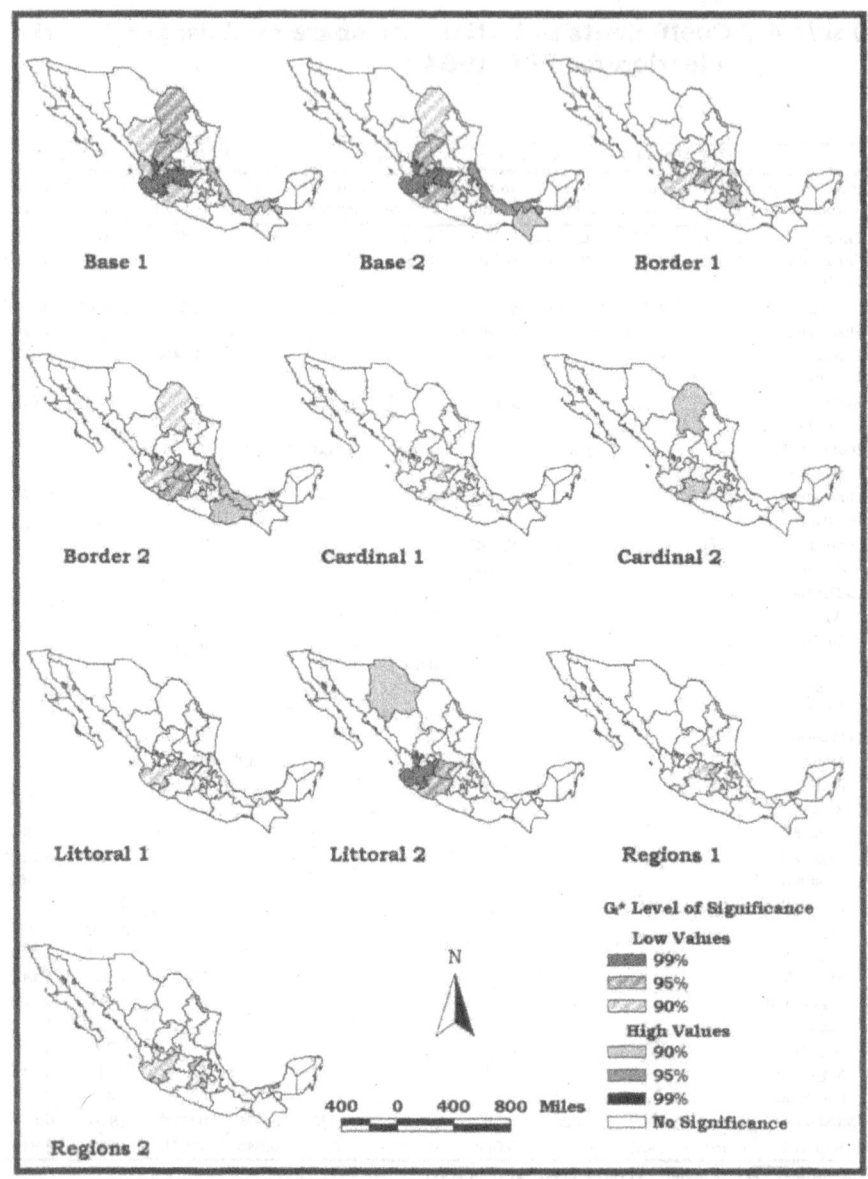

Figure 4.7 G_i^* test for residuals. PRI vote share presidential election 1964

Ending Conditions, PRI Presidential Elections

Table 4.8 shows the coefficients and the levels of significance for the ten models applied to the ending conditions for PRI. Clearly, the

Table 4.8 Coefficients in ending vote share models: presidential election for PRI, 2000

Independent Variables	BASE MODEL		BORDER		CARDINAL		LITTORAL		REGIONS	
	Socio Econ	Socio Spatial	Socio Border	Border Overall	Socio Cardinal	Cardinal Overall	Socio Littoral	Littoral Overall	Socio Regions	Regions Overall
Literacy	2.860	2.627	6.458	5.457	-2.181	-2.992	8.044[a]	10.410[a]	1.084	6.975
Gross State Product	-5.081	-5.721	-5.243	-5.329	-2.772	-8.470	-4.182	-6.467	-4.274	-6.244
Urbanization	-1.755	-1.773	-1.770	-1.583	-1.075	-1.411	-2.017	-2.360	0.161	-1.447
Hierarchical		1.537		3.288		5.787		1.281		-6.511
Population Potential		-0.048		-0.054		-0.097		-0.005		0.072
Relative Location		0.038		0.046		0.100		0.015		-0.057
Indigenous Language			3.921[a]	3.653	0.020	-1.357	4.073[a]	4.547[a]	2.721	1.833
Oil State			0.001	0.007	-0.005	-0.020	0.000	0.002	0.019	0.011
BORDER										
North			0.003	0.000						
South			-0.024	-0.038						
CARDINAL										
North					0.040	0.060				
South					0.009	0.018				
Central					0.084	0.095[a]				
West Central					-0.058	-0.088				
LITTORAL										
Atlantic							-0.038	0.056		
Pacific							0.025	0.043		
REGIONS										
Region I									0.006	0.048
Region II									-0.015	-0.008
Region III									0.064	0.047
Region IV									0.056	0.049
Region V									-0.016	0.002
Region VI									0.034	0.044
Region VII									0.163[b]	0.186[b]
Region VIII									0.043	0.056
Region IX									0.051	0.119
Region X									-0.033	0.052
Region XI									0.002	0.014
Region XII									0.044	0.121
Constant	2.696	-0.217	-0.084	-0.667	0.651	-0.757	-0.231	-0.722	0.225	0.648
R-Squared	0.212	0.242	0.328	0.343	0.488	0.540	0.358	0.376	0.699	0.725

[a] Significant at 0.1 level, [b] at 0.05 level, [c] at 0.01 level.

conditions surrounding the presidential vote for the PAN candidate had changed. Literacy emerged as significant and positive. PRI's vote shares were greater in states with a higher literacy level, a higher percent of monolingual indigenous population and along the Occidental Sierra Madre. The main change from initial to final conditions is the shift from negative to positive of the indigenous

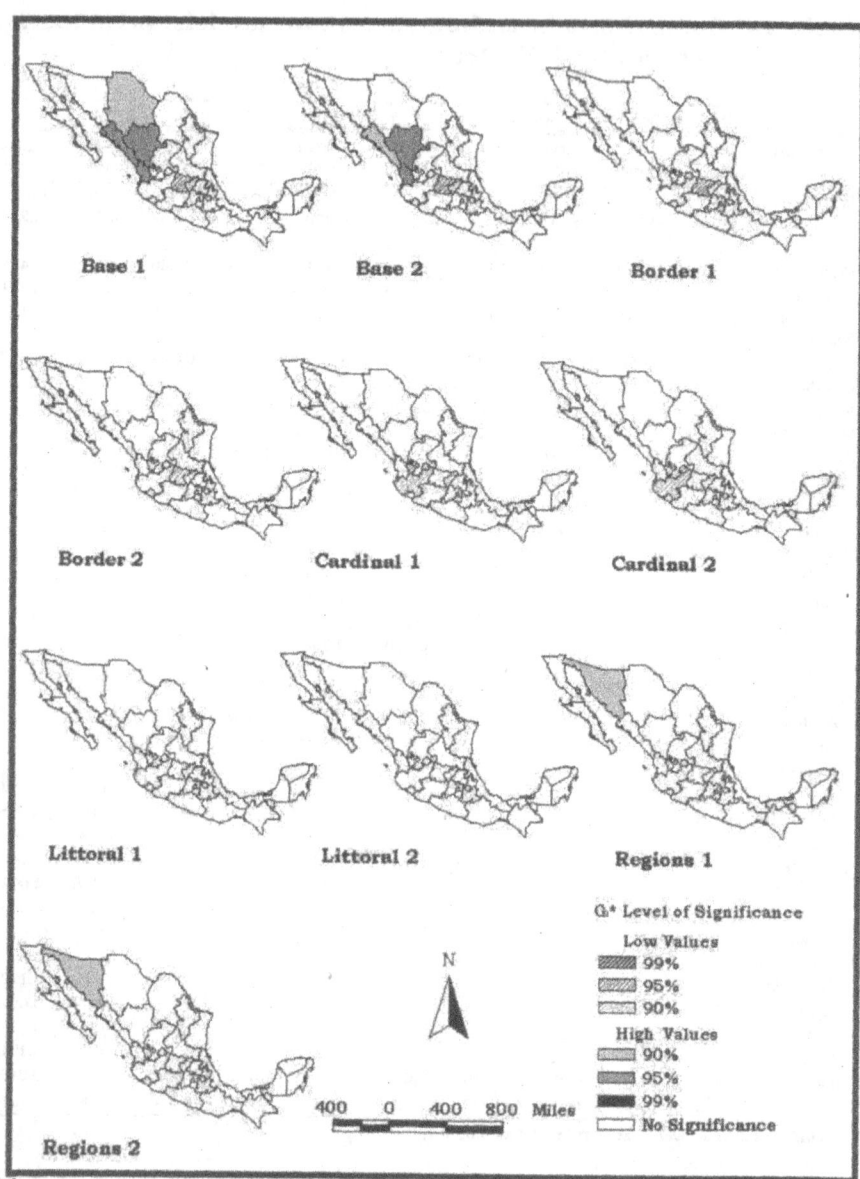

Figure 4.8 G_i^* test for residuals. PRI vote share presidential election 2000

language variable, reversing the pattern for PAN. Whereas initially, the indigenous population evidence anti-PRI sentiment, at the end of the period it was in indigenous areas that PRI held on to more support. The spatial process variables were not significant. Greater vote shares also remained in the central volcanic system states.

Test for spatial autocorrelation Figure 4.8 shows the G_i^* test of the residuals for the ten models. Strong clustering of high values prevailed in the northwestern states for the base models. There is a pocket of significant low values in central Mexico, specifically in Guanajuato and Queretaro. This cluster dissipated when regional controls were introduced.

The key conclusions for this period for vote share for PRI presidential elections thus are:

- pockets of low vote shares remaining in central west Mexico;
- shift of clusters from low values in northwestern states to high values in north central states in this period;
- a cluster of low values remained in central Mexico, but it decreased in significance.

Initial Conditions, PRI Senatorial Elections

Baja California Sur and Quintana Roo cast no votes for PRI in the senatorial election of 1964. The smallest share for PRI in this senatorial election, not including the states with null votes, was 68.4 percent in the Federal District. All other states cast more than 75 percent of the votes for PRI. Chiapas and Tamaulipas cast almost 100 percent of their vote for PRI in this election. In the 2000 elections the Federal District and Morelos cast less than 30 percent of their votes for PRI, while Nayarit (50.9 percent) and Sinaloa (60.4 percent) had the highest vote shares, as they did in the other two levels of representation.

Table 4.9 shows the coefficients and levels of significance. Higher vote shares for PRI were located in highly urbanized states and in their neighboring states, as well as in states with lower levels of literacy, low gross state product, low relative location values along the Yucatan and Baja California peninsulas. In addition, there is strong evidence of spatial diffusion processes in operation.

Test for spatial autocorrelation There are strong contrasts in the G_i^* statistics on residuals of these models. Figure 4.9 shows the clustering of high values in the northwestern states whereas clustering of low values in the extremities of the country, in both peninsulas, in the states of Yucatan and Quintana Roo and in Baja California Sur. The lack of votes in these entities might be explained at the local level. When spatial controls were applied to the base

Table 4.9 Coefficients in initial vote share models: senatorial election for PRI, 1964

Independent Variables	BASE MODEL Socio Econ	Socio Spatial	BORDER Socio Border	Border Overall	CARDINAL Socio Cardinal	Cardinal Overall	LITTORAL Socio Littoral	Littoral Overall	REGIONS Socio Regions	Regions Overall
Literacy	-11.869ᶜ	-4.727	-10.770ᵇ	-4.486	-12.924ᵇ	-7.075	-10.491ᵇ	-1.148	-11.008ᵃ	-2.410
Gross State Product	-7.315	-20.380ᶜ	-5.502	-18.137ᵇ	-7.691	-16.909ᵇ	-7.493	-20.249ᶜ	-14.232ᵇ	-21.898ᶜ
Urbanization	8.353ᵇ	6.039ᵃ	6.272	6.516ᵇ	8.656ᵇ	5.427ᵃ	7.854ᵃ	5.435	13.856ᶜ	10.186ᶜ
Hierarchical		10.767ᵃ		14.771ᵇ		17.473ᵇ		18.388ᶜ		12.627ᵇ
Population Potential		0.250ᶜ		0.266ᶜ		0.314ᶜ		0.316ᶜ		0.250ᶜ
Relative Location		-0.217ᶜ		-0.248ᶜ		-0.259ᶜ		-0.255ᶜ		-0.227ᶜ
Indigenous Language			-0.235	0.946	-0.829	-0.285	0.142	1.135	2.435	1.824
Oil State			0.106	0.118	0.133	0.082	0.091	0.132ᵃ	0.095	0.136
BORDER										
North			0.058	-0.005						
South			-0.151	-0.075						
CARDINAL										
North					-0.074	0.216				
South					-0.134	0.160				
Central					0.093	0.294ᵇ				
West Central					-0.137	0.005				
LITTORAL										
Atlantic							-0.091	0.085		
Pacific							-0.047	0.158ᵃ		
REGIONS										
Region I									-0.414ᵇ	-0.168
Region II									-0.078	-0.029
Region III									-0.198	-0.153
Region IV									0.030	0.017
Region V									-0.185	-0.200
Region VI									0.206	0.239
Region VII									0.248	0.213
Region VIII									0.074	0.151
Region IX									-0.021	0.238
Region X									0.012	0.167
Region XI									0.119	0.167
Region XII									-0.305ᵇ	-0.099
Constant	1.278ᶜ	3.280ᶜ	1.266ᶜ	3.544ᶜ	1.352ᶜ	3.581ᶜ	1.202ᶜ	3.124ᶜ	0.914ᶜ	2.896ᶜ
R-Squared	0.229	0.584	0.314	0.626	0.372	0.730	0.285	0.669	0.739	0.886

ᵃ Significant at 0.1 level, ᵇ at 0.05 level, ᶜ at 0.01 level.

model, the cluster of significant high values shifted to the southernmost states, Chiapas and Tabasco.

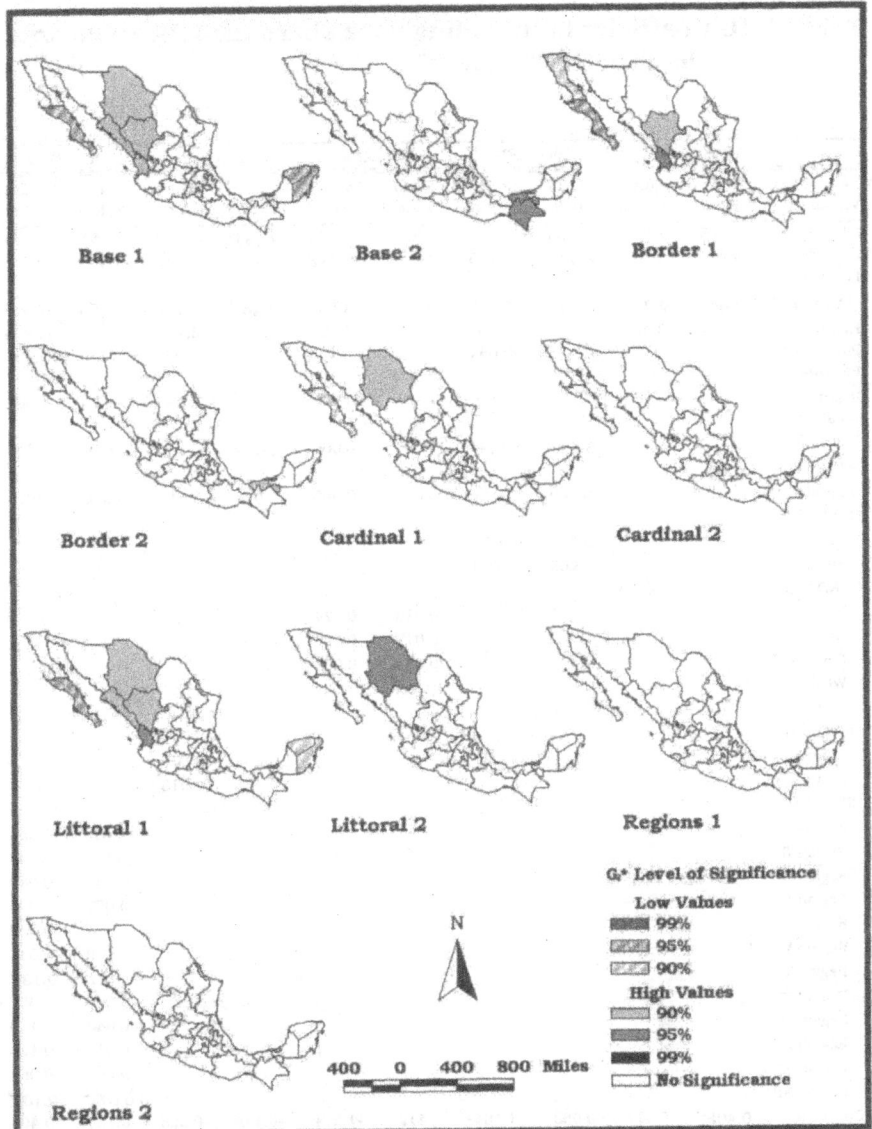

Figure 4.9 G_i^* test for residuals. PRI vote share senatorial election 1964

Ending Conditions, PRI Senatorial Elections

The ten models and the coefficients for the senatorial election models are presented in table 4.10. Low voteshares for PRI were found in the states with higher gross state products, higher levels of

Table 4.10 Coefficients in ending vote share models: senatorial election for PRI, 2000

	BASE MODEL		BORDER		CARDINAL		LITTORAL		REGIONS	
Independent Variables	Socio Econ	Socio Spatial	Socio Border	Border Overall	Socio Cardinal	Cardinal Overall	Socio Littoral	Littoral Overall	Socio Regions	Regions Overall
Literacy	2.176	1.726	5.766	4.186	1.233	-0.843	7.785ᵇ	8.360ᵃ	3.759	6.370
Gross State Product	-5.431ᵃ	-6.498	-5.265ᵃ	-5.788	-4.416	-9.932ᵇ	-4.919ᵃ	-6.759	-4.281	-6.718
Urbanization	-2.040ᵃ	-2.274ᵃ	-2.424ᵃ	-2.303	-1.600	-1.559	-2.449ᵇ	-2.487ᵃ	-1.465	-2.317
Hierarchical		3.573		7.566		7.760		3.434		-4.424
Population Potential		-0.079		-0.094		-0.130		-0.045		0.053
Relative Location		0.066		0.088		0.126		0.046		-0.035
Indigenous Language			3.738ᵃ	3.506ᵃ	1.390	0.066	4.649ᵇ	4.736ᵇ	2.996	0.748
Oil State			0.009	0.014	0.013	0.006	0.010	0.012	0.028	0.018
BORDER										
North			0.021	0.038						
South			0.005	-0.011						
CARDINAL										
North					0.016	0.024				
South					0.017	0.060				
Central					0.050	0.051				
West Central					-0.058	-0.092ᵇ				
LITTORAL										
Atlantic							0.043	0.046		
Pacific							0.011	0.016		
REGIONS										
Region I									-0.013	0.053
Region II									-0.011	-0.007
Region III									0.047	0.042
Region IV									0.069	0.066
Region V									-0.002	0.058
Region VI									0.009	0.041
Region VII									0.121ᵇ	0.180ᵇ
Region VIII									0.028	0.057
Region IX									0.040	0.116
Region X									0.012	0.120
Region XI									0.040	0.082
Region XII									0.071ᵃ	0.161ᵃ
Constant	0.408ᵃ	-0.477	0.053	-1.164	0.412	-1.274	-0.144	-0.905	0.135	0.404
R-Squared	0.370	0.416	0.494	0.521	0.608	0.657	0.532	0.540	0.771	0.787

ᵃ Significant at 0.1 level, ᵇ at 0.05 level, ᶜ at 0.01 level.

urbanization and in the central western states. In the other hand, higher vote shares emerged in states with higher literacy levels as well as in states with higher percentages of monolingual indigenous

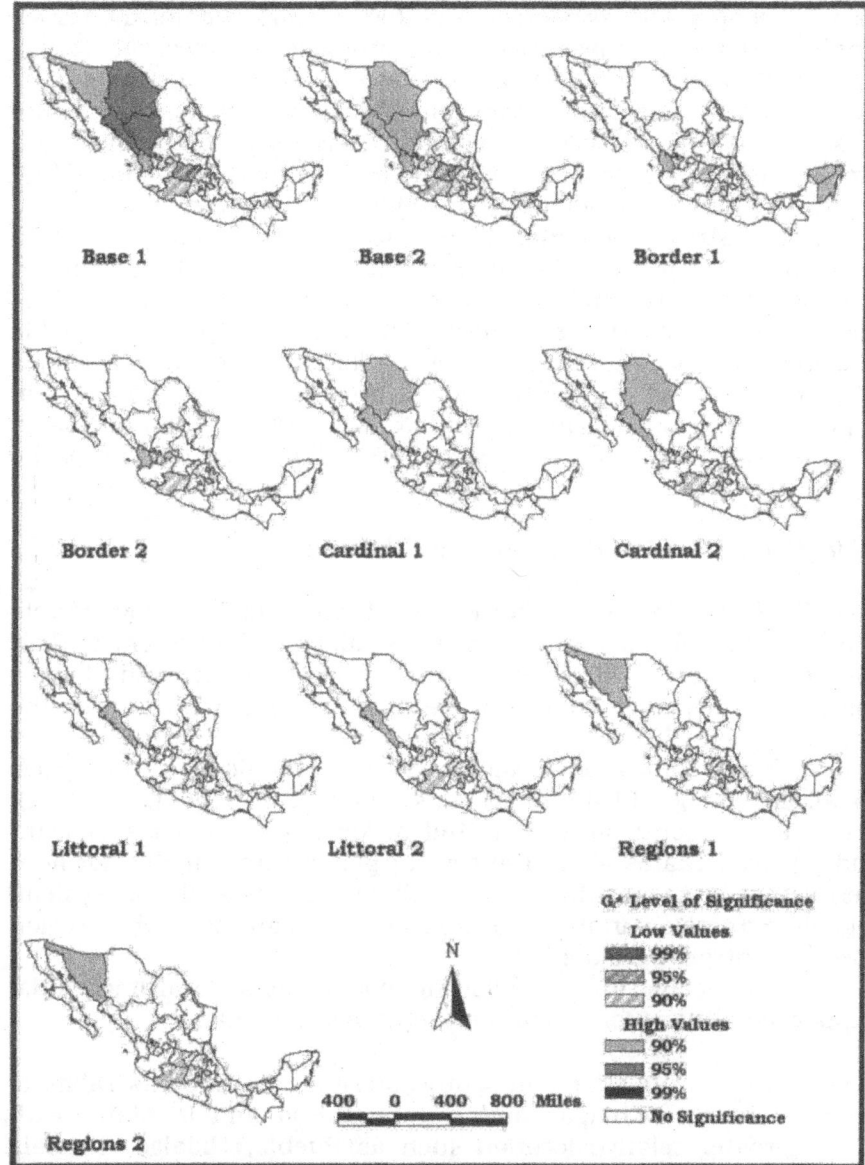

Figure 4.10 G_i^* test for residuals. PRI vote share senatorial election 2000

population and in states along the Occidental Sierra Madre. Spatial processes are no longer operating.

Test for spatial autocorrelation Clusters of high significant values emerged in the northwestern and southeastern states, whereas a cluster of low significant values remained in central western states. Once regional controls were implemented, as seen in figure 4.10, the clustering of high significant values prevailed in Chihuahua and Sinaloa while Michoacan retained low significant values. The Yucatan peninsula no longer has significant clustering.

The strong clustering in the northwestern states remained throughout the period. The effect of literacy on vote share changed through time. At the end of the process the higher the literacy levels, the greater the shares cast for PRI. The gross state product variable remained significant, with higher votes for PRI in the poorer states and in those states with higher proportions of monolingual population, such as Guerrero and Nayarit. Both spatial diffusion processes and regionalization effects were diluted by the end of the period.

Initial Conditions, PRI Representative Elections

Baja California Norte and the Federal District had the lowest vote shares while Tabasco and Chiapas cast almost 100 percent of their vote for PRI. In the 2000 election the Federal District and Morelos cast the lowest vote shares while Sinaloa and Nayarit cast the highest.

The urbanization variable remained significant and negative for all models so did the indigenous language variable (table 4.11). States in the south along the Gulf of Mexico remained significant and positive. States along the central plateau and in the northern sierras cast less votes than those in the central neo-volcanic system. The oil extractive variable appeared as significant only when region specific controls were applied.

This leads to the following conclusions regarding initial support conditions for PRI in representative elections:

- greater vote shares in southeastern states, such as Tabasco, Veracruz, Chiapas and Quintana Roo and in states with greater relative location such as Puebla, Hidalgo, Tlaxcala and Morelos;
- lower vote shares where urbanization or the proportion of monolingual indigenous population were greater, such as Tamaulipas, Coahuila or Chihuahua;

Test for spatial autocorrelation There is evidence of spatial diffusion processes in this period. There are strong clusters of both high and

Table 4.11 Coefficients in initial vote share models: representative election for PRI, 1964

Independent Variables	BASE MODEL		BORDER		CARDINAL		LITTORAL		REGIONS	
	Socio Econ	Socio Spatial	Socio Border	Border Overall	Socio Cardinal	Cardinal Overall	Socio Littoral	Littoral Overall	Socio Regions	Regions Overall
Literacy	0.201	0.075	0.170	0.053	0.063	0.271	0.132	1.015	3.402ᵇ	1.899
Gross State Product	-2.748	-1.951	-2.774	-1.757	-3.066	-2.531	-2.411	-2.351	-3.349ᵇ	-2.530
Urbanization	-2.437ᵇ	-2.294ᵇ	-2.488ᵇ	-3.210ᶜ	-2.507ᵇ	-3.284ᶜ	-2.663ᵇ	-2.861ᶜ	-3.434ᶜ	-2.611ᵇ
Hierarchical		0.833		0.443		3.038		2.252		1.197
Population Potential		-0.018		-0.023		0.006		-0.001		-0.014
Relative Location		0.030		0.051ᵇ		0.031		0.025		0.024
Indigenous Language			-0.861	-0.922	-1.403ᵃ	-1.458ᵇ	-0.689	-0.562	-0.181	0.175
Oil State			0.012	-0.008	0.017	-0.003	0.121	0.018	0.042ᵃ	0.036
BORDER										
North			0.004	0.065ᵃ						
South			0.054	0.085ᵇ						
CARDINAL										
North					0.004	0.106ᵇ				
South					0.034	0.106ᶜ				
Central					0.007	0.050				
West Central					-0.047	-0.023				
LITTORAL										
Atlantic							0.056ᵇ	0.081ᶜ		
Pacific							0.006	0.038		
REGIONS										
Region I									-0.107ᵇ	-0.085
Region II									-0.097ᵇ	-0.097ᵃ
Region III									-0.070	-0.043
Region IV									0.007	0.037
Region V									-0.175ᶜ	-0.126
Region VI									0.002	0.027
Region VII									-0.058	-0.028
Region VIII									0.014	0.008
Region IX									0.022	0.000
Region X									0.049	0.041
Region XI									-0.015	0.037
Region XII									0.012	0.016
Constant	0.996ᶜ	0.565ᵃ	1.009ᶜ	0.305	1.032ᶜ	0.418ᵃ	1.010ᶜ	0.492ᵃ	0.839ᶜ	0.528
R-Squared	0.521	0.585	0.622	0.730	0.664	0.814	0.640	0.736	0.854	0.882

ᵃ Significant at 0.1 level, ᵇ at 0.05 level, ᶜ at 0.01 level.

low significant values, in figure 4.11. Low significant values prevailed in the central-western states. Guanajuato is the state with the greatest level of significance in this cluster for the base model 1. High significant values are situated along the south of the Gulf of Mexico, in Veracruz and Tabasco. Once the spatial controls were

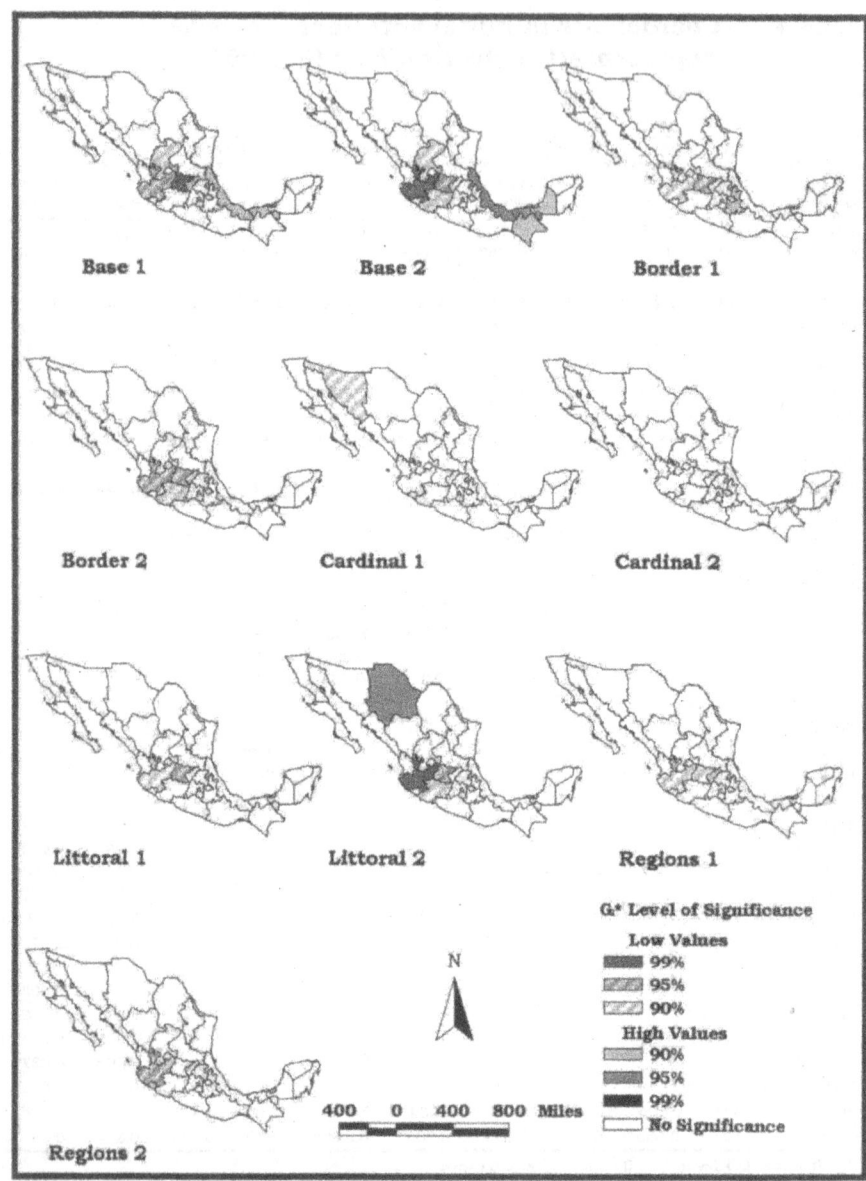

Figure 4.11 G_i^* **test for residuals. PRI vote share representative election 1964**

introduced, the cluster of low values expanded and its core shifted further west to Jalisco, while the cluster of high values increased in significance and expanded further south, to Chiapas and

Campeche. When region-specific controls are applied, the clustering of high values diluted significantly, but Jalisco, Guanajuato and Queretaro remained significant.

Ending Conditions, PRI Representative Elections

The ten models were applied to ending conditions for PRI. In this period the conditions surrounding the representative vote changed. Table 4.12 shows the coefficients and levels of significance of the models. Gross state product emerged as significant and negative, as did the central western states, while literacy and indigenous population had a significant positive effect on vote shares. In consequence, PRI had less votes in poorer states such as Baja California Sur and Aguascalientes and in central western states, such as Guanajuato and Michoacan and a greater vote share therefore in states with higher literacy levels, such as Coahuila, and with a greater percentage of monolingual indigenous population, like Guerrero, Nayarit and Hidalgo. Spatial controls were not significant in this period.

There is change in the variables that were significant in this time span. Urbanization in the initial conditions is displaced by gross state product, while literacy emerged as significant at the end. Regionalisms changed as well, from important border effects in support to pockets of low support in the central western region at the end of the period. The switch of sign of the indigenous language variable, from lower vote shares in the beginning to high vote shares at the end, the reverse of the pattern for PRI, is a phenomenon that must be explained.

Test for spatial autocorrelation Strong clustering in the northwestern states diluted when spatial controls were applied to the base models (figure 4.12). Sinaloa is the state where clustering of high values remained for most of the models while Guanajuato is the state where clustering of low values prevailed.

Clustering was quite different from initial to final conditions. The strong central western cluster of low values eroded, while the strong cluster of high values moved from the south Gulf to the northwestern states.

Summary: Vote Shares for PRI

The spatial processes that patterned the vote in the senatorial election of 1964 for PRI disappeared at the end of the period. The literacy variable remained significant through time, as the gross

Table 4.12 Coefficients in ending vote share models: representative election for PRI, 2000

Independent Variables	BASE MODEL		BORDER		CARDINAL		LITTORAL		REGIONS	
	Socio Econ	Socio Spatial	Socio Border	Border Overall	Socio Cardinal	Cardinal Overall	Socio Littoral	Littoral Overall	Socio Regions	Regions Overall
Literacy	0.744	0.951	3.961	3.049	-1.500	-2.329	6.665[a]	8.679[a]	1.356	7.517
Gross State Product	-5.813[b]	-6.981	-5.502[a]	-6.003	-4.483	-10.539[b]	-5.328[b]	-7.341	-5.020[a]	-7.787[a]
Urbanization	-1.365	-1.500	-1.648	-1.627	-0.717	-1.127	-1.496	-1.870	-0.225	-1.956
Hierarchical		0.131		5.176		0.811		-0.242		-5.119
Population Potential		-0.037		-0.059		-0.102		0.006		0.072
Relative Location		0.027		0.058		0.106		0.002		-0.047
Indigenous Language			3.650	3.561[a]	1.147	-0.342	4.865[b]	5.165[b]	3.324	2.429
Oil State			0.010	0.012	0.014	-0.002	0.014	0.011	0.026	0.012
BORDER										
North			0.035	0.051						
South			-0.007	-0.014						
CARDINAL										
North					0.031	0.056				
South					0.007	0.018				
Central					0.049	0.062				
West Central					-0.064	-0.094[b]				
LITTORAL										
Atlantic							0.045	0.061		
Pacific							0.011	0.024		
REGIONS										
Region I									-0.011	0.074
Region II									-0.025	-0.003
Region III									0.062	0.070
Region IV									0.096	0.115
Region V									0.007	0.067
Region VI									0.028	0.063
Region VII									0.120[b]	0.165[b]
Region VIII									0.041	0.066
Region IX									0.035	0.124
Region X									-0.018	0.097
Region XI									0.039	0.089
Region XII									0.053	0.159[a]
Constant	0.445[a]	0.104	0.135	-0.684	0.572	-0.931	-0.138	-0.360	0.238	0.405
R-Squared	0.296	0.339	0.464	0.476	0.564	0.632	0.491	0.509	0.771	0.806

[a] Significant at 0.1 level, [b] at 0.05 level, [c] at 0.01 level.

state product variable in some models. Cardinal differences remained through time, but regionalisms shifted. The strong party support in the northern states, switched to the states along Oriental Sierra Madre by the end of the time span. Low support remained in central western states, such as Guanajuato, Jalisco and Michoacan.

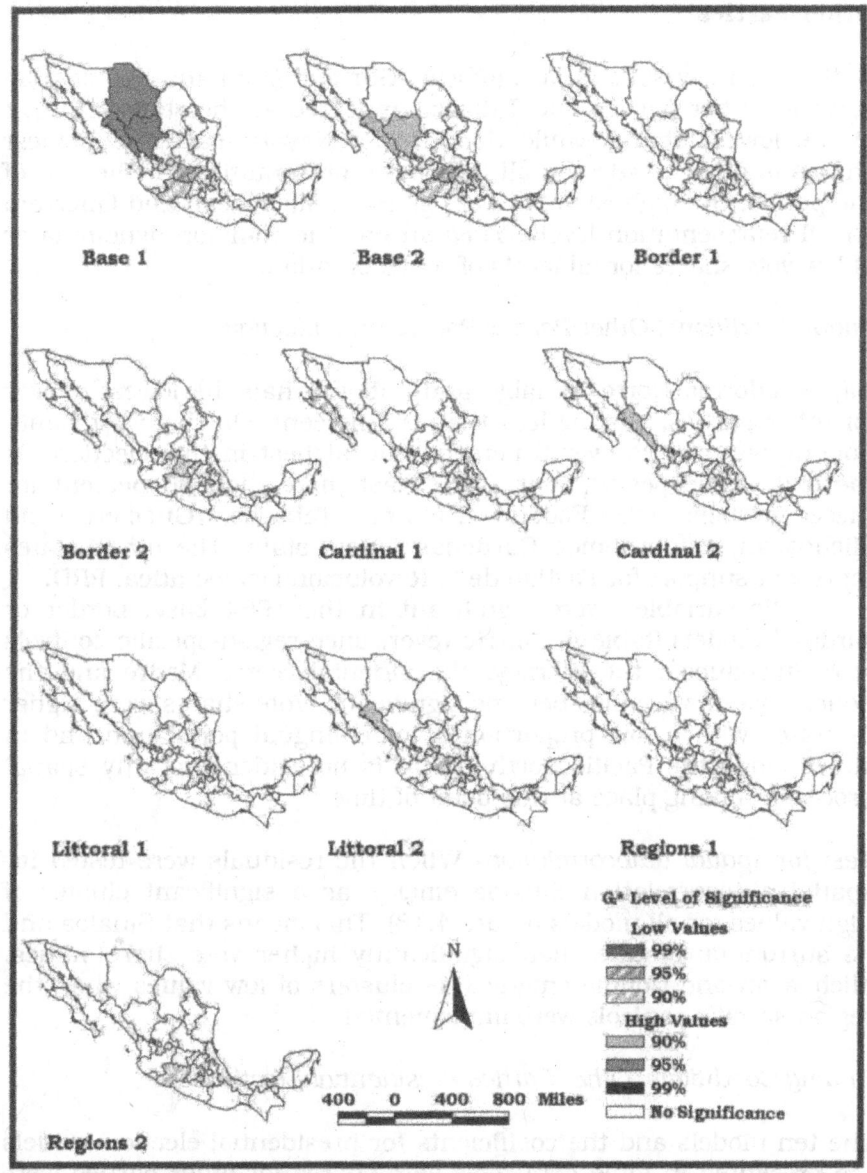

Figure 4.12 G_t^* **test for residuals. PRI vote share representative election 2000**

Overall the pattern for PRI is one of a retreat to residual bases of strength as PAN increased and extended its bases of support, and as other parties offered region-specific challenges to the PRI dominance that had existed in 1964, as we now shall see.

Other Parties

In the 1964 elections Baja California Sur and Quintana Roo cast no votes for other parties and Tabasco appeared as the state with one of the lowest shares while Sonora and Nayarit gave the highest shares to other parties on all levels of representation. At the end of the period, the highest votes were given in Michoacan and Guerrero for all representation levels. Yucatan has the common denominator of low vote shares for all levels of representation.

Initial Conditions, Other Parties Presidential Elections

Baja California Norte, Hidalgo and Tabasco had the lowest shares for other parties, casting less than 0.2 percent. On the other hand, Sonora cast a little over 6 percent, the highest in this election. At the end of the period, four states cast more than 30 percent for these parties: the Federal District, Tabasco, Guerrero and Michoacan, Cuahutemoc Cardenas' home state. The other states represent support for Partido de la Revolucion Democratica, PRD.

No variables were significant in the 1964 base, border or cardinal models (table 4.13). However, once region-specific controls were introduced, the literacy, the Oriental Sierra Madre and the Sonora plains variables became significant. Vote shares were higher in states with a low proportion of monolingual population and in states along the Pacific north. There is no evidence of any spatial processes taking place at this point of time.

Test for spatial autocorrelation When the residuals were tested for spatial autocorrelation Sinaloa emerge as a significant cluster of high values for all models (figure 4.13). This means that Sinaloa and its surrounding states had significantly higher vote share values. Michoacan and Colima emerged as clusters of low values when the region specific controls were implemented.

Ending Conditions, Other Parties Presidential Elections

The ten models and the coefficients for presidential election models are presented in table 4.14. Low vote shares for other parties were cast in highly urbanized areas, in oil extractive states, and states along the Occidental Sierra Madre. Higher vote shares also were cast in states with higher gross state product, such as the Federal District, in northern states such as Baja California Sur and Coahuila, and southern states such as Guerrero, Oaxaca and Michoacan. No spatial processes were present in the time span,

Table 4.13 Coefficients in initial vote share models: presidential election for other parties, 1964

Independent Variables	BASE MODEL		BORDER		CARDINAL		LITTORAL		REGIONS	
	Socio Econ	Socio Spatial	Socio Border	Border Overall	Socio Cardinal	Cardinal Overall	Socio Littoral	Littoral Overall	Socio Regions	Regions Overall
Literacy	0.094	0.155	-0.053	-0.008	-0.369	-0.319	0.103	0.303	-0.441	0.690[a]
Gross State Product	0.389	0.151	0.431	0.289	0.604	0.496	0.322	0.003	0.246	0.333
Urbanization	-0.017	-0.005	-0.175	-0.111	-0.110	-0.123	-0.092	-0.137	0.191	0.325
Hierarchical		0.319		0.309		0.580		0.436		0.402
Population Potential		0.006		0.004		0.008		0.008		-0.001
Relative Location		-0.008		-0.006		-0.008		-0.007		0.004
Indigenous Language			-0.274	-0.257	-0.296	-0.263	-0.301[a]	-0.278	-0.074	-0.008
Oil State			-0.005	-0.003	-0.005	-0.005	-0.001	-0.001	-0.004	-0.006
BORDER										
North			0.008	0.004						
South			-0.007	-0.009						
CARDINAL										
North					0.015	0.021				
South					-0.002	0.002				
Central					0.011	0.016				
West Central					0.002	0.007				
LITTORAL										
Atlantic							-0.006	-0.002		
Pacific							0.006	0.011		
REGIONS										
Region I									-0.002	0.009
Region II									0.002	0.004
Region III									-0.001	0.007
Region IV									0.004	0.013
Region V									0.005	0.019
Region VI									-0.002	0.006
Region VII									0.014[a]	0.022[a]
Region VIII									-0.008	-0.007
Region IX									-0.007	-0.008
Region X									-0.009	-0.007
Region XI									0.054[c]	0.069[c]
Region XII									-0.008	-0.002
Constant	0.003	0.097	0.294	0.101	0.043[a]	0.129	0.013	0.084	0.034	-0.031
R-Squared	0.062	0.133	0.232	0.266	0.262	0.331	0.263	0.344	0.768	0.815

[a] Significant at 0.1 level, [b] at 0.05 level, [c] at 0.01 level.

although changes were noticeable. From low vote shares in states with high monolingual indigenous populations there was a shift to states with oil extractive industry and states with lower urbanization levels. The gross state product variable became important at the end of the period, as did cardinal variables.

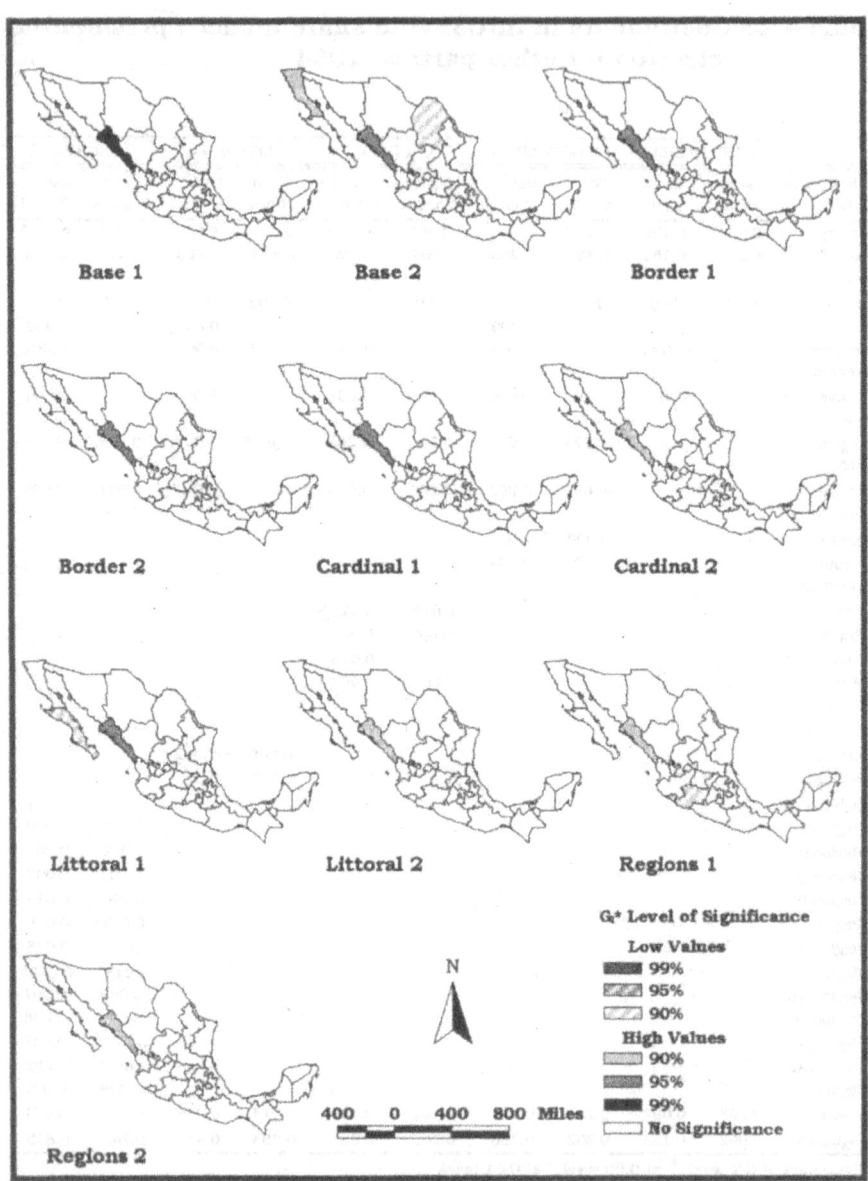

Figure 4.13 G_i^* test for residuals. Other parties vote share presidential election 1964

Test for spatial autocorrelation The significant G_i^* statistics for each of the regression models are shown in figure 4.14. There is a significant clustering of high values in states along the south Pacific, specifically in Guerrero, in all but the regions models. A

Table 4.14 Coefficients in ending vote share models: presidential election for other parties, 2000

Independent Variables	BASE MODEL		BORDER		CARDINAL		LITTORAL		REGIONS	
	Socio Econ	Socio Spatial	Socio Border	Border Overall	Socio Cardinal	Cardinal Overall	Socio Littoral	Littoral Overall	Socio Regions	Regions Overall
Literacy	-7.620	-1.847	-4.791	-5.018	5.841	8.432	-3.646	0.688	8.128	-1.446
Gross State Product	6.352	10.177	1.204[a]	10.479	7.491	16.040[c]	7.747[a]	9.234	4.806	11.133
Urbanization	-1.863	-1.517	-2.427	-2.786	-4.086[a]	-7.169[c]	-2.289	-2.602	-5.425	-2.648
Hierarchical		-0.842		1.047		-0.048		-2.363		5.628
Population Potential		0.069		0.060		0.198		0.100		-0.028
Relative Location		-0.057		-0.039		-0.130		-0.075		0.011
Indigenous Language			-2.658	-1.988	0.643	0.788	-2.298	-0.684	2.343	4.311
Oil State			-0.068[a]	-0.074	-0.074[b]	-0.112[c]	-0.054	-0.041	-0.051	-0.032
BORDER										
North			0.022	0.079						
South			0.029	0.043						
CARDINAL										
North					0.027	0.270[c]				
South					0.058	0.212[c]				
Central					-0.066	0.053				
West Central					0.090	0.196[c]				
LITTORAL										
Atlantic							0.008	0.047		
Pacific							0.012	0.055		
REGIONS										
Region I									-0.032	-0.100
Region II									-0.119	-0.132
Region III									-0.082	-0.063
Region IV									-0.074	-0.065
Region V									-0.107	-0.140
Region VI									-0.021	-0.034
Region VII									-0.199[a]	-0.231
Region VIII									-0.125	-0.149
Region IX									-0.033	-0.146
Region X									-0.201	-0.344
Region XI									-0.104	-0.112
Region XII									-0.083	-0.203
Constant	0.365	1.190	0.806	1.237	-0.068	1.246	0.687	1.227	-0.095	0.411
R-Squared	0.120	0.182	0.224	0.288	0.393	0.682	0.215	0.276	0.498	0.565

[a] Significant at 0.1 level, [b] at 0.05 level, [c] at 0.01 level.

cluster of significantly low values located in northern states emerged when cardinal and spatial controls were implemented. When region-specific controls are introduced, the clusters of high and low significant values disappeared from the models.

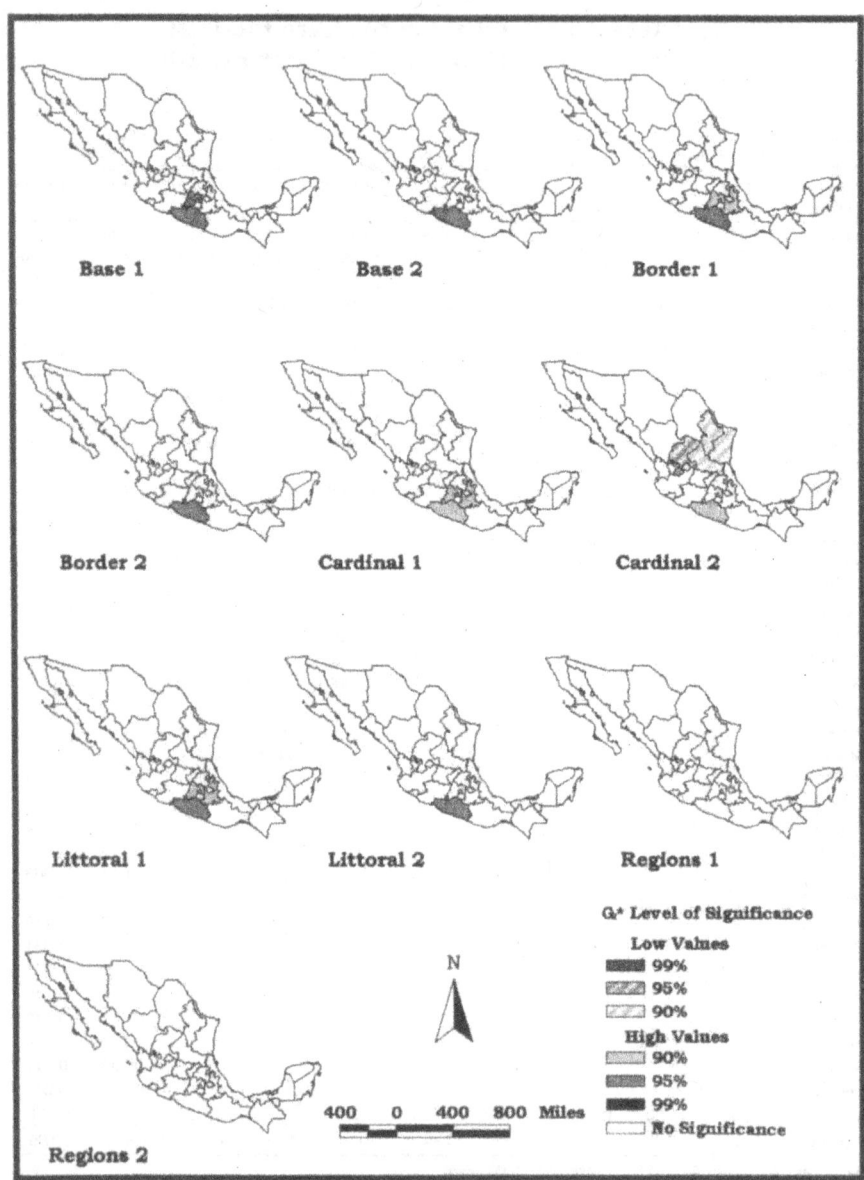

Figure 4.14 G_i^* test for residuals. Other parties vote share presidential election 2000

Initial Conditions, Other Parties Senatorial Elections

Less than half of the states had vote shares higher than 0.01 percent in this category of representation in the initial conditions. Sonora had the highest with 9 percent. At the end of the period, only Chihuahua and Yucatan cast less than 10 percent of their votes for other parties, while Baja California Sur and Michoacan cast a little over 40 percent, evidence of growth of party competition.

As in the preceding analyses, the ten models were estimated and their coefficient values are listed in table 4.15. Higher vote shares were cast in states with higher population potential, greater hierarchical level and along the north Pacific, mainly in Sonora, whereas low vote shares were present in states with high relative location and greater proportions of monolingual indigenous populations. There is some evidence of spatial diffusion in the models.

Test for spatial autocorrelation Clustering of highly significant values are present in Sinaloa and Baja California Norte for the base model (figure 4.15). Once spatial controls are introduced to the base model, Coahuila and the states surrounding it emerged as a significant cluster of low values, while Sinaloa disappeared as significant. When region-specific controls are applied the significant values switch from high values in Sinaloa to low values in Coahuila, to insignificant in the models containing the overall region variables.

Ending Conditions, Other Parties Senatorial Elections

Table 4.16 shows the coefficients and the levels of significance for the ten models. Greater vote shares were cast in states with greater gross domestic product, such as the Federal District, with certain cardinal characteristics, such as Baja California Sur. Lower vote shares where cast in states with higher urbanization levels, in states with an oil extractive industry, in states along the Oriental and Occidental Sierras and in the central plateau. There is no evidence of spatial diffusion, the proportion of monolingual population is no longer significant, and oil states emerged as significant and negative.

Test for spatial autocorrelation Figure 4.16 shows the G_i^* statistic for residuals of the ten models. There is a strong cluster of high values in Guerrero and Puebla. Some northeastern states had clusters highly significant values. Once spatial controls are implemented, the significance of the clusters both with high and low

Table 4.15 Coefficients in initial vote share models: senatorial election for other parties, 1964

Independent Variables	BASE MODEL		BORDER		CARDINAL		LITTORAL		REGIONS	
	Socio Econ	Socio Spatial	Socio Border	Border Overall	Socio Cardinal	Cardinal Overall	Socio Littoral	Littoral Overall	Socio Regions	Regions Overall
Literacy	0.265	0.340	-0.032	0.083	-0.331	-0.228	0.251	0.593	-0.252	-0.344
Gross State Product	0.392	0.001	0.537	0.276	0.394	0.205	0.312	-0.208	0.178	0.042
Urbanization	-0.111	-0.043	-0.351	-0.286	-0.159	-0.207	-0.209	-0.240	0.091	0.184
Hierarchical		0.820		0.814		1.016		1.075		1.158[b]
Population Potential		0.012[a]		0.010		0.013		0.016[b]		0.009
Relative Location		-0.014[a]		-0.010		-0.013		-0.014[a]		-0.002
Indigenous Language			-0.410	-0.372	-0.497[a]	-0.445	-0.418	-0.367	-0.117	-0.025
Oil State			-0.009	-0.006	-0.007	-0.007	-0.002	0.001	-0.006	-0.006
BORDER										
North			0.017	0.016						
South			-0.002	-0.003						
CARDINAL										
North					0.013	0.026				
South					-0.006	0.003				
Central					0.004	0.014				
West Central					-0.011	-0.002				
LITTORAL										
Atlantic							-0.004	0.001		
Pacific							0.008	0.016		
REGIONS										
Region I									-0.006	0.020
Region II									0.000	0.005
Region III									-0.004	0.011
Region IV									0.008	0.021
Region V									-0.001	0.021
Region VI									0.003	0.016
Region VII									0.009	0.021
Region VIII									-0.007	-0.003
Region IX									-0.007	0.001
Region X									-0.005	0.003
Region XI									0.081[c]	0.107[c]
Region XII									-0.009	0.008
Constant	-0.005	0.161	0.036	0.131	0.051	0.177	0.010	0.141	0.025	0.000
R-Squared	0.042	0.159	0.218	0.279	0.217	0.308	0.191	0.326	0.728	0.811

[a] Significant at 0.1 level, [b] at 0.05 level, [c] at 0.01 level.

values decrease only in the base models but increase or shift for the other models. A cluster of low values in Aguascalientes emerges when region-specific controls are implemented.

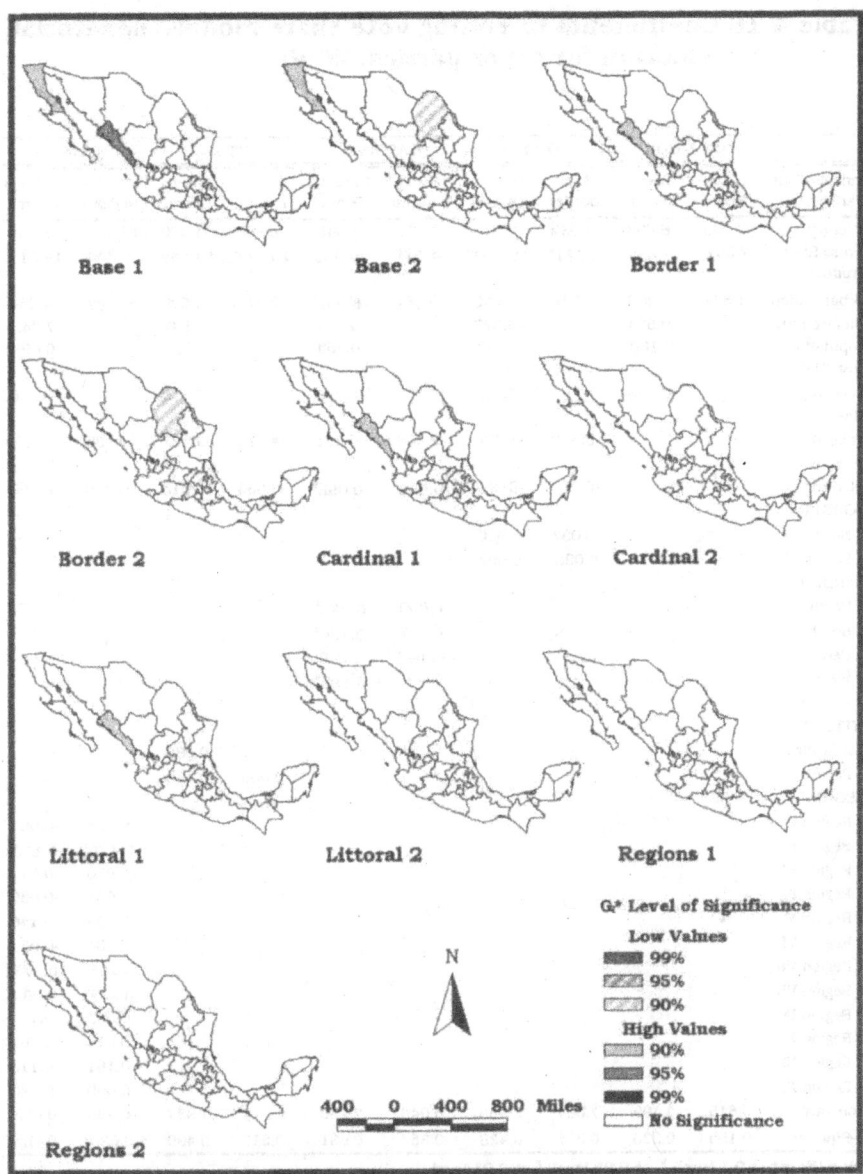

Figure 4.15 G_i^* test for residuals. Other parties vote share senatorial election 1964

Overall, the strong cluster of high values in Sinaloa disappeared in this time span. The clustering of low values in central Mexico only emerges at the end of the period.

Table 4.16 Coefficients in ending vote share models: senatorial election for other parties, 2000

Independent Variables	BASE MODEL		BORDER		CARDINAL		LITTORAL		REGIONS	
	Socio Econ	Socio Spatial	Socio Border	Border Overall	Socio Cardinal	Cardinal Overall	Socio Littoral	Littoral Overall	Socio Regions	Regions Overall
Literacy	-3.185	-6.808	-7.032	-8.211	0.296	1.945	-6.966	-1.990	12.3688	-1.058
Gross State Product	7.502	17.652[b]	8.871[a]	16.106[b]	8.763	23.559[c]	10.123[b]	16.138[b]	6.240	16.011[b]
Urbanization	-1.834	-0.906	-1.714	-1.752	-3.587	-6.001[b]	-2.710	-2.529	-6.287[b]	-4.354
Hierarchical		-0.524		-5.377		-2.595		-0.947		7.248
Population Potential		0.109		0.150		0.253		0.153		0.009
Relative Location		-0.098		-0.133		-0.194		-0.115		-0.016
Indigenous Language			-3.828	-3.136	-2.488	-0.951	-4.912	-2.127	-0.885	2.232
Oil State			-0.070	-0.067	-0.078[a]	-0.095[b]	-0.053	-0.015	-0.070	-0.050
BORDER										
North			-0.032	0.010						
South			0.093	0.092						
CARDINAL										
North					0.009	0.230[a]				
South					0.077	0.204[b]				
Central					-0.047	0.056				
West Central					0.054	0.189[b]				
LITTORAL										
Atlantic							0.041	0.088		
Pacific							0.056	0.119		
REGIONS										
Region I									-0.028	-0.067
Region II									-0.170[a]	-0.170[a]
Region III									-0.070	-0.014
Region IV									-0.084	-0.037
Region V									-0.153	-0.146
Region VI									-0.038	-0.021
Region VII									-0.261[b]	-0.275[b]
Region VIII									-0.227[b]	-0.208[b]
Region IX									-0.005	-0.141
Region X									-0.013	-0.182
Region XI									-0.161	-0.113
Region XII									-0.060	-0.190
Constant	0.615	2.199	1.004	2.955	0.046	2.780	1.046[b]	1.937	-0.190	0.856
R-Squared	0.155	0.335	0.361	0.428	0.357	0.631	0.317	0.490	0.630	0.765

[a] Significant at 0.1 level, [b] at 0.05 level, [c] at 0.01 level.

Initial Conditions, Other Parties Representative Elections

Eight states cast less than 10 percent of their votes for other parties in the initial representative elections. Although none of the states

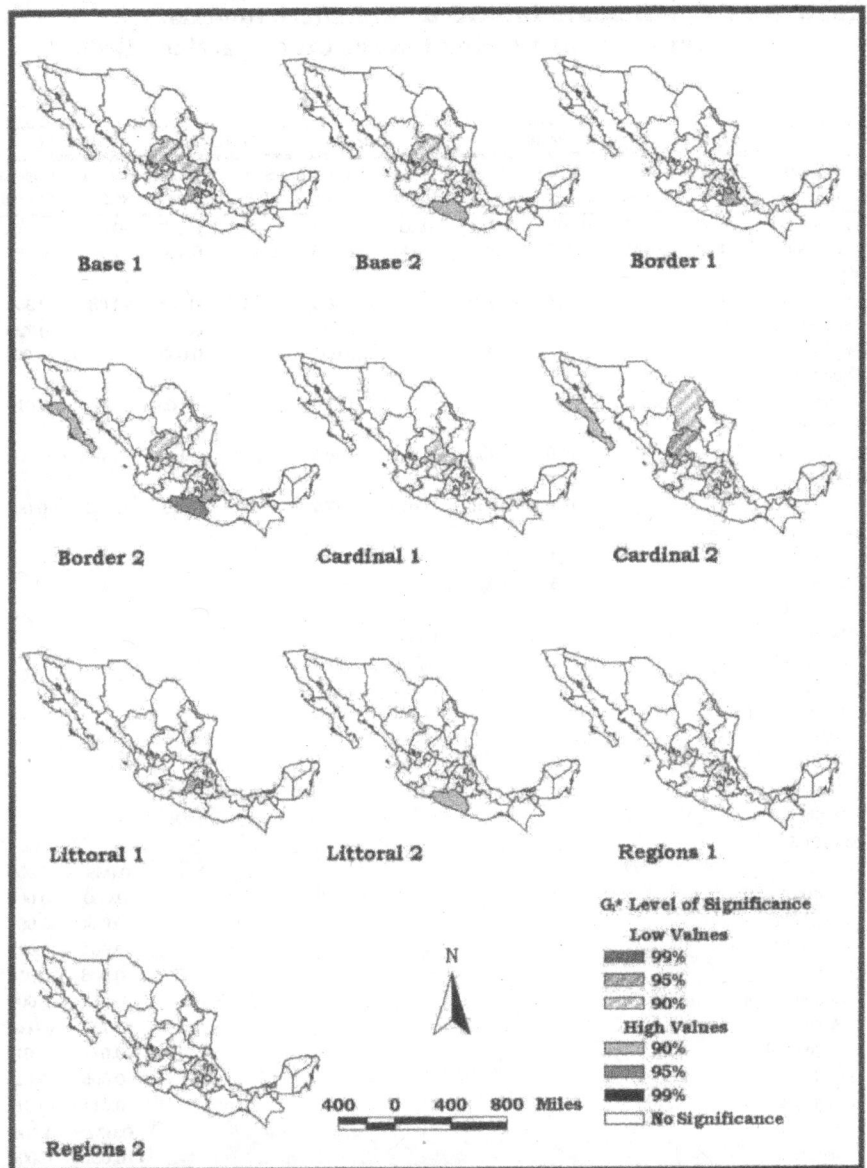

Figure 4.16 G_i^* **test for residuals. Other parties vote share senatorial election 2000**

surpassed the 10 percent share for senatorial elections, Baja California Sur, Nayarit and Sonora cast the highest, with a little over 7 percent. At the end of the time span conditions were different,

Table 4.17 Coefficients in initial vote share models: representative election for other parties, 1964

	BASE MODEL		BORDER		CARDINAL		LITTORAL		REGIONS	
Independent Variables	Socio Econ	Socio Spatial	Socio Border	Border Overall	Socio Cardinal	Cardinal Overall	Socio Littoral	Littoral Overall	Socio Regions	Regions Overall
Literacy	0.747[a]	0.483	0.591	0.278	-0.032	-0.270	0.800[a]	0.827	-0.091	-0.705
Gross State Product	0.458	0.685	0.384	0.859	0.742	1.086	0.457	0.444	0.501	0.782
Urbanization	0.295	-0.115	-0.418	-0.212	-0.401	-0.267	-0.441	-0.355	-0.033	0.302
Hierarchical		0.330		0.370		0.551		0.728		0.725
Population Potential		0.001		-0.001		0.001		0.005		-0.004
Relative Location		-0.004		-0.004		-0.003		-0.005		0.010
Indigenous Language			-0.386	-0.403	-0.508	-0.459	-0.496[a]	-0.468[a]	-0.146	0.009
Oil State			-0.008	-0.001	-0.010	-0.007	0.000	0.002	0.002	-0.001
BORDER										
North			0.004	0.000						
South			0.006	-0.021						
CARDINAL										
North					0.025	0.028				
South					0.001	-0.001				
Central					0.015	0.017				
West Central					-0.002	0.002				
LITTORAL										
Atlantic							-0.006	-0.005		
Pacific							0.020[b]	0.023[b]		
REGIONS										
Region I									0.033[a]	0.050
Region II									0.000	0.002
Region III									-0.014	0.001
Region IV									-0.001	0.015
Region V									-0.008	0.018
Region VI									-0.013	0.002
Region VII									0.023	0.039[a]
Region VIII									-0.011	-0.011
Region IX									-0.005	-0.011
Region X									-0.011	-0.011
Region XI									0.074[c]	0.102[c]
Region XII									-0.002	0.006
Constant	-0.015	0.057	0.014	0.095	0.050	0.096	-0.005	0.035	-0.003	-0.111
R-Squared	0.139	0.183	0.242	0.308	0.309	0.337	0.416	0.441	0.678	0.752

[a] Significant at 0.1 level, [b] at 0.05 level, [c] at 0.01 level.

Michoacan and Baja California Sur cast the highest votes with more than 40 percent, while Yucatan, Chihuahua and Nuevo Leon had cast less than 10 percent. Table 4.17 shows the coefficients for the

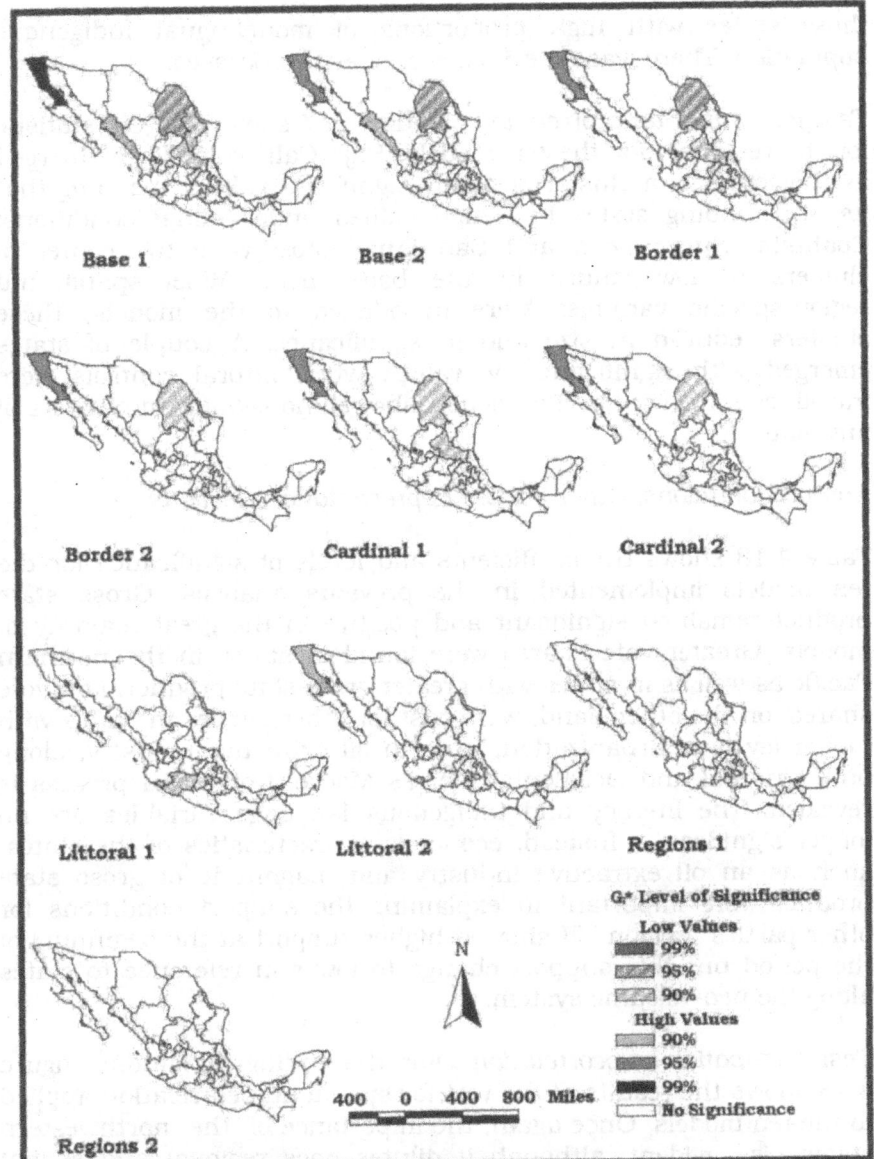

Figure 4.17 G_i^* test for residuals. Other parties vote share representative election 1964

ten models and their levels of significance. Greater vote shares occurred where literacy levels were higher, mainly in the Baja California peninsula as well as in Sonora. Low vote shares were in those states with high proportions of monolingual indigenous population. There was no evidence of spatial processes.

Test for spatial autocorrelation Figure 4.17 shows the G_i^* statistic for the residuals for the ten models. Baja California Norte emerged as the center of a cluster of highly significant values, meaning that its surrounding states had high values under initial conditions; Coahuila, Nuevo Leon and San Luis Potosi were the center of clusters of low values in the base model. When spatial and region-specific variables were introduced to the models, these clusters reduced in size and in significance. A couple of states emerged with significant low values when littoral controls were introduced. Region-specific models showed no significant clusters of any value.

Ending Conditions, Other Parties Representative Elections

Table 4.18 shows the coefficients and levels of significance for the ten models implemented in the previous analysis. Gross state product remained significant and positive in the great majority of models. Greater vote shares were found in states in the northern Pacific as well as in states with greater gross state product. Low vote shares, on the other hand, were cast for other parties in states with higher levels of urbanization, with an oil extractive industry, along both Oriental and Occidental Sierras Madre. No spatial process is revealed. The literacy and indigenous language variables are no longer significant. Instead, economic characteristics of the states, such as an oil extractive industry and magnitude of gross state product were important in explaining the support conditions for other parties. Region VII showed higher support at the beginning of the period but this support change to lower in reference to states along the neo-volcanic system.

Test for spatial autocorrelation For the ending conditions, figure 4.18 shows the results of the test for spatial autocorrelation applied to the ten models. Once again, the importance of the northwestern states is evident, although it dilutes once regional and spatial controls are introduced. Baja California Sur and Guerrero remained significant in a cluster of high values for some of the models. There are some scattered clusters of low significant values based in San Luis Potosi and Zacatecas throughout the models.

The strong evidence of support for other parties in the northern states remained significant from the beginning to the end.

Table 4.18 Coefficients in ending vote share models: representative election for other parties, 2000

Independent Variables	BASE MODEL Socio Econ	Socio Spatial	BORDER Socio Border	Border Overall	CARDINAL Socio Cardinal	Cardinal Overall	LITTORAL Socio Littoral	Littoral Overall	REGIONS Socio Regions	Regions Overall
Literacy	-0.243	-3.622	-3.664	-4.985	2.337	2.811	-3.770	0.263	12.5486	10.098
Gross State Product	8.767ª	17.758ᵇ	10.080ᵇ	16.478ᵇ	10.681ᵇ	23.927ᶜ	11.239ᵇ	16.159ᵇ	8.021	16.287ᵇ
Urbanization	-3.226	-2.374	-3.184	-3.129	-5.171ᵇ	-7.30ᶜ	-4.042ª	-3.840ª	-8.902ᵇ	-9.583ᵇ
Hierarchical		0.295		-4.243		0.238		0.129		-5.305
Population Potential		0.083		0.118		0.199		0.116		8.031
Relative Location		-0.076		-0.106		-0.146		-0.086		-0.013
Indigenous Language			-3.031	-2.538	-1.965	0.735	-4.444	-2.117	-0.405	0.005
Oil State			-0.075ª	-0.069	-0.088ᵇ	-0.103ᵇ	-0.056	-0.024	-0.074	2.366
BORDER										-0.057
North			-0.031	0.001						
South			0.067	0.060						
CARDINAL										
North					0.027	0.237ᵇ				
South					0.066	0.177ᵇ				
Central					-0.037	0.058				
West Central					0.067	0.187ᶜ				
LITTORAL										
Atlantic							0.022	0.061		
Pacific							0.059	0.111ᵇ		
REGIONS										
Region I									0.001	-0.031
Region II									-0.138	-0.136
Region III									-0.082	-0.026
Region IV									-0.083	-0.036
Region V									-0.135	-0.124
Region VI									-0.050	-0.033
Region VII									-0.233ᵇ	-0.245ᵇ
Region VIII									-0.199ᶜ	-0.216ᶜ
Region IX									-0.014	-0.137
Region X									-0.026	-0.178
Region XI									-0.125	-0.081
Region XII									-0.072	-0.191
Constant	0.442	1.698	0.796	2.400	0.372	2.109	0.847	1.437	-0.180	0.486
R-Squared	0.204	0.350	0.382	0.428	0.410	0.650	0.377	0.505	0.663	0.773

ª Significant at 0.1 level, ᵇ at 0.05 level, ᶜ at 0.01 level.

Low support was situated in a belt extending from the central northern states to the central southwestern states.

Baja California states had highly significant positive values in the initial period whereas the south showed significant low values at the end of the period.

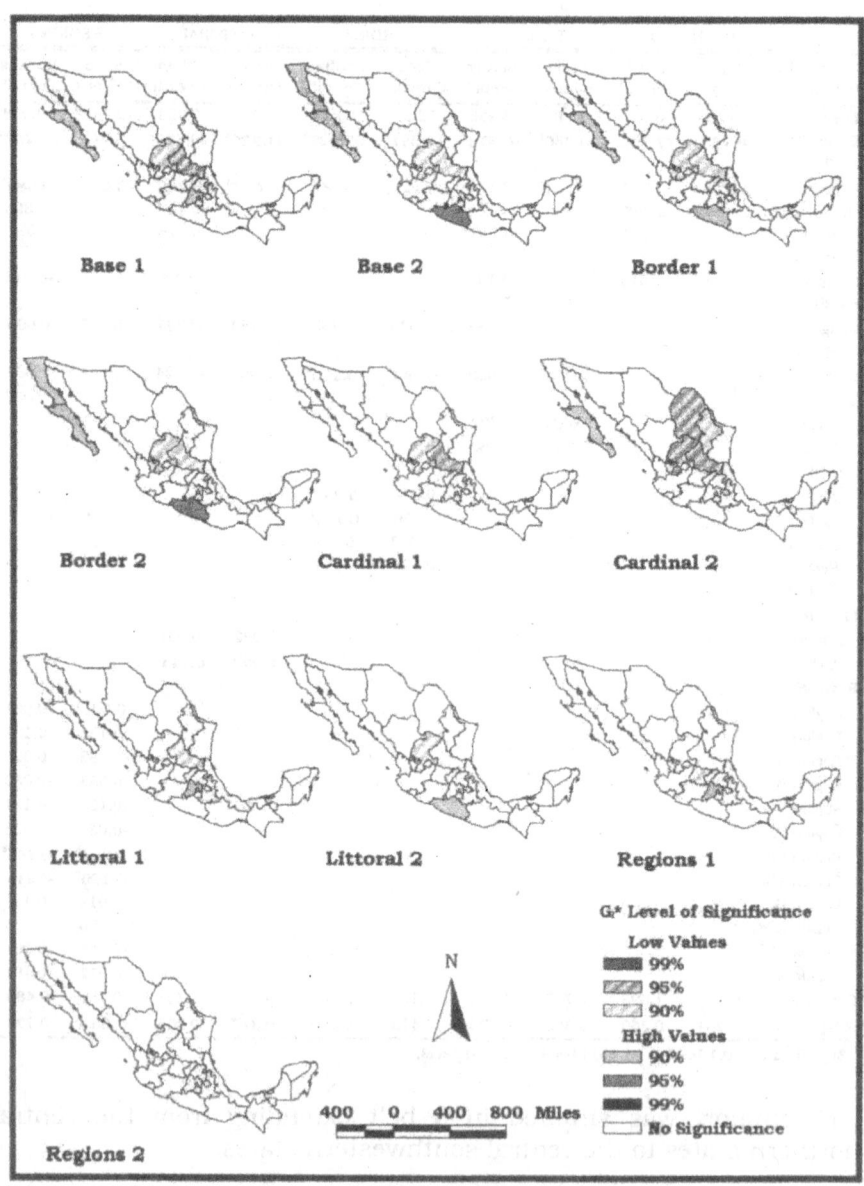

Figure 4.18 G_i^* test for residuals. Other parties vote share representative election 2000

Summary: Vote Shares for Other Parties

The support for other parties in Mexico's political landscape has changed substantially over the last three decades. Vote shares were low in the 1960s, although somewhat higher where literacy levels were greater. By the end of the time period, more support for other parties was found where gross state product was the greatest, whereas in states with an extractive oil industry, lower levels of urbanization, or along both main sierras had the lowest support.

Overview of Comparative Statistics: 1964-2000 Shifts in Voting Patterns

Drawing together the findings in this chapter, at the beginning of the study period there was PRI dominance at all levels of representation. To the extent that PAN offered a challenge to PRI it was where urbanization levels were the greatest, the proportion of the dialectically monolingual indigenous population was greater and in oil extractive states. Other parties challenged PAN in states where the literacy was the greatest.

At the end of the time span, PRI's dominance had been eroded, especially at the presidential level although less so in senatorial and representative elections. PAN support had increased strongly in oil extractive states and the support was greater in the central plateau than in states along the neo-volcanic system which divides Mexico at its center. Support for other parties not only remained in states with the highest literacy level but also in states with the highest gross state product, the best instance being the Federal District. PRI support remained stronger in states with a greater proportion of non-Spanish speaking indigenous population and in states with higher literacy levels but low gross state product.

There was some evidence of spatial diffusion at the beginning of the time span, with strongest significant values for senatorial elections for PRI and to a lesser degree for other parties and PAN. These initial signs had vanished at the end of the period, however. On the other hand, there was regional vote concentration for PAN in the central plateau and in some states along the Oriental Sierra Madre and for other parties in the southernmost states along the Pacific and in central Mexico, while a regional concentration remained in states along the Occidental Sierra Madre for PRI.

Important switches of support occurred: in the strong initial support for PAN in states with the greatest indigenous monolingual population to residual support at the end of the time span in the same area for PRI, and influence of literacy at the beginning negative for PAN but at the end positive and highly significant.

PAN's base of support was overwhelmingly middle-class. This was reflected in the significance of the urbanization variable. From 1987 to 1990 Luis H. Alvarez, (PAN's national president from 1987-1993) had wanted to broaden the party's base in squatter settlements and other low-income peripheral urban neighborhoods and rural areas (Chand, p. 130) but the scarcity of full-time PAN workers trying to organize the party in these regions plus the high level of regime control over urban workers and *campesinos* made that task almost impossible. On the other hand, Cuauhtemoc Cardenas' impressive performance in the 1988 presidential campaign, attracting a large working-class population, as well as strong support in "poverty stricken states, like Morelos" (Chand, p. 131) gave PAN leaders a wake-up call to focus party support on these two main areas.

The electoral system opened up as a result of a series of electoral reforms between 1989 and 1996. The most important step in this process of democratization was the "citizen-run Federal Election Institute (IFE), reformed in 1996 to exclude political party representatives from all decision making and controlled by citizens councilors approved by the three major political parties" (Chand, p. 291). With PRI's lock on the political process, both PAN and other parties, especially PRD could launch organized challenges. Under the leadership of Vicente Fox, PAN had a strong power base centering in Guanajuato and was able to appeal to votes in areas where the level of urbanization was higher and in oil extractive states. The power base of the PRD derived from the strength of Cuauhtemoc Cardenas in his home state of Michoacan, but extended to a strong appeal in workers in the southern states Guerrero and Tabasco, in Baja California Sur and in the Federal District. In the faces of these challenges, PRI retreated to residual party strengths in states with greatest proportion of monolingual indigenous population such as Chiapas, Oaxaca or Hidalgo on one hand, and in more urbanized states such as Sinaloa, Chihuahua or Yucatan. These changes appear to be understood in terms of the influence of significant social and economic variables (urbanization, indigenous population, oil industry) and the regional power bases of charismatic party leaders (Fox and Cardenas). The comparative statistics (1964 vs. 2000) provided no evidence that spatial diffusion may have molded the change. The next chapter explores whether the same conclusions apply to the dynamics of rates of changes.

Chapter 5

Change in Shares of the Popular Vote

Whereas the previous chapter documented factors associated with variations in vote shares at initial and end-point time periods, this chapter focuses upon the dynamic of vote share changes between initial and ending conditions for PAN, PRI and other parties in presidential, senatorial and representative elections. Following the methodology of chapter four, the same ten models were calibrated to capture the effects of different sets of variables on PAN, PRI and other parties' votes. The difference is that the dependent variable is measured as the vote share change between initial and ending conditions and the independent variables are measured as changes in literacy levels, in gross state product shares, in urbanization, in hierarchical level, in population potential, in relative location and in the proportion of the dialectically monolingual population. The dummy variables for oil, border, cardinal, littoral and regions remained, of course, the same.

Partido Accion Nacional, PAN

Changes of support for PAN over the 36-year period went from less than seven to close to 50 percent points. The states where changes of support were least were the Federal District, Guerrero and Michoacan for the three party categories, while the two states with the greatest changes were Sonora and Aguascalientes.

PAN Presidential Elections

Table 5.1 shows the coefficients and the levels of significance for the ten presidential models. The only circumstance in which significant coefficients are observed is where there is a full set of regional controls, in which case changes in support were shown to be inversely proportional to changes in literacy levels. When region-specific controls were introduced, states along the Oriental Sierra Madre emerged as significant in relation to states situated in the neo-volcanic system that is, in the central states.

Table 5.1 Coefficients for change in vote share models: presidential elections for PAN, 1964-2000

Independent Variables	BASE MODEL Socio Econ	Socio Spatial	BORDER Socio Border	Border Overall	CARDINAL Socio Cardinal	Cardinal Overall	LITTORAL Socio Littoral	Littoral Overall	REGIONS Socio Regions	Regions Overall
Literacy	-2.555	-4.021	-1.517	-1.149	-1.529	-1.035	-2.785	-3.066	-5.435ª	-6.946ª
Gross State Product	4.826	6.694	2.595	2.866	4.876	4.529	5.915	6.104	7.803	7.384
Urbanization	2.073	0.789	2.989	1.849	2.266	1.146	1.897	1.260	2.719	4.311
Hierarchical		-4.811		0.736		-1.074		-2.042		-1.294
Population Potential		0.036		0.066		0.046		0.018		-0.013
Relative Location		-0.019		-0.043		-0.028		-0.013		0.014
Indigenous Language			1.468	1.836	2.043	1.966	1.522	1.489	3.173	2.435
Oil State			0.038	0.028	0.045	0.033	0.013	0.012	0.043	0.087
BORDER										
North			0.054	0.104						
South			-0.015	0.001						
CARDINAL										
North					0.017	0.069				
South					-0.056	-0.022				
Central					-0.007	0.017				
West Central					-0.043	-0.026				
LITTORAL										
Atlantic							-0.001	0.000		
Pacific							-0.062	-0.059		
REGIONS										
Region I									-0.057	-0.042
Region II									0.080	0.043
Region III									-0.053	-0.134
Region IV									0.088	0.008
Region V									-0.108	-0.161
Region VI									-0.044	-0.086
Region VII									-0.099	-0.083
Region VIII									0.117ᵇ	0.106
Region IX									-0.016	-0.006
Region X									-0.018	-0.048
Region XI									0.127	0.139
Region XII									0.010	0.023
Constant	0.328ᶜ	0.567	0.281ᶜ	0.797ª	0.331ᵇ	0.631	0.379ᶜ	0.557	0.405ᶜ	0.115
R-Squared	0.118	0.170	0.225	0.294	0.244	0.270	0.635	0.272	0.639	0.665

ª Significant at 0.1 level, ᵇ at 0.05 level, ᶜ at 0.01 level.

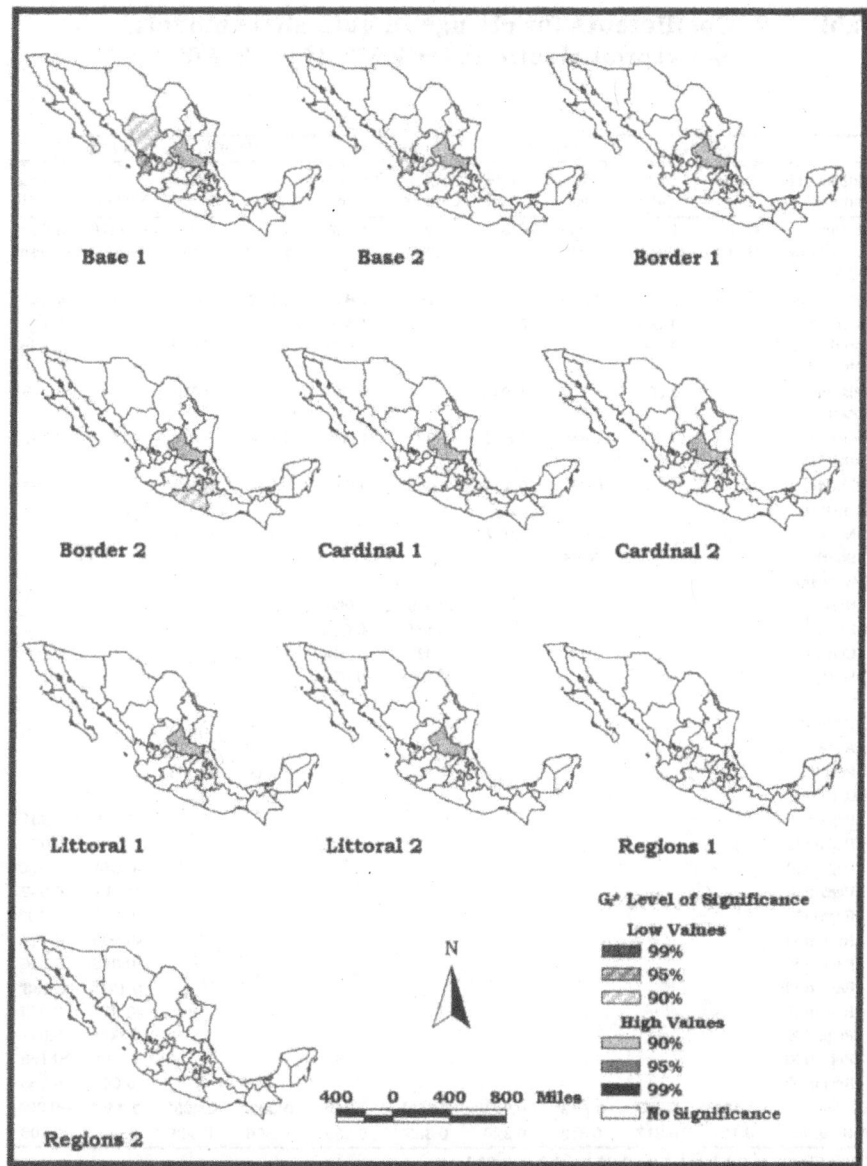

Figure 5.1 G_i^* test for residuals. Change in vote share for PAN presidential elections 1964-2000

Test for spatial autocorrelation Residuals from each of the regressions were tested using the G_i^* statistic in order to determine whether the variables in the models captured the spatial behavior of the dependent variable. Figure 5.1 shows these residuals for all ten

Table 5.2 Coefficients for change in vote share models: senatorial elections for PAN, 1964-2000

Independent Variables	BASE MODEL		BORDER		CARDINAL		LITTORAL		REGIONS	
	Socio Econ	Socio Spatial	Socio Border	Border Overall	Socio Cardinal	Cardinal Overall	Socio Littoral	Littoral Overall	Socio Regions	Regions Overall
Literacy	-2.653	-3.634	-1.611	-1.319	-0.256	-0.107	-3.055	-2.719	-4.7176	-6.939ª
Gross State Product	8.369	9.943ª	6.509	6.407	7.060	7.172	9.745ª	9.430	10.961ª	11.273ª
Urbanization	1.722	1.466	2.566	2.174	1.780	1.842	1.503	1.891	2.200	4.566
Hierarchical		-1.601		0.887		1.406		0.776		0.146
Population Potential		0.006		0.029		0.008		-0.017		-0.015
Relative Location		0.003		-0.019		-0.003		0.010		0.026
Indigenous Language			1.446	1.658	1.893	1.908	1.448	1.471	3.326	2.392
Oil State			0.037	0.034	0.042	0.037	0.012	0.013	0.039	0.084
BORDER										
North			0.053	0.077						
South			-0.050	-0.042						
CARDINAL										
North					0.049	0.066				
South					-0.056	-0.042				
Central					0.025	0.034				
West Central					-0.030	-0.028				
LITTORAL										
Atlantic							-0.023	-0.027		
Pacific							-0.060	-0.066		
REGIONS										
Region I									-0.039	0.031
Region II									0.097	0.077
Region III									-0.044	-0.130
Region IV									0.126	0.049
Region V									-0.075	-0.107
Region VI									-0.065	-0.082
Region VII									-0.045	0.006
Region VIII									0.121ᵇ	0.133ª
Region IX									-0.025	0.023
Region X									0.000	0.011
Region XI									0.117	0.165
Region XII									-0.005	0.055
Constant	0.294ᶜ	0.229	0.252ᶜ	0.481	0.253ª	0.249	0.352ᶜ	0.225ᶜ	0.353ᶜ	-0.204
R-Squared	0.187	0.217	0.312	0.326	0.335	0.339	0.308	0.303	0.649	0.700

ª Significant at 0.1 level, ᵇ at 0.05 level, ᶜ at 0.01 level.

models. Clustering of low values for changes in vote shares emerged in Durango and Nayarit for the base model and a cluster of high values is present in San Luis Potosi and states surrounding it.

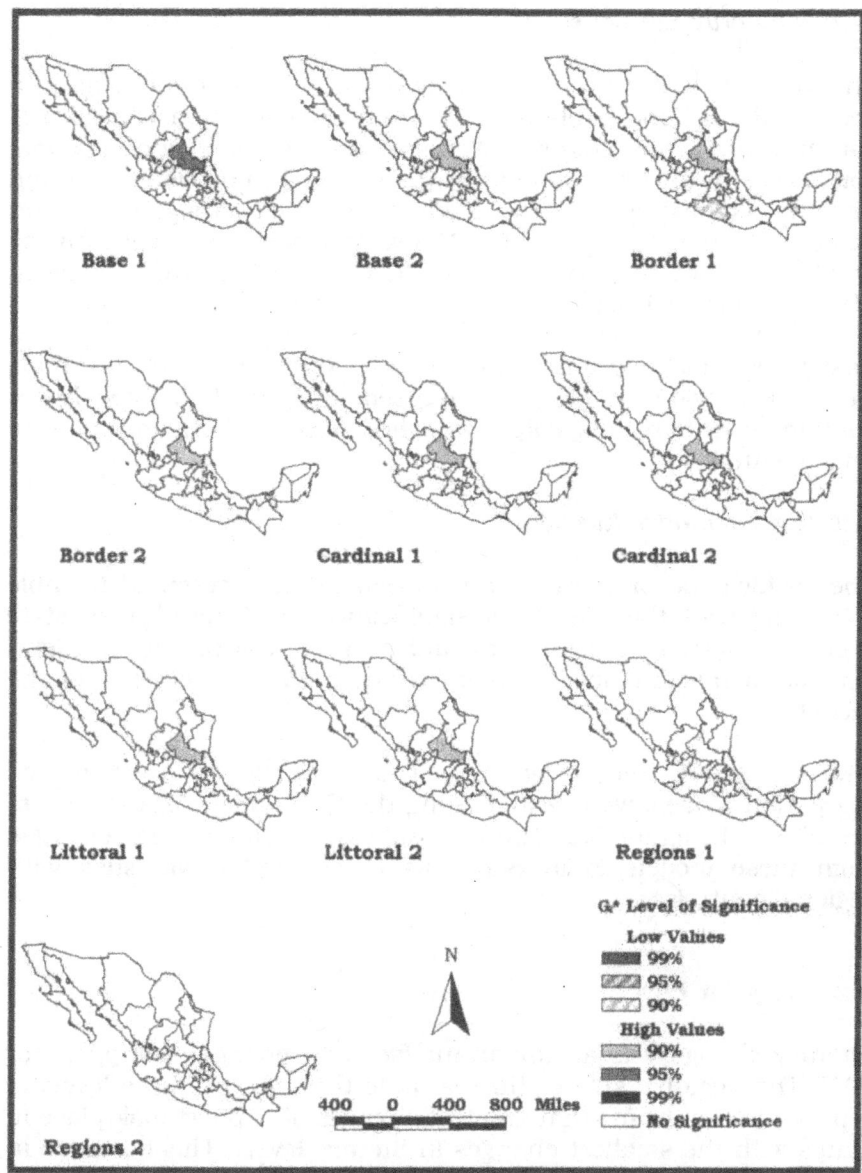

Figure 5.2 G_1^* test for residuals. Change in vote share for PAN senatorial elections 1964-2000

Once regional controls were implemented, the cluster of low values vanished: spatial autocorrelation resulted not from spatial diffusion processes but from the presence of regional change concentrations.

PAN Senatorial Elections

The next models were implemented for vote share changes in senatorial elections (table 5.2). The only significant variable in the earlier models was change in gross state product. Once regional controls were introduced literacy was revealed to be significant and negative whereas gross state product remained as significant and positive. Change in support for PAN was greatest in states with the greatest change in gross state product, and where the change in literacy level was least.

Test for spatial autocorrelation The G_i^* statistic for the residuals from the previous models are mapped in figure 5.2. The cluster containing in San Luis Potosi vanished once spatial controls were implemented.

PAN Representative Elections

The coefficients for representative elections are presented in table 5.3 along with their levels of significance. As before, gross state product emerged as significant and positive whereas literacy level became significant once regional controls were introduced to the models.

Test for spatial autocorrelation The residuals for each of the regression models were tested using the G_i^* statistic. These results are shown in figure 5.3. The only significant cluster that emerged from these models is in San Luis Potosi and it vanishes with regional controls.

Summary for PAN

Literacy change was an important factor in change of support for PAN. The negative sign of this variable through the three levels of representation means that greatest changes of support took place in states with the smallest changes in literacy levels. This occurred in the states that were the levels of literacy were already high, that is, in main urbanized areas, such as Baja California Norte, Coahuila or Nuevo Leon. Changes in gross state product were directly proportional to changes in the support for PAN. States with these characteristics are: Jalisco, Quintana Roo and Queretaro.

Table 5.3 Coefficients for change in vote share models: representative elections for PAN, 1964-2000

Independent Variables	BASE MODEL		BORDER		CARDINAL		LITTORAL		REGIONS	
	Socio Econ	Socio Spatial	Socio Border	Border Overall	Socio Cardinal	Cardinal Overall	Socio Littoral	Littoral Overall	Socio Regions	Regions Overall
Literacy	-2.473	-3.638	-1.668	-1.587	-1.247	-1.222	-2.743	-2.575	-4.8716	-7.041[a]
Gross State Product	8.257	9.830[a]	6.512	6.808	7.390	7.519	9.914[a]	9.670	10.387[a]	9.995
Urbanization	1.902	0.942	2.683	1.734	2.249	1.597	1.530	1.200	2.660	4.429
Hierarchical		-4.436		-0.972		-1.709		-2.059		-4.155
Population Potential		0.021		0.042		0.018		-0.003		-0.017
Relative Location		-0.009		-0.028		-0.011		-0.001		0.020
Indigenous Language			1.428	1.604		1.793	1.530	1.498	2.997	1.714
Oil State			0.034	0.028		0.038	0.007	0.006	0.040	0.098
BORDER										
North			0.044	0.071						
South			-0.021	-0.018						
CARDINAL										
North					0.019	0.036				
South					-0.048	-0.036				
Central					0.019	0.027				
West Central					-0.031	-0.025				
LITTORAL										
Atlantic							-0.011	-0.018		
Pacific							-0.067[a]	-0.074		
REGIONS										
Region I									-0.065	-0.043
Region II									0.087	0.038
Region III									-0.025	-0.138
Region IV									0.077	-0.033
Region V									-0.090	-0.159
Region VI									-0.056	-0.113
Region VII									-0.056	-0.025
Region VIII									0.110[a]	0.096
Region IX									-0.027	-0.008
Region X									-0.001	-0.051
Region XI									0.108	0.131
Region XII									0.020	0.045
Constant	0.286[c]	0.403	0.251[c]	0.600	0.270[b]	0.398	0.350[c]	0.394	0.344[c]	-0.058
R-Squared	0.187	0.222	0.273	0.300	0.295	0.301	0.327	0.333	0.608	0.654

[a] Significant at 0.1 level, [b] at 0.05 level, [c] at 0.01 level.

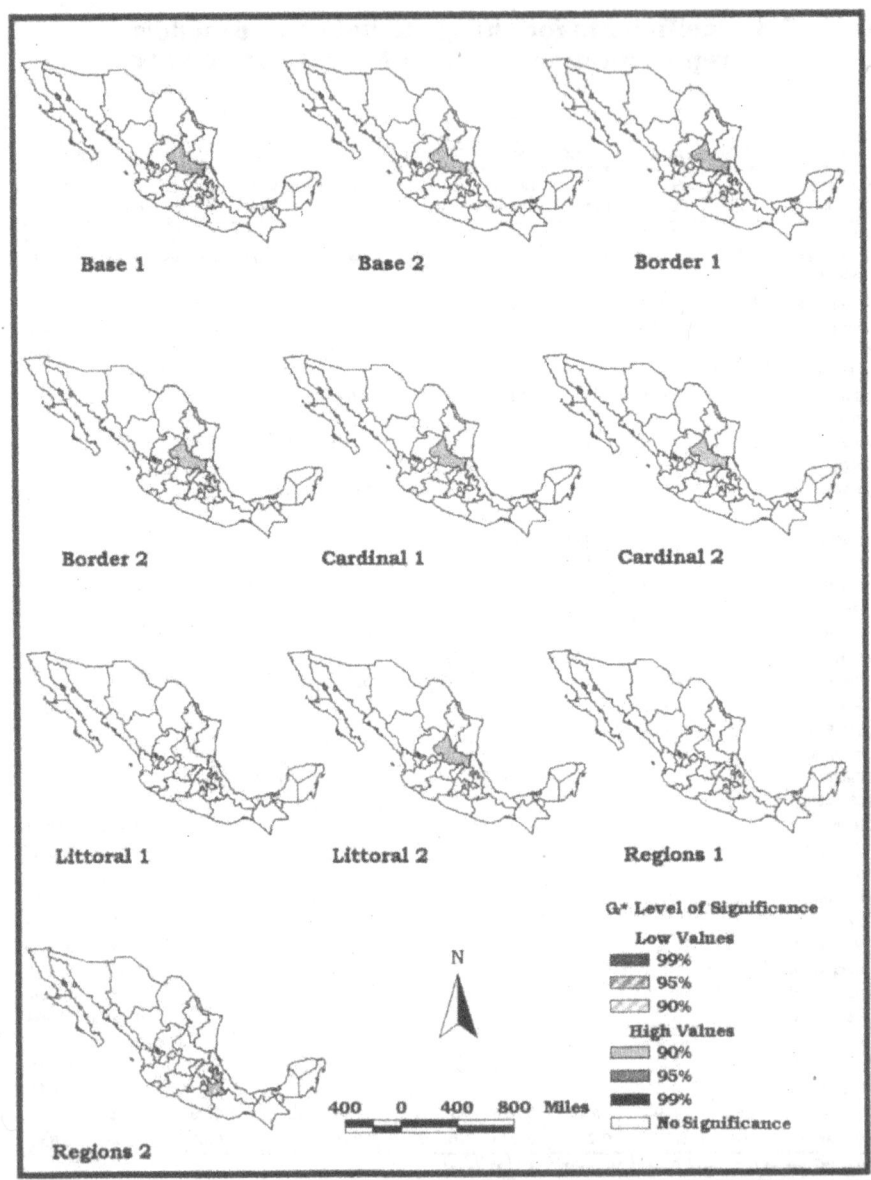

Figure 5.3 G_i^* test for residuals. Change in vote share for PAN representative elections 1964-2000

Table 5.4 Coefficients for change in vote share models: presidential elections for PRI, 1964-2000

Independent Variables	BASE MODEL Socio Econ	Socio Spatial	BORDER Socio Border	Border Overall	CARDINAL Socio Cardinal	Cardinal Overall	LITTORAL Socio Littoral	Littoral Overall	REGIONS Socio Regions	Regions Overall
Literacy	-1.950	-0.544	-1.803	-1.729	-0.672	-1.744	-1.970	-0.433	2.1262	2.364
Gross State Product	3.840	2.537	6.386	5.364	6.433	7.572	6.892	5.242	1.801	3.909
Urbanization	-3.557^b	-1.261	-4.503^b	-2.933	-4.583^b	-1.711	-4.727^b	-2.525	-4.670^c	-5.441^c
Hierarchical		8.613^a		1.345		4.541		6.289		14.256
Population Potential		-0.059^a		-0.068^a		-0.105^a		-0.071^b		0.009
Relative Location		0.039^a		0.043^a		0.067^c		0.044^b		0.008
Indigenous Language			-0.369	-0.573	-0.044	0.148	-0.388	-0.103	-0.822	-0.654
Oil State			-0.035	-0.021	-0.033	-0.008	-0.044	-0.035	-0.053	-0.103^b
BORDER										
North			-0.007	-0.050						
South			-0.066	-0.079						
CARDINAL										
North					-0.009	-0.116				
South					-0.047	-0.111^c				
Central					0.029	-0.019				
West Central					-0.049	-0.092^a				
LITTORAL										
Atlantic							-0.047	-0.066		
Pacific							-0.014	-0.038		
REGIONS										
Region I									0.043	0.133^a
Region II									0.032	0.110^a
Region III									0.144^a	0.226^b
Region IV									0.035	0.135
Region V									0.210^c	0.317^c
Region VI									-0.023	0.074
Region VII									0.159^c	0.220^c
Region VIII									-0.013	0.049
Region IX									-0.008	0.064
Region X									-0.028	0.077
Region XI									-0.034	0.034
Region XII									0.030	0.116^b
Constant	-0.378^c	-0.926^c	-0.338^c	-0.867^c	-0.353^c	-1.117^c	-0.321^c	-0.896^c	-0.465	-0.658^c
R-Squared	0.214	0.355	0.362	0.462	0.395	0.598	0.340	0.474	0.774	0.862

^a Significant at 0.1 level, ^b at 0.05 level, ^c at 0.01 level.

Partido Revolucionario Institucional, PRI

In the period from 1965 to 2000 PRI lost support in every state. Morelos was the state in which support for PRI decreased the most

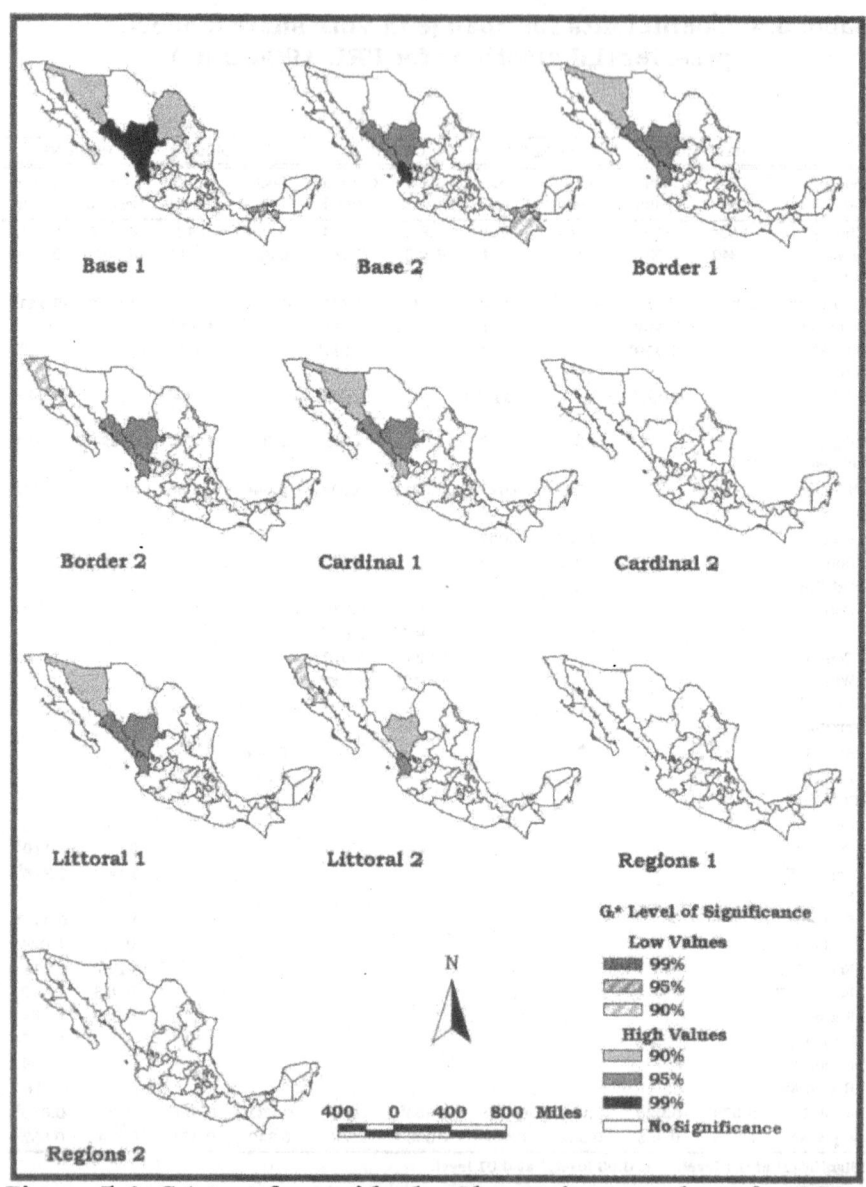

Figure 5.4 G₁* test for residuals. Change in vote share for PRI presidential elections 1964-2000

for all levels of representation, while Quintana Roo and Baja California Sur were added to Morelos for presidential and representative elections and Estado de Mexico and Veracruz for senatorial elections. On the other hand, Nayarit and Chihuahua were the states that lost least support for all levels of representation. Baja California Norte joined them for senatorial and representative elections and Sinaloa for presidential elections.

PRI Presidential Elections

The coefficients and levels of significance of the ten models are in table 5.4. The vote change for PRI was lowest (i.e. the party's residual strengths were greater where urbanization and population potential levels increased most rapidly, in the densely populated core of the country.

Test for spatial autocorrelation Figure 5.4 shows the G_i^* statistic for the coefficients of the ten models. Strong clustering of high values appeared in the northwestern and north central states, and a cluster of low values is present in Tabasco. When spatial and regional controls were introduced, the core of the cluster with high significant values shifted south, from Sinaloa and Durango to Nayarit, while the cluster of low values expanded to Chiapas. Once region-specific controls were implemented the cluster of low values disappeared.

PRI Senatorial Elections

The greatest changes took place in states where the literacy levels, gross state product and population potentials changed the least and where urbanization changed the most. Table 5.5 shows the coefficients and their levels of significance. Clearly spatial diffusion processes are operating.

Test for spatial autocorrelation Figure 5.5 shows the G_i^* statistic results for residuals from the previous regressions. There are clusters of high values in the two extremes of the country, in Baja California Sur and in the Yucatan peninsula, for the base and littoral models. When spatial and regional controls are introduced clusters of significantly low values emerged in the northwestern states of Chihuahua and Sinaloa and in central Mexico, in Puebla, Estado de Mexico and Morelos.

PRI Representative Elections

The change on support for PRI representatives is inversely proportional to literacy change, urbanization change and population potential change, similar to the previous analysis. Changes in gross

Table 5.5 Coefficients for change in vote share models: senatorial elections for PRI, 1964-2000

Independent Variables	BASE MODEL Socio Econ	Socio Spatial	BORDER Socio Border	Border Overall	CARDINAL Socio Cardinal	Cardinal Overall	LITTORAL Socio Littoral	Littoral Overall	REGIONS Socio Regions	Regions Overall
Literacy	-9.352[b]	-2.257	-11.136[a]	-5.133	-8.788	-5.981	-8.041[b]	-2.333	-2.387	-3.650
Gross State Product	-13.978	-24.493[c]	-14.014	-27.751[c]	-18.891	-28.896[c]	-20.969[a]	-31.582[c]	-30.316[c]	-31.983[c]
Urbanization	15.972[c]	19.040[c]	15.516[c]	22.487[c]	17.486[c]	22.435[c]	17.762[c]	22.107[c]	17.409[c]	22.370[c]
Hierarchical		11.915		18.456[a]		15.136		15.682		153.587
Population Potential		-0.100[a]		-0.145[b]		-0.116		-0.099		-0.019
Relative Location		0.024		0.060		0.031		0.021		0.015
Indigenous Language			-2.844	-0.971	-3.114	-0.780	-3.047	-0.286	-3.428	-2.454
Oil State			-0.032	0.073	-0.034	0.084	0.020	0.098	0.052	0.123
BORDER										
North			-0.080	-0.102						
South			0.190[a]	0.119						
CARDINAL										
North					0.062	-0.081				
South					0.201[a]	0.038				
Central					0.039	-0.053				
West Central					-0.007	0.018				
LITTORAL										
Atlantic							0.148[a]	0.029		
Pacific							0.137[a]	0.033		
REGIONS										
Region I									0.473[c]	0.493[c]
Region II									0.100	0.041
Region III									0.179	0.093
Region IV									-0.070	-0.166
Region V									0.220	0.137
Region VI									0.068	0.019
Region VII									0.221[b]	0.178
Region VIII									0.068	0.047
Region IX									0.144	0.121
Region X									0.162	0.197
Region XI									0.080	0.049
Region XII									0.448[c]	0.418
Constant	-0.629[c]	-0.808	-0.618[c]	-1.340[b]	-0.788[c]	-0.902	-0.839[c]	-0.904	-1.050[c]	-1.413[c]
R-Squared	0.449	0.683	0.568	0.764	0.582	0.736	0.555	0.718	0.866	0.910

[a] Significant at 0.1 level, [b] at 0.05 level, [c] at 0.01 level.

state product, in hierarchical levels and in relative locations were directly tied to changes in vote share for PRI representatives during this period. Table 5.6 shows the coefficients and the levels of significance of the ten models implemented. There was a reduction of the spatial frame of support for PRI.

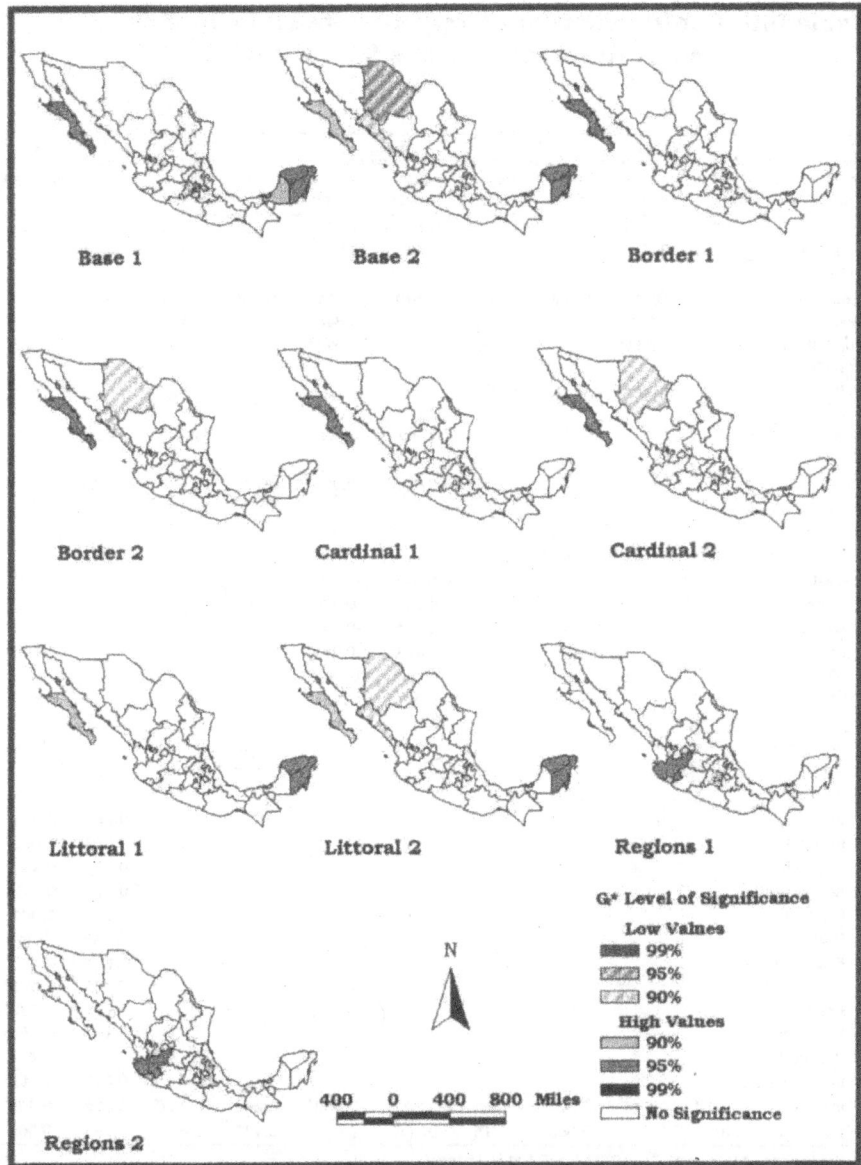

Figure 5.5 G_1^* test for residuals. Change in vote share for PRI senatorial elections 1964-2000

Test for spatial autocorrelation Clusters of significantly high values were present in the northwestern states, and of low values in the southern states. When control variables for spatial diffusion and regionalization were implemented in the models, the cluster of high

Table 5.6 Coefficients for change in vote share models: representative elections for PRI, 1964-2000

Independent Variables	BASE MODEL Socio Econ	Socio Spatial	BORDER Socio Border	Border Overall	CARDINAL Socio Cardinal	Cardinal Overall	LITTORAL Socio Littoral	Littoral Overall	REGIONS Socio Regions	Regions Overall
Literacy	-2.356^a	-1.190	-1.126	-0.573	0.105	-0.458	-2.430^a	-1.164	1.4423	1.682
Gross State Product	3.408	2.424	5.404	4.052	6.221	6.960	6.324	5.013	3.081	5.264^a
Urbanization	-4.436^c	-2.352	-5.298^c	-3.795^b	-5.880^c	-3.459^b	-5.456^c	-3.397^a	-6.006^c	-6.424^c
Hierarchical		7.609^a		3.844		5.645		6.301		34.214
Population Potential		-0.055^b		-0.043		-0.074^b		-0.062^b		0.009
Relative Location		0.037^b		0.026		0.049^a		0.040^b		0.009
Indigenous Language			0.312	0.379	0.692	0.923	0.253	0.504	0.003	0.357
Oil State			-0.037	-0.025	-0.037	-0.020	-0.037	-0.029	-0.046	-0.098^c
BORDER										
North			0.035	0.019						
South			-0.063^a	-0.062						
CARDINAL										
North					-0.051	-0.036				
South					0.030	-0.084				
Central					-0.046	-0.011				
West					0.019	-0.081^a				
Central					-0.051					
LITTORAL										
Atlantic							-0.043	-0.056		
Pacific							-0.008	-0.026		
REGIONS										
Region I									0.063	0.164^c
Region II									0.013	0.096^a
Region III									0.112	0.199^c
Region IV									0.073	0.179^b
Region V									0.194^c	0.307^c
Region VI									-0.042	0.063
Region VII									0.113^c	0.175^c
Region VIII									0.005	0.071^b
Region IX									0.002	0.078^a
Region X									-0.045	0.077b
Region XI									0.003	0.073
Region XII									0.020	0.111^b
Constant	-0.323^c	-0.845^c	-0.307^c	-0.652^b	-0.307^c	-0.903^c	-0.264^c	-0.791^c	-0.376^c	-0.609^c
R-Squared	0.389	0.519	0.560	0.615	0.558	0.693	0.491	0.611	0.794	0.901

^{a} Significant at 0.1 level, ^{b} at 0.05 level, ^{c} at 0.01 level.

values was reduced in size and in significance while the cluster of low values disappeared in all but the base models. Figure 5.6 shows the G_i^* statistic for the residuals of the models: again, with regional controls, autocorrelations are gone.

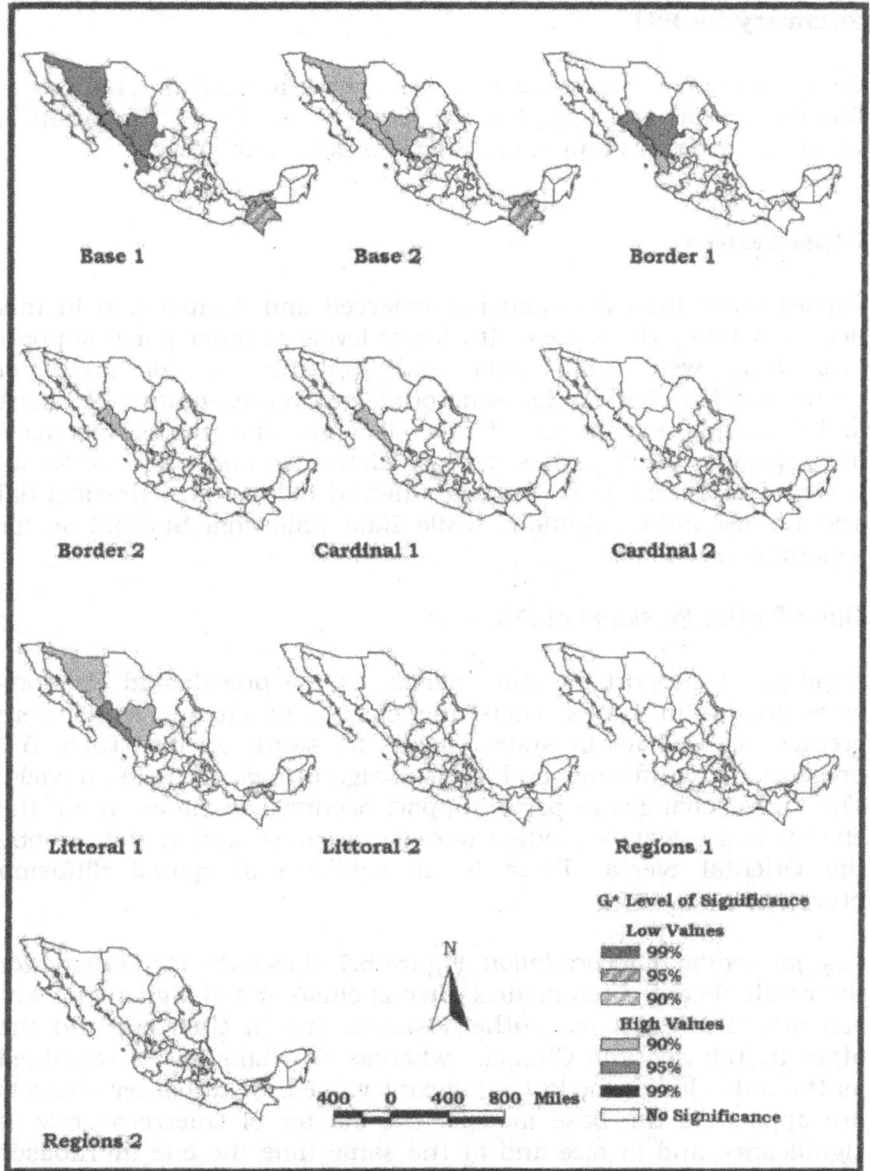

Figure 5.6 G_i^* test for residuals. Change in vote share for PRI representative elections 1964-2000

Summary for PRI

Bases of support remained in states with the smallest changes in literacy levels and gross state product such as Tamaulipas, Veracruz or Sonora and in areas with rapid urban growth.

Other Parties

Parties other than PAN and PRI emerged and disappeared in this period of time. The states with lower levels of other party support over time were Chihuahua and Yucatan for all levels of representation, Sonora for senatorial and representative elections and Guanajuato in the presidential elections. The greatest increases of support for other parties were in Michoacan and Guerrero for all levels of representation. Tabasco showed increases in presidential and representative elections while Baja California Sur did so for senatorial elections.

Other Parties Presidential Elections

Changes in support for other parties in the presidential elections were greater in states where the change in literacy levels were greater, as well as in states along the south Pacific. Table 5.7 presents the coefficients and levels of significance of the ten models. The lowest changes in party support occurred in states where the change in gross state product were the greatest, and in states along the Oriental Sierra. There is no evidence of spatial diffusion processes.

Test for spatial autocorrelation Figure 5.7 shows the G_i^* statistic for the residuals of the ten models. Strong clustering of high significant values was present in southern states, one in Guerrero and the other in Tabasco and Chiapas, whereas San Luis Potosi remained as the only cluster for low significant values. Once border controls are applied to the base models, the cluster of Guerrero grew in significance and in size and at the same time the one in Tabasco and Chiapas disappeared. After introducing cardinal controls the cluster of high significant values was dissolved, leaving two clusters of low significant values one in San Luis Potosi and the other in the Yucatan peninsula. These vanished when regional controls were imposed.

Change in Shares of the Popular Vote

Table 5.7 Coefficients for change in vote share models: presidential elections for other parties, 1964-2000

Independent Variables	BASE MODEL		BORDER		CARDINAL		LITTORAL		REGIONS	
	Socio Econ	Socio Spatial	Socio Border	Border Overall	Socio Cardinal	Cardinal Overall	Socio Littoral	Littoral Overall	Socio Regions	Regions Overall
Literacy	4.101	4.092[a]	2.938	2.380	1.945	2.456	4.348[b]	3.015	2.942	4.095
Gross State Product	-9.122[a]	-9.555[a]	-9.2976	-8.369	-11.840[a]	-12.435	-13.062[b]	-11.414[a]	-9.695	-11.302[a]
Urbanization	1.891	0.907	1.888	1.367	2.668	0.900	3.168	1.586	2.237	1.422
Hierarchical		-3.747		-2.632		-3.572		-4.353		-6.365
Population Potential		0.022		0.001		0.058		0.053		0.003
Relative Location		-0.019		0.001		-0.038		-0.031		-0.020
Indigenous Language			-1.034	-1.245	-1.967	-2.117	-1.094	-1.399	-2.270	-1.800
Oil State			-0.002	-0.007	-0.013	-0.027	0.029	0.020	0.006	0.013
BORDER										
North			-0.046	-0.055						
South			0.073	0.069						
CARDINAL										
North					-0.005	0.051				
South					0.101[a]	0.134[a]				
Central					-0.018	0.007				
West Central					0.095	0.120				
LITTORAL										
Atlantic							0.046	0.066		
Pacific							0.075[a]	0.097[b]		
REGIONS										
Region I									0.011	-0.090
Region II									-0.110	-0.150
Region III									-0.089	-0.093
Region IV									-0.121	-0.143
Region V									-0.100	-0.153
Region VI									0.069	0.015
Region VII									-0.063	-0.134
Region VIII									-0.106[a]	-0.154[a]
Region IX									0.022	-0.055
Region X									0.033	-0.041
Region XI									-0.093	-0.167
Region XII									-0.046	-0.140
Constant	0.027	0.318	0.037	0.044	-0.004	0.444	-0.077	0.301	0.043	0.496
R-Squared	0.208	0.239	0.327	0.332	0.439	0.493	0.335	0.393	0.576	0.624

[a] Significant at 0.1 level, [b] at 0.05 level, [c] at 0.01 level.

Other Parties Senatorial Elections

The vote share for other parties in senatorial elections increased most notably in states with greater changes in literacy levels, urbanization, population potential and in the south Pacific, (table 5.8). Changes were inversely proportional to changes in gross state product and relative location.

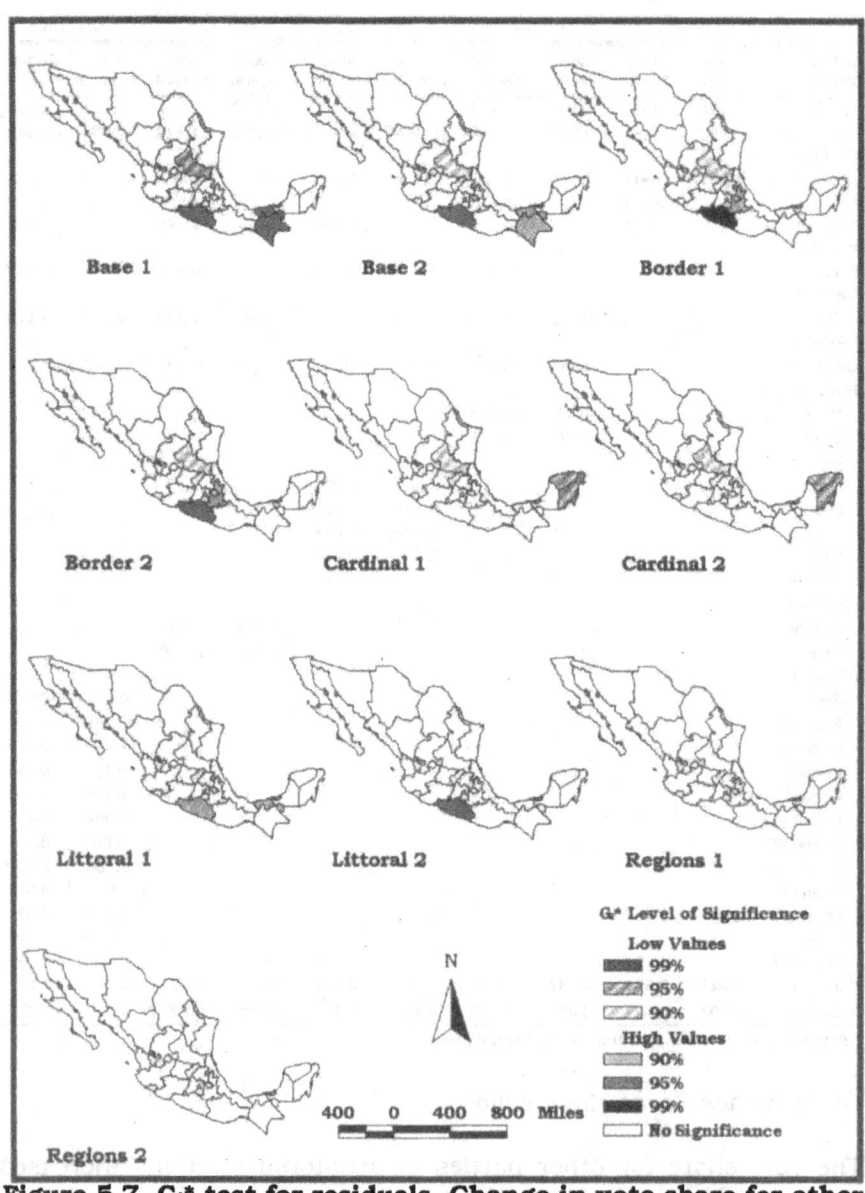

Figure 5.7 G_1^* test for residuals. Change in vote share for other parties presidential elections 1964-2000

Table 5.8 Coefficients for change in vote share models: senatorial elections for other parties, 1964-2000

Independent Variables	BASE MODEL Socio Econ	Socio Spatial	BORDER Socio Border	Border Overall	CARDINAL Socio Cardinal	Cardinal Overall	LITTORAL Socio Littoral	Littoral Overall	REGIONS Socio Regions	Regions Overall
Literacy	3.635	3.450	1.266	0.909	-0.189	0.914	4.087ᵃ	2.225	2.384	4.177
Gross State Product	-12.546ᵇ	-13.082ᵇ	-12.754ᵇ	-12.022ᵃ	-15.369ᵇ	-17.027ᵇ	-17.837ᶜ	-15.980ᵇ	-14.329ᵇ	-16.831ᵇ
Urbanization	3.721	2.176	3.884ᵃ	3.162	5.073ᵇ	2.770	5.367ᵇ	3.282	4.373	3.552
Hierarchical		-4.167		-2.287		-3.490		-4.268	-3.257	13.351
Population Potential		0.048		0.016		0.086		0.088ᵃ		0.004
Relative Location		-0.039		-0.010		-0.058ᵃ		-0.053ᵃ		-0.031
Indigenous Language		-1.359	-1.040		-2.391	-2.427	-1.516	-1.689	-2.754	-1.803
Oil State		0.009	0.004		-0.003	-0.017	0.038	0.030	0.011	0.024
BORDER										
North			-0.088	-0.085						
South			0.092	0.090						
CARDINAL										
North					-0.043	0.041				
South					0.114ᵃ	0.159ᵇ				
Central					-0.031	0.005				
West Central					0.099	0.139ᵃ				
LITTORAL										
Atlantic							0.075	0.102		
Pacific							0.088ᵇ	0.121ᵇ		
REGIONS										
Region I									0.020	-0.128
Region II									-0.120	-0.181
Region III									-0.076	-0.079
Region IV									-0.147	-0.176
Region V									-0.130	-0.209
Region VI									0.093	0.014
Region VII									-0.081	-0.194ᵃ
Region VIII									-0.130ᵃ	-0.201ᵇ
Region IX									0.031	-0.086
Region X									0.024	-0.075
Region XI									-0.152	-0.267ᵃ
Region XII									-0.022	-0.165
Constant	0.028	0.582	0.057	0.193	0.017	0.700ᵃ	-0.110	0.546	0.032	0.701
R-Squared	0.210	0.272	0.399	0.404	0.459	0.543	0.356	0.456	0.628	0.707

ᵃ Significant at 0.1 level, ᵇ at 0.05 level, ᶜ at 0.01 level.

Test for spatial autocorrelation Guerrero remained as the state with low significant values for changes in support for other parties, (figure 5.8). Clusters of high significant values emerged in the northwestern states, such as Sonora, Chihuahua and Sinaloa, in San Luis Potosi as well as in states belonging to the Yucatan peninsula. Tabasco and Chiapas formed a cluster of high significant values only in the base models. When regions-specific controls were introduced these clusters disappeared.

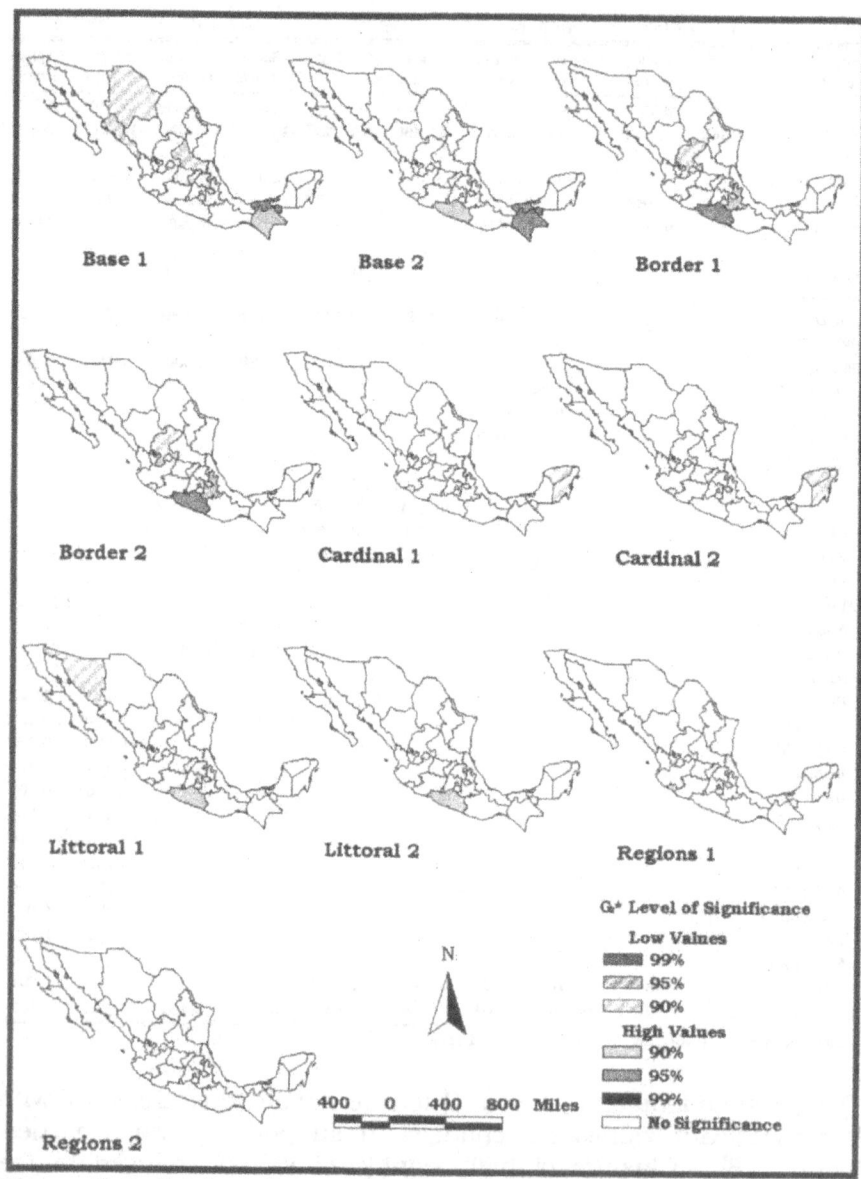

Figure 5.8 G_i^* test for residuals. Change in vote share for other parties senatorial elections 1964-2000

Table 5.9 Coefficients for change in vote share models: representative elections for other parties, 1964-2000

	BASE MODEL		BORDER		CARDINAL		LITTORAL		REGIONS	
Independent Variables	Socio Econ	Socio Spatial	Socio Border	Border Overall	Socio Cardinal	Cardinal Overall	Socio Littoral	Littoral Overall	Socio Regions	Regions Overall
Literacy	4.323^b	4.276^a	2.297	1.533	0.887	1.360	4.664^b	3.148	3.0096	4.759
Gross State Product	-12.249^b	-12.715^b	-12.376^b	-11.141	-14.523^b	-15.204^a	-16.720^b	-14.942^a	-13.723^b	-15.441^b
Urbanization	3.065	2.003	3.122	2.521	4.108^a	2.380	4.419^a	2.720	3.723	2.454
Hierarchical		-2.895		-3.422		-3.860		-4.184		2.486
Population Potential		0.031		-0.002		0.054		0.063		0.007
Relative Location		-0.025		0.004		-0.036		-0.037		-0.027
Indigenous Language			-1.712	-2.018	-2.645^a	-2.782	-1.797	-2.077	-2.953	-2.147
Oil State			0.003	-0.004	-0.009	-0.020	0.029	0.019	0.002	-0.002
BORDER										
North			-0.078	-0.093						
South			0.074	0.068						
CARDINAL										
North					-0.043	0.006				
South					0.094	0.121				
Central					-0.031	-0.010				
West Central					0.090	0.114				
LITTORAL										
Atlantic							0.052	0.075		
Pacific							0.075	0.102		
REGIONS										
Region I									0.000	-0.117
Region II									-0.098	-0.133
Region III									-0.086	-0.067
Region IV									-0.146	-0.147
Region V									-0.104	-0.149
Region VI									0.099	0.051
Region VII									-0.061	-0.148
Region VIII									-0.118	-0.169^a
Region IX									0.021	-0.068
Region X									0.031	-0.041
Region XI									-0.112	-0.200
Region XII									-0.049	-0.158
Constant	0.010	0.380	0.031	0.003	0.002	0.444	-0.110	0.336	0.013	0.605
R-Squared	0.237	0.269	0.398	0.406	0.457	0.497	0.357	0.416	0.614	0.665

^{a} Significant at 0.1 level, ^{b} at 0.05 level, ^{c} at 0.01 level.

Other Parties Representative Elections

Support for other parties' representatives was greater in states with the greatest changes in literacy levels and urbanization. Table 5.9 shows the coefficients and levels of significance.

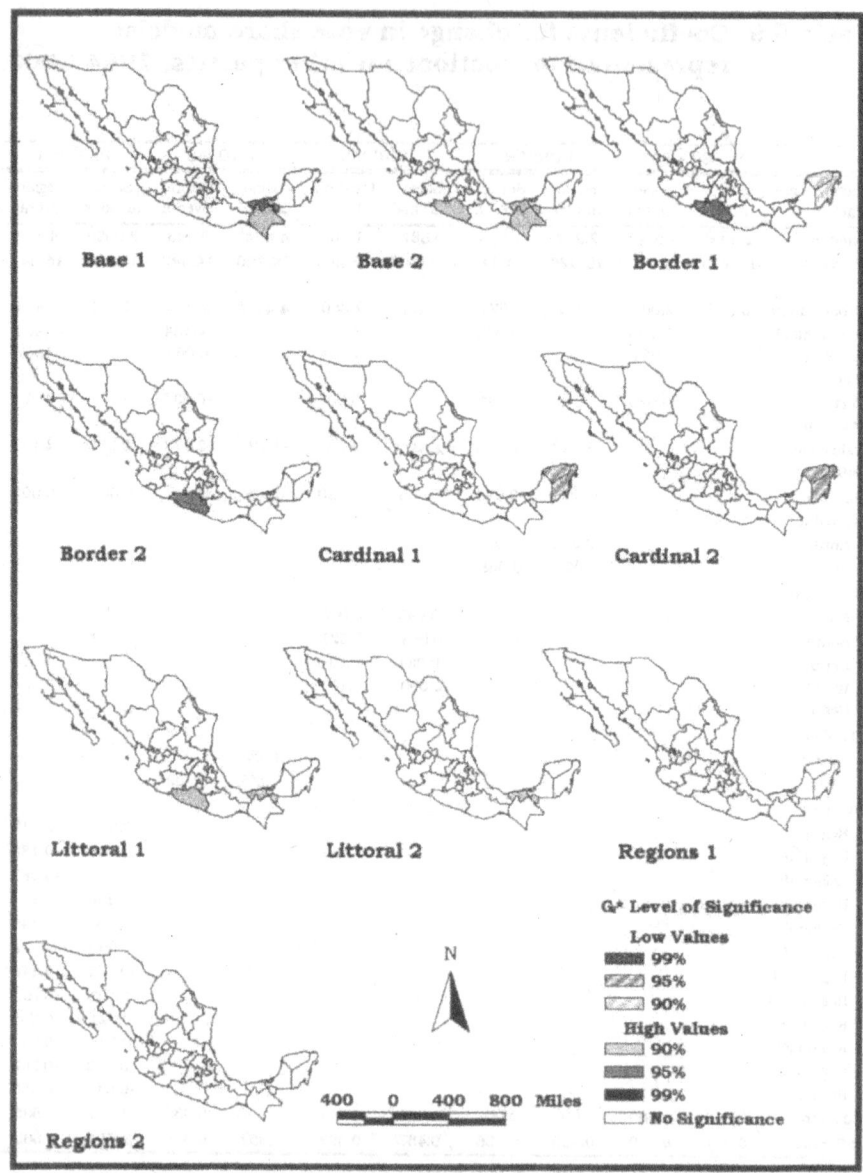

Figure 5.9 G_1^* **test for residuals. Change in vote share for other parties representative elections 1964-2000**

Support decreased in states with greater changes in gross state product and in the monolingual indigenous population. Once region-specific controls were introduced, decrease of support for PRI representatives was greater in the Great North American plains and in the over all south, from the Yucatan peninsula all the way to Veracruz in the central east Mexico, to Michoacan in the southwest but excluding Tabasco. Little evidence of spatial processes is present for other representatives' support.

Test for spatial autocorrelation Figure 5.9 show the G_i^* statistic values. A cluster of highly significant values situated in the southern states Tabasco, Chiapas and Michoacan and a cluster of low significant values in the Yucatan peninsula vanished once a full set of regional controls was introduced.

Summary for Other Parties

Support changes for parties other than PAN or PRI was the greatest in southern Pacific states, which happened to be the states with greatest changes in literacy levels as well as urbanization, such as Guerrero or Oaxaca, and in states where gross state product change the least and are situated in the most central area, such as the Federal District.

Overview of the Dynamics of Vote Share Changes

Increase of party support for any party is directly related to decrease on support for some other party. What occurred in Mexico for PRI was a contraction of support in the face of increased support for PAN among the more professional working class, especially in both emerging and existing industrial zones. States such as Jalisco, Nuevo Leon or Guanajuato fit these characteristics. The increase of support for other parties was strong in extreme conditions, especially in the poorest, less literate and urbanized states lying in the periphery of the country, such as Guerrero, Oaxaca and Michoacan, together with the Federal District, to which has been rapid migration and where PRD was able to make major inroads by radicalizing the working poor. Of course, expansion of support for PAN and PRD is a mirror image of vote change for PRI.

Chapter 6

Change in the Dissimilarity Index

I now turn to changes in dissimilarity indices for PAN and for other parties between the initial conditions of 1964 and ending conditions of 2000 at the three electoral levels. The dissimilarity index can be regarded as a measure of the dispersion of vote shares about the overall vote for the party under study. It is described by Duncan (1957 p.30) as "the sum of the positive differences between the two percentage distributions." Thus, I computed the dissimilarity index as the sum of positive differences between the percentage of votes for minority party members (PAN or other parties) and the percentage of PRI voters, at both initial and ending conditions. The dependent variable is the change between these indices from 1964 to 2000. A decrease implies more competitive party politics. An increase represents the increasing concentration of support in a state. As in chapter five, ten models are calibrated using the same independent variables. Because the dissimilarity index is an absolute value, the direction of change is not captured. It does not tell us which accounts for any increased concentration that may be discovered. For purpose of analysis I first explore changes in dissimilarity indices for PAN's presidential elections. The comparison is repeated for the PAN senatorial and representative elections. The discussion then turns to dissimilarity indices for the set of other parties, where the sequence of analyses is repeated.

Partido Accion Nacional, PAN

Jalisco was the state that had the greatest increase in dissimilarity indices for PAN for all levels of representation, meaning that there was a greater increase of support for PAN in Jalisco than nationwide. The Federal District and Veracruz were the two states with the lowest changes.

PAN Presidential Elections

The Federal District had the lowest index change at the presidential level, but the Estado de Mexico, the Federal District's neighboring state, had the greatest change, followed close by Jalisco.

Table 6.1 Coefficients for change in dissimilarity index models: presidential elections for PAN, 1964-2000

Independent Variables	BASE MODEL		BORDER		CARDINAL		LITTORAL		REGIONS	
	Socio Econ	Socio Spatial	Socio Border	Border Overall	Socio Cardinal	Cardinal Overall	Socio Littoral	Littoral Overall	Socio Regions	Regions Overall
Literacy	-0.703^b	-0.370	-0.589^a	-0.277	-0.257	0.007	-0.533^a	-0.431	-0.396	-0.252
Gross State Product	7.463^c	6.824^c	8.620^c	7.980^c	8.220^c	7.489^c	8.447^c	8.027^c	8.657^c	8.045^c
Urbanization	0.201	0.117	-0.295	-0.386	-0.190	-0.353	-0.222	-0.359	-0.153	-0.202
Hierarchical		0.257		-0.063		-0.218		-0.198		-5.083
Population Potential		0.005		0.008		0.007		0.007		-0.001
Relative Location		-0.006^a		-0.008^b		-0.007^b		-0.007^b		-0.004^b
Indigenous Language			0.024	0.178	0.112	0.205	0.041	0.176	0.155^a	0.545^b
Oil State			-0.021^c	-0.017^c	-0.018^c	-0.014^b	-0.019^c	-0.015^c	-0.019^c	-0.011
BORDER										
North			-0.002	0.005						
South			0.007	0.001						
CARDINAL										
North					0.005	0.008				
South					0.001	-0.002				
Central					0.011	0.011				
West Central					-0.004	0.003				
LITTORAL										
Atlantic							0.002	-0.002		
Pacific							0.004	0.001		
REGIONS										
Region I									0.006	-0.024
Region II									0.028^b	0.009^b
Region III									0.012	-0.001
Region IV									0.018	0.000
Region V									-0.007	-0.031^b
Region VI									0.000	-0.023^b
Region VII									0.013	-0.007
Region VIII									0.010	-0.007
Region IX									0.009	-0.014
Region X									0.013	-0.016
Region XI									0.012	-0.009
Region XII									0.009	-0.019^b
Constant	-0.004	0.092^a	0.015	0.125^c	0.002	0.106^b	0.009	0.118^c	0.006	0.108^c
R-Squared	0.810	0.876	0.893	0.927	0.902	0.939	0.889	0.926	0.938	0.978

^{a} Significant at 0.1 level, ^{b} at 0.05 level, ^{c} at 0.01 level.

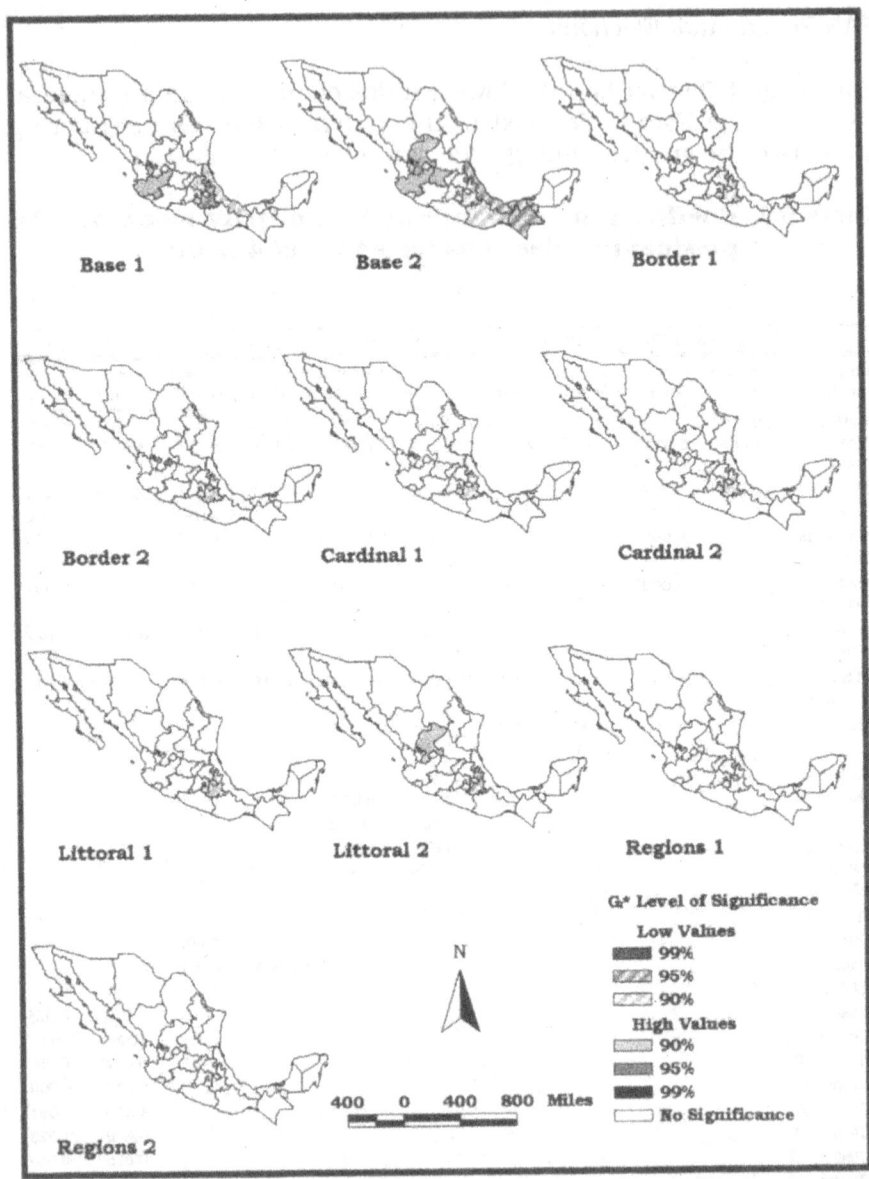

Figure 6.1 G₁* test for residuals. Change in dissimilarity index for PAN presidential elections 1964-2000

The increase for Sinaloa was for PRI rather than PAN. When the ten models were applied to this variable, it was evident that changes in gross state product were significant through all the models. In the base models the greatest increases in support for PAN were in states with the greatest changes in gross state product. PAN's rise to majority status was least in states where the changes in literacy and relative location were the greatest (table 6.1). The negative sign on relative location variable reinforces the notion that PAN was least able to make progress in traditional core areas that have been bases of PRI support. Once spatial and region-specific controls were implemented, states with oil extraction industry and in the central plateau had significantly greater changes than the states along the neo-volcanic system.

Test for spatial autocorrelation Residuals from each of the regressions were tested using the G_i^* statistic in order to determine whether the variables in the models captured the spatial behavior of the dependent variable. These statistics are shown in figure 6.1. Clusters of high values initially emerged in Jalisco together with low values in central Gulf states. Once regional controls were implemented, spatial autocorrelation vanishes.

PAN Senatorial Elections

Veracruz and Tamaulipas, two neighboring states had low dissimilarity index change while Zacatecas and Queretaro had the greatest changes.
    Coefficients and the levels of significance are captured in table 6.2. for the ten models. The results are virtually identical to those for presidential elections.

Test for spatial autocorrelation G_i^* statistic appear in figure 6.2. Initial clusters of high values emerged in Jalisco, Nayarit and Guanajuato and of low values in Veracruz and Puebla before the introduction of regional controls. Once these controls were implemented, spatial autocorrelations were eliminated.

PAN Representative Elections

Veracruz and Hidalgo are neighboring states with the lowest values of changes in dissimilarity index. On the other hand, Nayarit and Aguascalientes were among the states with the highest changes in dissimilarity indices. Table 6.3 summarizes the models, which again are virtually identical to these for presidential and senatorial elections.

Table 6.2 Coefficients for change in dissimilarity index models: senatorial elections for PAN, 1964-2000

	BASE MODEL		BORDER		CARDINAL		LITTORAL		REGIONS	
Independent Variables	Socio Econ	Socio Spatial	Socio Border	Border Overall	Socio Cardinal	Cardinal Overall	Socio Littoral	Littoral Overall	Socio Regions	Regions Overall
Literacy	-0.081[b]	-0.298	-0.614	-0.147	-0.420	-0.067	-0.550[a]	-0.329	-0.261	-0.101
Gross State Product	9.345[c]	8.417[c]	10.561[c]	9.649[c]	10.434[c]	9.466[c]	10.461[c]	9.797[c]	10.573[c]	9.849[c]
Urbanization	0.134	0.133	-0.456	-0.455	-0.362	-0.474	-0.411	-0.483	-0.324	-0.238
Hierarchical		0.937		0.464		0.064		0.058		-0.144
Population Potential		0.004		0.009[a]		0.007		0.006		-0.001
Relative Location		-0.008[a]		-0.009[b]		-0.008[b]		-0.007[b]		-0.005[b]
Indigenous Language		-0.284		-0.065	-0.174	-0.035	-0.260	-0.060	0.247	0.334
Oil State		-0.027[c]		-0.021[c]	-0.024[c]	-0.018[c]	-0.025[c]	-0.020[c]	-0.028[c]	-0.016[c]
BORDER										
North			-0.001	0.009						
South			0.011	0.004						
CARDINAL										
North					0.002	0.005				
South					0.002	-0.003				
Central					0.006	0.006				
West Central					-0.008	0.001				
LITTORAL										
Atlantic							0.005	-0.003		
Pacific							0.002	-0.003		
REGIONS										
Region I									0.009	-0.026[b]
Region II									0.033[b]	0.010
Region III									0.019	0.002
Region IV									0.017	-0.006
Region V									0.003	-0.028[b]
Region VI									0.013	-0.016
Region VII									0.014	-0.012
Region VIII									0.011	-0.009
Region IX									0.008	-0.020[b]
Region X									0.015	-0.017
Region XI									0.019	-0.008
Region XII									0.014	-0.020[b]
Constant	-0.001	0.113	0.015	0.139[c]	0.009	0.126	0.011	0.130	0.002	0.118[c]
R-Squared	0.816	0.902	0.910	0.946	0.909	0.947	0.903	0.943	0.943	0.985

[a] Significant at 0.1 level, [b] at 0.05 level, [c] at 0.01 level.

Test for spatial autocorrelation G_i^* statistics are presented in figure 6.3. Again, clusters dilute once the spatial and region-specific controls are introduced into the models.

Change in the Dissimilarity Index 131

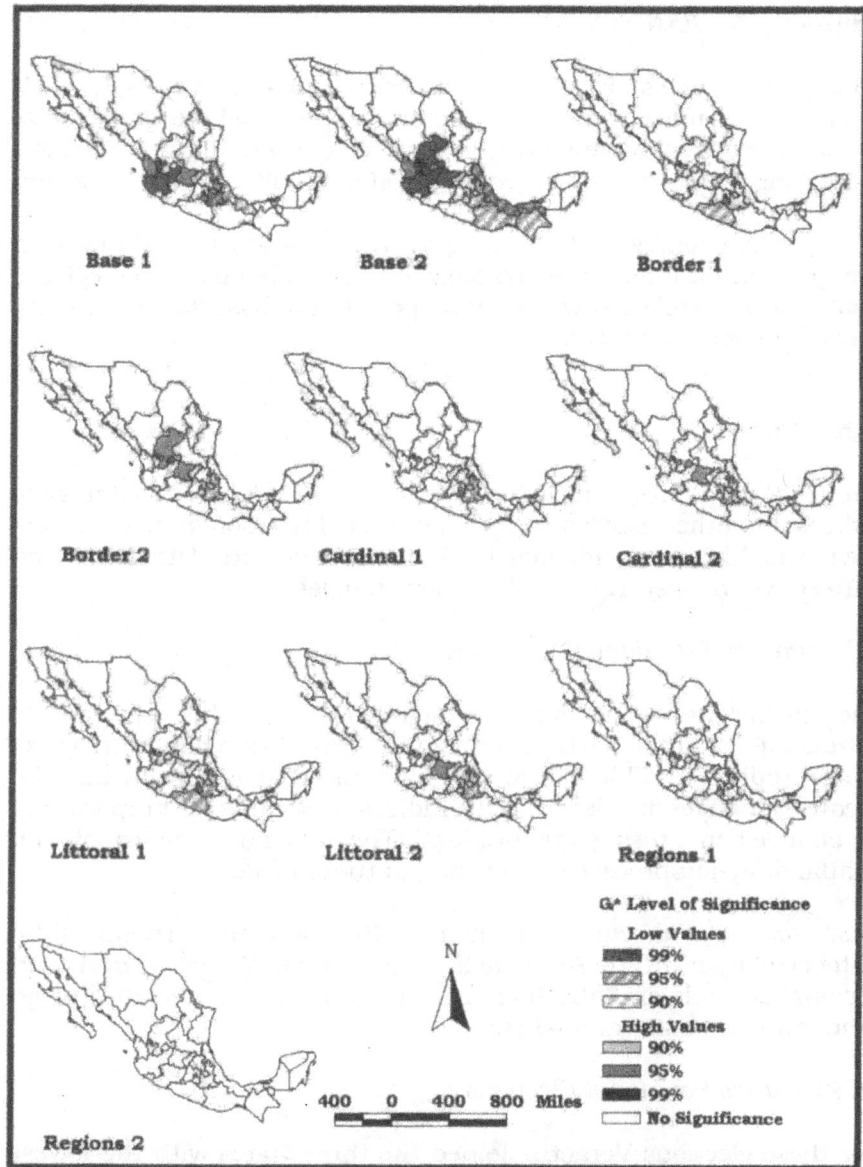

Figure 6.2 G_1^* **test for residuals. Change in dissimilarity index for PAN senatorial elections 1964-2000**

Summary for PAN

What these models show is that concentrations of support for PAN strengthened most significantly in those states where gross state product also grew more rapidly, consistent with the idea that PAN's increasing support was among Queretaro, Jalisco and Quintana Roo.

PAN's relative vote share growth was weakest in states with the greatest oil industry expansion and in traditional core regions. Spatial autocorrelation was region-specific, not associated with any process of spatial diffusion.

Other Parties

The Federal District had the lowest changes in its dissimilarity indices for other parties largely because PRD dominance in this area was high and unchallenged by PAN or PRI. Otherwise, no pattern can be discerned in the index changes.

Other Parties Presidential Elections

The coefficients and levels of significance of the ten models estimated for other parties are in table 6.4. The change in gross state product variable is the only variable that is significant: the greatest changes in dissimilarity indices were directly proportional to changes in gross state product. There is no evidence of any spatial diffusion processes operating in these models.

Test for spatial autocorrelation G_i^* statistics reveal little autocorrelation in these models (figure 6.4). When spatial and regional controls are introduced, Colima remains significant, but no other autocorrelation remains.

Other Parties Senatorial Elections

For these elections Veracruz joined the three states with the lowest changes in dissimilarity indices, while Baja California Sur, Puebla and Tamaulipas had the greatest changes. In these latter states PRI lost significant support.

The strongest changes in dissimilarity indices for other parties took place in states where the gross state product changed the most (table 6.5). No spatial diffusion processes are evident.

Test for spatial autocorrelation Figure 6.5 shows the G_i^* statistics. After spatial and regional controls were introduced all clusters vanished.

Table 6.3 Coefficients for change in dissimilarity index models: representative elections for PAN, 1964-2000

Independent Variables	BASE MODEL Socio Econ	Socio Spatial	BORDER Socio Border	Border Overall	CARDINAL Socio Cardinal	Cardinal Overall	LITTORAL Socio Littoral	Littoral Overall	REGIONS Socio Regions	Regions Overall
Literacy	-0.824[b]	-0.420	-0.608[a]	-0.195	-0.408	-0.074	-0.580[a]	-0.471	-0.297	-0.135
Gross State Product	9.265[c]	8.512[c]	10.315[c]	9.573[c]	10.198[c]	9.384[c]	10.222[c]	9.758[c]	10.528[c]	9.850[c]
Urbanization	0.115	0.097	-0.405	-0.441	-0.332	-0.485	-0.364	-0.465	-0.348	-0.276
Hierarchical		0.878		0.538		0.114		0.051		0.069
Population Potential		0.006		0.011[b]		0.009		0.007		-0.001
Relative Location		-0.007		-0.010[b]		-0.008[b]		-0.008[b]		-0.005[b]
Indigenous Language			-0.261	-0.059	-0.157	-0.043	-0.254	-0.096	0.234	0.328
Oil State			-0.024[c]	-0.020[c]	-0.021[c]	-0.017	-0.022[c]	-0.018[c]	-0.028[c]	-0.015[c]
BORDER										
North			0.000	0.011						
South			0.009	0.004						
CARDINAL										
North					0.003	0.010				
South					0.001	0.000				
Central					0.007	0.008				
West Central					-0.008	0.000				
LITTORAL										
Atlantic							0.005	0.001		
Pacific							0.002	0.000		
REGIONS										
Region I									0.005	-0.029
Region II									0.028[a]	0.007[b]
Region III									0.019	0.003
Region IV									0.026	0.004
Region V									-0.001	-0.030[b]
Region VI									0.008	-0.018[a]
Region VII									0.011	-0.014
Region VIII									0.008	-0.011
Region IX									0.007	-0.020[b]
Region X									0.011	-0.018
Region XI									0.016	-0.010
Region XII									0.010	-0.022[b]
Constant	0.000	0.109	0.013	0.139	0.007	0.122	0.010	0.124[b]	0.006	0.116[b]
R-Squared	0.835	0.902	0.911	0.944	0.915	0.944	0.909	0.938	0.943	0.982

[a] Significant at 0.1 level, [b] at 0.05 level, [c] at 0.01 level.

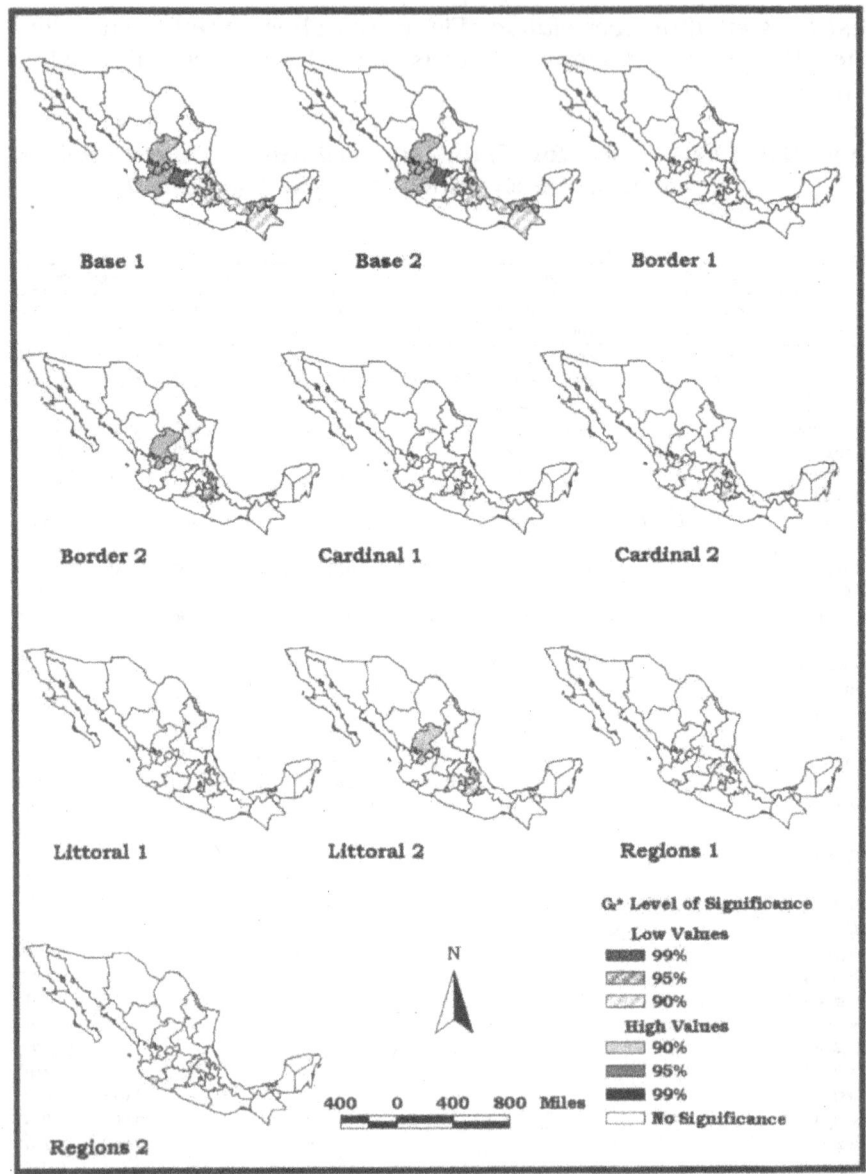

Figure 6.3 G_1^* test for residuals. Change in dissimilarity index for PAN representative elections 1964-2000

Table 6.4 Coefficients for change in dissimilarity index models: presidential elections for other parties, 1964-2000

Independent Variables	BASE MODEL		BORDER		CARDINAL		LITTORAL		REGIONS	
	Socio Econ	Socio Spatial	Socio Border	Border Overall	Socio Cardinal	Cardinal Overall	Socio Littoral	Littoral Overall	Socio Regions	Regions Overall
Literacy	-0.444	-0.609	-0.630	-0.996	-0.388	-0.536	-0.364	-0.682	0.106	0.048
Gross State Product	5.234ᶜ	5.480ᶜ	5.480ᶜ	6.423ᶜ	5.262ᶜ	5.680ᶜ	5.676ᶜ	6.256ᶜ	6.302ᶜ	6.128ᶜ
Urbanization	0.157	-0.088	-0.007	-0.307	0.048	-0.152	-0.033	-0.261	-0.321	-0.399
Hierarchical		-0.284		-1.691		-0.812		-0.775		-10.782
Population Potential		0.002		-0.001		0.003		0.006		-0.001
Relative Location		0.000		0.002		-0.001		-0.001		-0.001
Indigenous Language			0.108	-0.036	0.034	-0.066	0.047	-0.099	0.559	0.439
Oil State			-0.004	-0.007	-0.005	-0.009	-0.008	-0.012	-0.022ᵇ	-0.017
BORDER										
North			-0.008	-0.015						
South			-0.010	-0.013						
CARDINAL										
North					0.000	0.003				
South					-0.001	0.004				
Central					0.008	0.010				
West Central					0.009	0.007				
LITTORAL										
Atlantic							0.002	0.009		
Pacific							0.000	0.006		
REGIONS										
Region I									-0.003	-0.013
Region II									0.009	0.001
Region III									0.022	0.012
Region IV									0.033	0.022
Region V									0.023	0.013
Region VI									-0.004	-0.015
Region VII									-0.008	-0.012
Region VIII									-0.015	-0.022
Region IX									-0.006	-0.012
Region X									-0.020	-0.035
Region XI									-0.068ᶜ	-0.073ᶜ
Region XII									-0.007	-0.015
Constant	-0.001	0.002	0.014	0.005	0.001	0.002	0.006	0.011	0.021	0.043
R-Squared	0.580	0.588	0.611	0.640	0.616	0.631	0.596	0.628	0.859	0.870

ᵃ Significant at 0.1 level, ᵇ at 0.05 level, ᶜ at 0.01 level.

Other Parties Representative Elections

Hidalgo was among the states with the lowest changes in dissimilarity indices, while Michoacan, Tamaulipas and Guanajuato experienced the greatest changes.

Table 6.6 shows the coefficients and the levels of significance for the ten models. The results are the same as in the presidential and senatorial elections.

Test for spatial autocorrelation Figure 6.6 shows the G_i^* statistics. There are initial clusters of significantly high values but they vanished when region-specific controls were applied.

Summary for Other Parties

Changes on gross state product were the most relevant influence on concentration of support for other parties. There was no evidence of spatial diffusion processes.

Overview of the Dynamics of Dissimilarity Index Changes

Increased concentration of support as represented by increases in dissimilarity indices, was mostly driven by changes in gross state product for both PAN and other parties, particularly PRD.

Changes in vote concentration were least in the country's traditional core areas, long bastions of PRI support. There was no evidence of spatial diffusion processes. Spatial autocorrelations were removed by regional controls, consistent with the notion that Mexican politics remains marked by strong regional-based party affiliations.

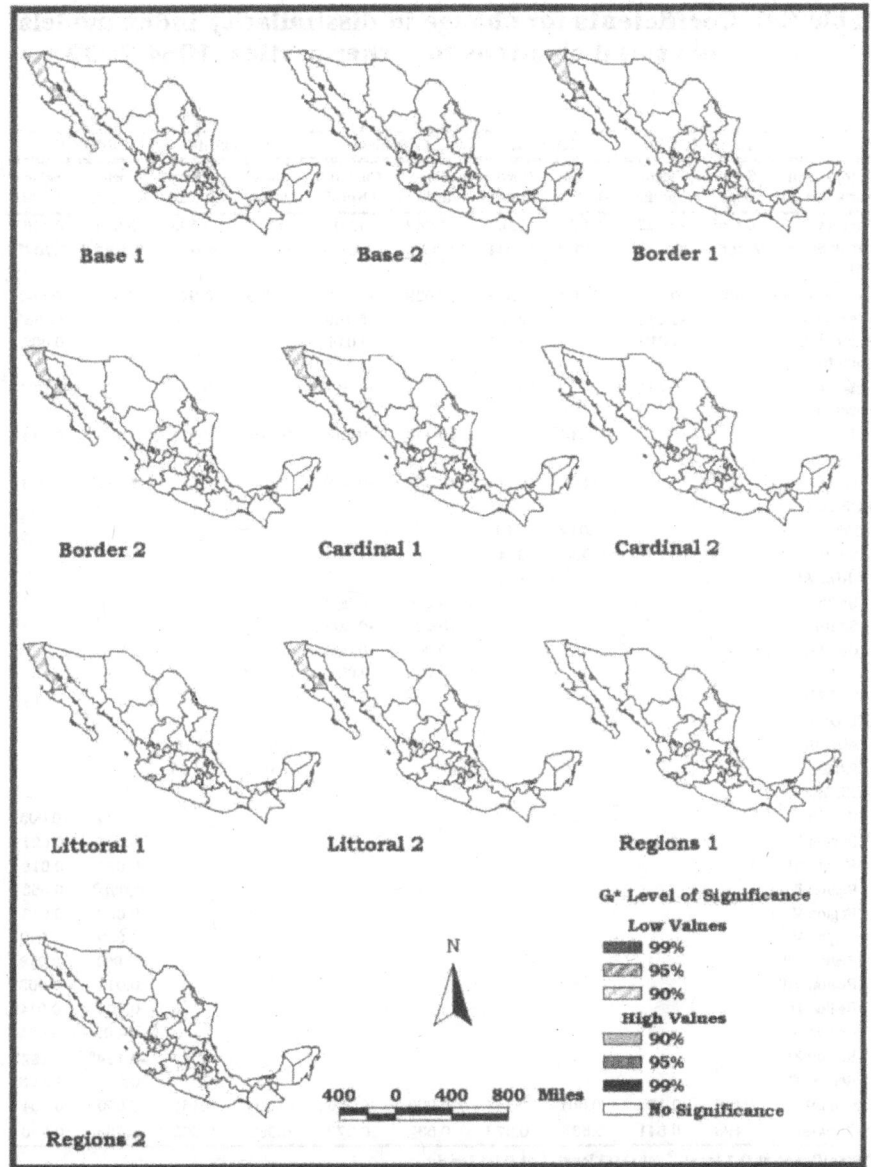

Figure 6.4 G_1^* test for residuals. Change in dissimilarity index for other parties presidential elections 1964-2000

Table 6.5 Coefficients for change in dissimilarity index models: senatorial elections for other parties, 1964-2000

Independent Variables	BASE MODEL Socio Econ	BORDER Socio Spatial	BORDER Socio Border	BORDER Border Overall	CARDINAL Socio Cardinal	CARDINAL Cardinal Overall	LITTORAL Socio Littoral	LITTORAL Littoral Overall	REGIONS Socio Regions	REGIONS Regions Overall
Literacy	-0.635	-0.722	-0.873	-1.055	-1.049	-1.001	-0.373	-0.595	-0.034	0.116
Gross State Product	7.488^c	7.368^c	7.805^c	8.004^c	8.125^c	7.915^c	8.011^c	8.167^c	8.179^c	7.707^c
Urbanization	0.057	-0.417	-0.107	-0.756	-0.029	-0.673	-0.309	-0.923	-0.339	-0.554
Hierarchical		-1.116		-2.612		-2.199		-2.195		-11.582
Population Potential		0.016		0.013		0.014		0.015		0.000
Relative Location		-0.013		-0.010		-0.011		-0.011		-0.004
Indigenous Language			-0.513	-0.534	-0.446	-0.518	0.529	-0.577	0.576	0.544
Oil State			-0.008	-0.008	-0.007	-0.009	-0.017	-0.018	-0.027^b	-0.021
BORDER										
North			-0.012	-0.011						
South			0.006	-0.005						
CARDINAL										
North					-0.016	-0.008				
South					-0.005	-0.003				
Central					-0.006	-0.003				
West Central					-0.006	0.000				
LITTORAL										
Atlantic							0.013	0.013		
Pacific							-0.011	-0.010		
REGIONS										
Region I									0.024	-0.005
Region II									0.037	0.021
Region III									0.029	0.018
Region IV									0.070^b	0.055
Region V									0.033	0.012
Region VI									0.009	-0.012
Region VII									-0.001	-0.018
Region VIII									0.012	-0.003
Region IX									0.006	-0.014
Region X									-0.002	-0.031
Region XI									-0.114^c	-0.132^c
Region XII									0.016	-0.008
Constant	-0.007	0.170	-0.001	0.147	0.006	0.155	-0.004	0.151	0.000	0.104
R-Squared	0.496	0.541	0.538	0.573	0.532	0.570	0.560	0.600	0.858	0.880

^{a} Significant at 0.1 level, ^{b} at 0.05 level, ^{c} at 0.01 level.

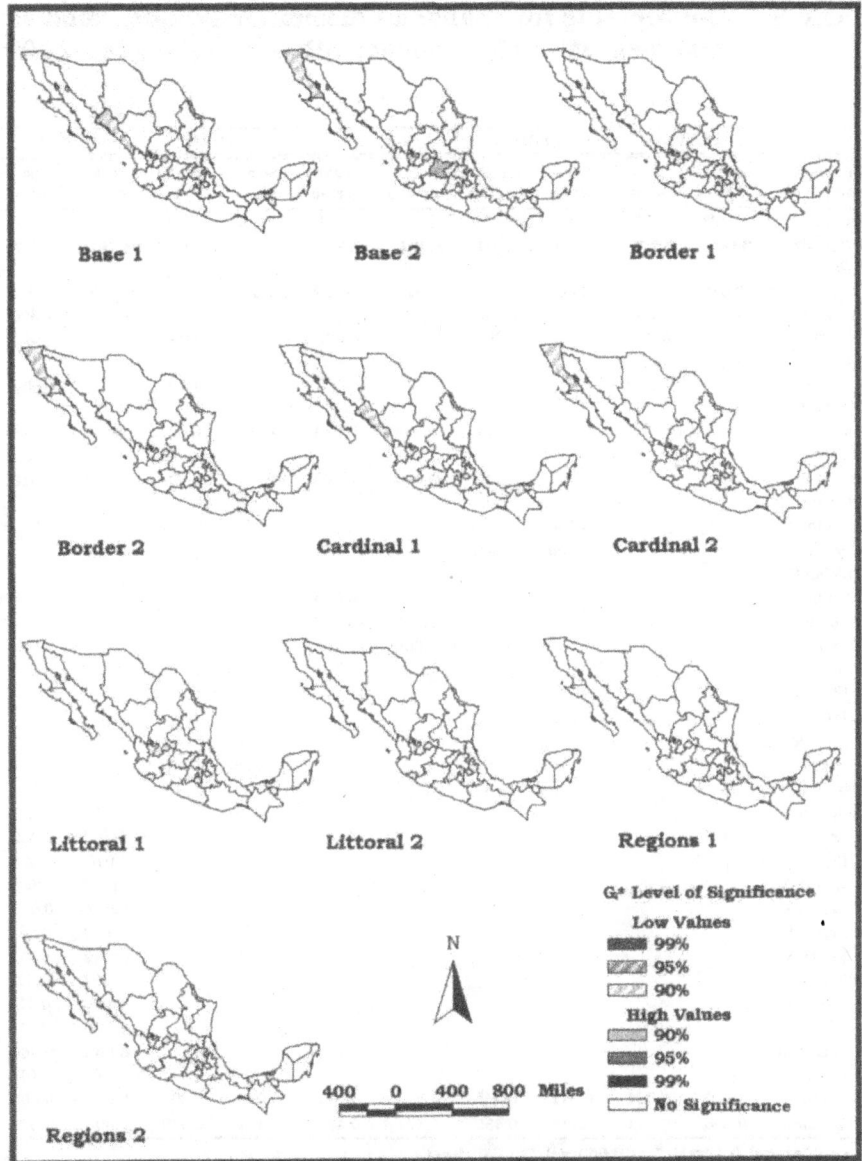

Figure 6.5 G_1^* test for residuals. Change in dissimilarity index for other parties senatorial elections 1964-2000

Table 6.6 Coefficients for change in dissimilarity index models: representative elections for other parties, 1964-2000

Independent Variables	BASE MODEL		BORDER		CARDINAL		LITTORAL		REGIONS	
	Socio Econ	Socio Spatial	Socio Border	Border Overall	Socio Cardinal	Cardinal Overall	Socio Littoral	Littoral Overall	Socio Regions	Regions Overall
Literacy	-0.392	-0.576	-0.515	-0.653	-0.714	-0.674	-0.349	-0.508	-0.053	0.110
Gross State Product	3.007^c	3.297^c	3.204^c	3.592^c	3.232^c	3.250^c	3.430^c	3.707^c	3.851^b	3.797^b
Urbanization	-0.036	-0.019	-0.061	-0.146	-0.123	-0.132	-0.211	-0.209	-0.339	-0.355
Hierarchical		0.399		0.050		0.270		0.241		7.576
Population Potential		0.003		0.003		0.003		0.003		0.001
Relative Location		-0.001		0.000		-0.001		0.000		-0.002
Indigenous Language			0.068	0.021	-0.025	-0.024	0.040	-0.006	0.653	0.794^b
Oil State			0.001	-0.003	-0.001	-0.002	-0.006	-0.007	-0.015	-0.018^a
BORDER										
North			-0.004	-0.003						
South			-0.008	-0.003						
CARDINAL										
North					-0.007	-0.003				
South					-0.005	-0.002				
Central					-0.006	-0.003				
West Central					0.012	0.012				
LITTORAL										
Atlantic							0.001	0.005		
Pacific							-0.008	-0.004		
REGIONS										
Region I									-0.001	-0.005
Region II									0.021^a	0.022
Region III									0.016	0.023
Region IV									0.036^b	0.041^a
Region V									0.017	0.019
Region VI									-0.003	-0.001
Region VII									-0.012	-0.017
Region VIII									-0.007	-0.007
Region IX									-0.006	-0.010
Region X									-0.016	-0.013
Region XI									-0.052^c	-0.056^c
Region XII									-0.005	-0.010
Constant	0.005	0.004	0.011	0.008	0.017	0.022	0.014	0.003	0.023	0.056
R-Squared	0.386	0.424	0.414	0.435	0.479	0.485	0.431	0.460	0.809	0.821

^{a} Significant at 0.1 level, ^{b} at 0.05 level, ^{c} at 0.01 level.

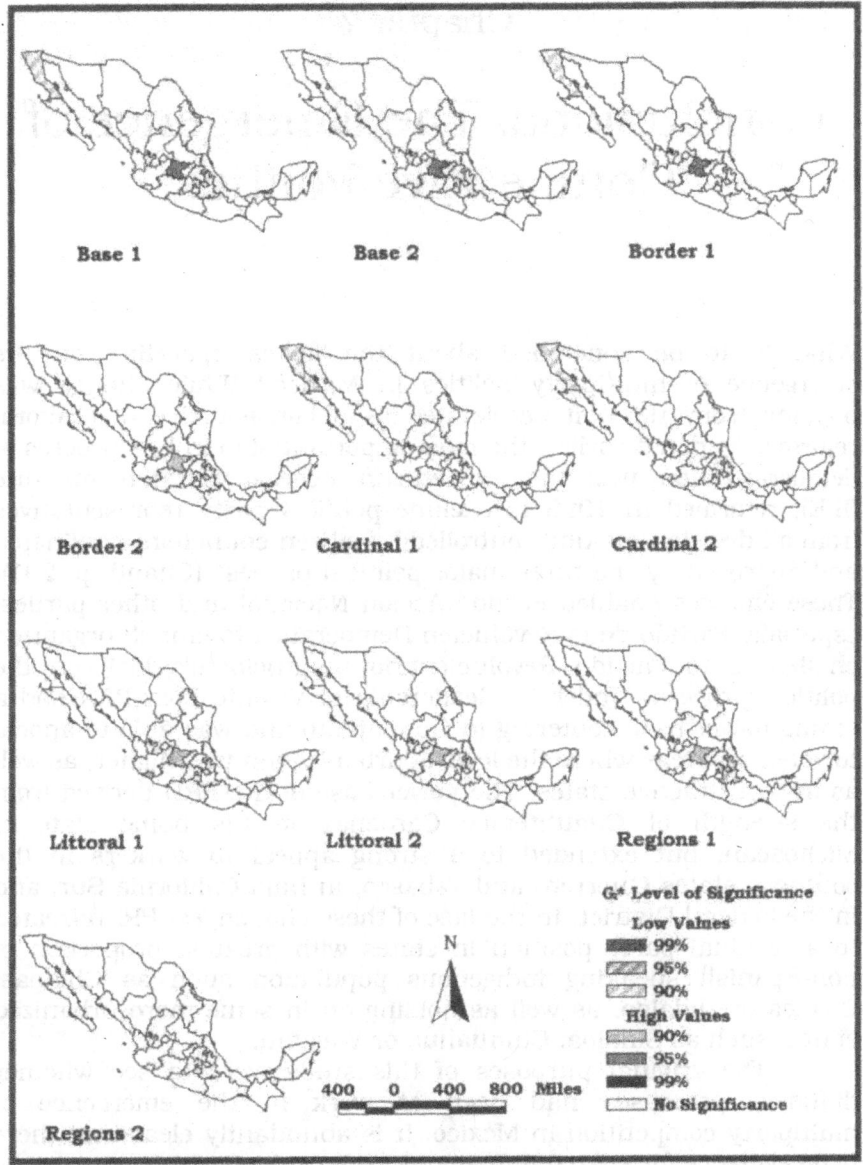

Figure 6.6 G_1* test for residuals. Change in dissimilarity index for other parties representative elections 1964-2000

Chapter 7

Conclusions: The Emergence of Competitive Politics

What is to be concluded about the forces operating on the emergence of multiparty politics in Mexico? While change was ongoing from 1964, it accelerated as a consequence of electoral reforms. As noted earlier, the most important step in this process of democratization was the "citizen-run Federal Election Institute (IFE), reformed in 1996 to exclude political party representatives from all decision making controlled by citizen councilors nominated and approved by the three major political parties" (Chand, p. 291). These changes enabled Partido Accion Nacional and other parties, especially Partido de la Revolucion Democratica to launch organized challenges to Partido Revolucionario Institucional's lock on the political process. Under the leadership of Vicente Fox, PAN had a strong power base centering in Guanajuato and was able to appeal to voters in areas where the level of urbanization was higher, as well as in oil extractive states. The power base of the PRD derived from the strength of Cuauhtemoc Cardenas in his home state of Michoacan, but extended to a strong appeal to workers in the southern states Guerrero and Tabasco, in Baja California Sur, and in the Federal District. In the face of these challenges, PRI retreated to a residual party position in states with greatest proportion of non-Spanish speaking indigenous population such as Chiapas, Oaxaca or Hidalgo, as well as holding on in some more urbanized states, such as Sinaloa, Chihuahua or Yucatan.

The original purposes of this study were to see whether diffusion processes had been at work in the emergence of multiparty competition in Mexico. It is abundantly clear that there is no evidence for spatial diffusion: that hypothesis fails.

I thus turn to the alternative, that the operation of broad national processes of change has unfolded across an uneven socioeconomic map, and that Mexican politics remain marked by some other forms of regionalism.

With respect of socioeconomic influences, the analyses point to the following conclusions.

PAN strength grew where gross state product changes were the greatest, in places like Jalisco, Aguascalientes or Queretaro, where industrialization took off over the last three decades and where there were increasing income and the emergence of a large middle class. Because these places already had some urban infrastructure, their changes on literacy levels were smaller than states in the south for instance Guerrero, where literacy increased rapidly, but in spite of this the level was still among the lowest in 2000.

Other parties, particularly PRD, established positions in states with characteristics contrasting with those giving PAN support. These included states with the greatest changes in literacy levels, or in urbanization, rural states that were integrated to the political context over the last decades, together with the Federal District, to which many rural residents had migrated. The same states showed little growth of the gross state product or had the smallest change in the proportion of non-Spanish speaking population. The best example of the latter is the Federal District. Support for PRD was strongest in the poorest states and in the Federal District, with its great extremes of wealth and poverty.

PRI's residual strength was in states with a greater proportion of non-Spanish speaking indigenous population and states with higher literacy levels but low gross state product. The power base for PRI remained in Sinaloa and Nayarit, two neighboring states, and to a lower degree in Yucatan, Campeche and Durango. PRI used its organization and power to retain control of those least integrated into the emergent competitive party politics, contrasting with PAN's appeal to the middle and business classes and PRD's appeal to the working poor.

Spatial autocorrelation was present in many initial models. Variables suggested by diffusion theory failed to remove it. Nor were cardinal or littoral controls particularly useful. However, regional controls did remove the spatial autocorrelations, pointing to the importance of more localized regionalism in party support alongside the socioeconomic influences.

A belt of growth of support for PAN was evident in states along the Oriental Sierra Madre, in Sonora and in the easternmost state of Quintana Roo. At the core of this concentration was Vicente Fox's home-state strength in Guanajuato.

The growth of support for other parties, in particular for PRD, was evident in two extreme conditions. One was in the south Pacific, most markedly in the states of Guerrero, Tabasco, Oaxaca, and especially in Cuauhtemoc Cardenas' home state Michoacan. Two other concentrations of support were in Baja California Sur (in the north of Mexico) and in the Federal District, where left-wing political activation of the working poor was most evident.

PRI retained power in the central Pacific (Sinaloa and Nayarit) and in the east of the Gulf of Mexico in Yucatan and Campeche. In contrast to the PAN and PRD regionalizations derived from charismatic leadership, these residual strengths were, however, dictated by PRI's remaining socioeconomic base.

The resulting picture is thus, quite different than that pointed for the emergence of democracy on a global map by O' Loughlin et al (1998) and Gleditsch and Ward (2000). They claimed evidence for spatial diffusion. Within Mexico, however, the emergence of competitive party politics depended upon successful challenges to PRI autocracy among middle and business classes on the one hand and the Spanish-speaking poor in the other, complemented by the strong regional power bases of Vicente Fox and Cuauhtemoc Cardenas. Little if any case can be made for the spatial diffusion of party competition as the democratization of Mexican politics unfolds.

Bibliography

Barro, Robert J. (1999), "Determinants of Democracy." *Journal of Political Economy* 107(6). December.

Berry, Brian J. L. (1972), "Hierarchical Diffusion: The Basis of Developmental Filtering and Spread in a System of Growth Centers," pp. 108-138. In *Growth Centers in Regional Economic Development*, edited by Niles M. Hansen. New York: The Press Free.

Berry, Brian J. L., Shane Hall, Rodolfo Hernandez-Guerrero and Patricia H. Martin. (2000), "Mexico's Demographic Transition: Public Policy and Spatial Process." *Population and Environment* 21(4). March.

Brown, Lawrence A. (1968), *Diffusion Processes and Location*. Philadelphia: Regional Science Research Institute.

Castellanos Hernandez, Eduardo and Fernando Zertuche Muñoz. (1997), *Legislacion y Estadisticas Electorales, 1814-1997*. Mexico: Centro de Investigaciones Legislativas del Instituto Federal Electoral.

Chand, Vikram K. (2001), *Mexico's Political Awakening*. Indiana: University of Notre Dame Press.

Cliff, Andrew D., Peter Haggett, J. K. Ord and G. R. Versey. (1981), *Spatial Diffusion: A Historical Geography of Epidemics in an Island Community*. Cambridge: Cambridge University Press.

Duncan, Otis D. (1957), "The Measurement of Population Distribution." *Population Studies* 11(1). 27-45.

Getis, Arthur and J. K. Ord. (1992), "The Analysis of Spatial Association by Use of Distance Statistics." *Geographical Analysis* 24(3). July.

Gleditsch, Kristian S. and Michael D. Ward. (2000), "War and Peace in Space and Time." *International Studies Quarterly* 44(March). 1-29.

Haggett, Peter, Andrew D. Cliff and Allan Frey. (1977), "Diffusion" in *Locational Analysis in Human Geography*. New York: John Wiley and Sons.

Hägerstrand, Torsten. (1967), *Innovation Diffusion as a Spatial Process*. Chicago: The University of Chicago Press.

Hollifield, James F. and Calvin Jillson. (2000), *The Political Economy of Democratic Transitions*. London: Routledge.

Jaggers, Keith and Ted Robert Gurr. (1996), *Polity III: Regime Change and Political Authority, 1800-1994*, second release. Ann Arbor: Inter-University Consortium for Political Science and Social Research.

Lipset, Seymour M. (1959), "Some Social Requisites of Democracy: Economic Development and Political Legitimacy." *The American Political Science Review* 53(1). 96-105.

Massey, Douglas and Nancy Denton. (1987), "Trends in the Residential Segregation of Blacks, Hispanics and Asians: 1970-1980." *American Sociological Review* 52(December). 802-825.

———. (1989), "Hypersegregation in U.S. Metropolitan Areas: Black and Hispanic Segregation Along Five Dimensions." *Demography* 26(3). 373-391.

O' Laughlin, John, et al. (1998), "The Diffusion of Democracy, 1964-1994." *Annals of the Association of American Geographers* 88(4). 545-574.

Ord, J. K. and Arthur Getis. (1995), "Local Spatial Autocorrelation Statistics: Distributional Issues and an Application." *Geographical Analysis* 27(4). October.

Pye, Lucian W. (2000), "Democracy and Its Enemies," in *Pathways to Democracy: The Political Economy of Democratic Transitions*, edited by James F. Hollifield and Calvin Jillson. London: Routledge.

Schatz, Sara. (2000), *Elites, Masses, and the Struggle for Democracy in Mexico, A Culturalist Approach*. Westport, CT: Praeger Publishers.

Schumpeter, Joseph A. (1975), *Capitalism, Socialism and Democracy*. 3rd ed. New York: Harper.

Shin, Doh Chull. (1994), "On the Third Wave of Democratization: A Synthesis and Evaluation of Recent Theory and Research." *World Politics* 47(1). 135-170.

Singer, J. D. and M Small. (1994), *Correlates of War Project: International and Civil War Data, 1816-1992 (ICPSR 9905)*. Interuniversity Consortium of Political Science Research. Ann Harbor, Michigan.

Index

Barro, Robert, 8
Berry, Brian, 5, 48
Brown, Lawrence, 1, 3

Cardenas, Cuauhtemoc, 68, 86, 102, 142, 144
Chand, Vikram, 102, 144
Cliff, Andrew, 3, 4, 5
COW-IW, 12

Dahl, Robert, 7
Democracy, 1, 6, 7, 8, 9, 10, 11, 12, 13, 144
Denton, Nancy, 15
Diffusion
  barriers, 6
  democracy, 10
  hierarchical, 5
  innovation, 5
  model, 5
  process, 1, 3, 4, 6, 10, 14, 30, 47
  theory, 51
Dissimilarity index, 15
Duncan, Otis, 15, 126

Elections
  presidential, 1, 15, 16, 17, 18, 19, 20, 21, 22, 24, 25, 27, 28, 31, 32, 35, 38, 41, 44, 51, 52, 53, 54, 55, 56, 57, 58, 59, 68, 71, 72, 73, 74, 75, 86, 87, 88, 89, 90, 101, 102, 103, 104, 105, 111, 112, 113, 118, 119, 120, 126, 127, 128, 129, 135, 136, 137
  representatives, 6, 15, 16, 18, 21, 24, 27, 31, 51, 53, 62, 65, 66, 67, 69, 70, 80, 81, 82, 83, 84, 85, 94, 96, 97, 99, 100, 101, 103, 108, 109, 110, 112, 113, 116, 117, 118, 123, 124, 126, 133, 134, 140, 141
  senatorial, 15, 16, 17, 18, 20, 21, 23, 24, 26, 27, 29, 31, 33, 36, 39, 42, 45, 51, 53, 57, 60, 61, 62, 63, 64, 75, 76, 77, 78, 79, 83, 92, 93, 94, 95, 101, 103, 106, 107, 108, 112, 113, 114, 115, 118, 119, 121, 122, 126, 129, 130, 131, 136, 138, 139
ESDA, 11

Fox, Vicente, , 31, 53, 56, 68, 102, 142, 143, 144

Getis, Arthur 30, 31, 50
Gi*, 11, 13, 30, 31, 32, 33, 34, 35, 36, 38, 39, 41, 42, 44, 45, 47, 50, 52, 53, 55, 56, 57, 59, 62, 64, 66, 70, 72, 74, 75, 77, 79, 82, 85, 88, 90, 91, 93, 95, 97, 98, 100, 105, 107, 108, 110, 112, 113, 115, 116, 117, 118, 120, 122, 124, 125, 128, 129, 130, 131, 132, 133, 134, 136, 137, 139, 141
Gleditsch, Kristian, 12, 144
Gurr, 10, 12

Hägerstrand, Torsten, 3, 4
Haggett, Peter, 3, 4, 5
Hollifield, James, 9

IFE. See Insituto Federal Electoral
Instituto Federal Electoral, 14

Jaggers, Keith, 10, 12

Lipset, Seymour, 8, 9
Logistic
  curve, 4
  model, 4

Massey, Douglas, 15
Mexico, 1, 2, 9, 10, 14, 22, 27, 31, 34, 48, 50, 60, 67, 75, 80, 81, 93, 100, 101, 127, 142, 144
  Gulf of, 80, 81
Mexican States
  Aguascalientes, 53, 63, 83, 92, 103, 129, 143
  Baja California Norte, 18, 53, 57, 61, 80, 86, 91, 98, 108, 113
  Baja California Sur, 23, 57, 61, 75, 83, 86, 91, 95, 96, 98, 102, 112, 113, 118, 132, 142, 144
  Campeche, 83, 143, 144
  Chiapas, 18, 23, 31, 34, 68, 71, 75, 76, 80, 82, 102, 113, 118, 122, 125, 142
  Chihuahua, 15, 31, 53, 57, 61, 67, 80, 91, 96, 102, 112, 113, 118, 121, 142
  Coahuila, 15, 25, 56, 60, 67, 69, 80, 83, 86, 91, 98, 108
  Colima, 58, 86, 132
  Durango, 31, 106, 113, 143
  Federal District, 21, 24, 27, 37, 57, 62, 68, 75, 80, 86, 91, 101, 102, 103, 125, 126, 127, 132, 142, 143, 144
  Guanajuato, 31, 53, 56, 57, 60, 61, 63, 67, 68, 69, 71, 75, 81, 83, 84, 102, 118, 125, 129, 135, 142, 143
  Guerrero, 23, 34, 53, 56, 57, 63, 80, 83, 86, 88, 91, 98, 102, 103, 118, 121, 125, 142, 143
  Hidalgo, 68, 80, 83, 86, 102, 129, 135, 142
  Jalisco, 15, 53, 56, 57, 60, 63, 67, 69, 71, 82, 84, 108, 125, 126, 128, 129, 132, 143
  Michoacan, 18, 22, 31, 56, 58, 60, 69, 80, 83, 84, 86, 91, 96, 102, 103, 118, 125, 135, 142, 144
  Morelos, 22, 75, 80, 102, 111, 112, 113
  Nayarit, 21, 25, 31, 68, 75, 80, 83, 86, 95, 106, 112, 113, 129, 143, 144
  Nuevo Leon, 31, 67, 96, 98, 125
  Oaxaca, 23, 31, 59, 67, 68, 86, 102, 125, 142, 143
  Puebla, 59, 67, 68, 80, 91, 113, 129, 132
  Queretaro, 58, 63, 71, 75, 83, 108, 129, 132, 143
  Quintana Roo, 57, 61, 75, 80, 86, 108, 112, 132, 143
  San Luis Potosi, 31, 98, 106, 108, 118, 121
  Sinaloa, 21, 31, 68, 75, 80, 83, 86, 91, 93, 102, 113, 121, 128, 142, 143, 144
  Sonora, 53, 86, 91, 95, 97, 103, 118, 121, 143
  Tabasco, 23, 31, 34, 53, 57, 59, 61, 63, 67, 68, 71, 76, 80, 81, 86, 102, 113, 118, 122, 125, 142, 143
  Tamaulipas, 31, 57, 75, 80, 118, 129, 132, 135
  Veracruz, 59, 67, 71, 80, 81, 112, 118, 125, 126, 129, 132
  Yucatan, 27, 75, 80, 86, 91, 96, 102, 113, 118, 121, 125, 142, 143, 144
  Zacatecas, 56, 67, 68, 69, 98, 129

Ord, J. K., 30, 31, 50
O' Loughlin, John, 4, 10, 12, 31, 144

Partido Accion Nacional, PAN, 14, 15, 16, 17, 18, 21, 24, 25, 26, 31, 32, 33, 34, 41, 42, 47, 51, 52, 53, 54, 55, 56, 57, 58, 59, 60, 61, 62, 63,

64, 65, 66, 67, 69, 70, 73, 74, 85, 101, 102, 103, 104, 105, 106, 107, 108, 109, 110, 118, 125, 126, 127, 128, 129, 130, 131, 132, 133, 134, 136, 142, 143, 144

Political
  change, 14, 15
  development theories, 6
  dynamics, 2
Polity III, 10, 12
Partido de la Revolucion Democratica, PRD, 24, 27, 37, 86, 102, 125, 132, 136, 142, 143, 144
Partido Revolucionario Institucional, PRI, 14, 15, 18, 19, 20, 21, 31, 35, 36, 47, 51, 53, 68, 71, 72, 73, 74, 75, 76, 77, 78, 79, 80, 81, 82, 83, 84, 85, 101, 102, 103, 111, 112, 113, 114, 115, 116, 117, 118, 125, 126, 128, 129, 132, 136, 142, 143, 144
Pye, Lucian, 6, 7, 8

Schatz, Sara, 8, 9
Schumpeter, Joseph, 7

Shin, Doh, 8, 9
Sierra Madre, 60, 73, 79, 84, 86, 101, 104, 143
Singer, J. D., 12
Single-party systems, 9
Small, M., 12
Spatial
  autocorrelation, 30, 31, 46, 47, 52, 53, 56, 57, 60, 66, 67, 69, 75, 80, 83, 86, 88, 91, 98, 105, 107, 108, 113, 115, 118, 121, 125, 129, 130, 132, 133, 136, 143
  clustering, 13
  controls, 50, 53, 56, 58, 60, 65, 66, 67, 68, 70, 71, 75, 80, 81, 83, 86, 89, 91, 92, 98, 103, 104, 106, 108, 113, 116, 118, 122, 124, 125, 129, 130, 132, 133, 136, 143
  diffusion, 1, 2, 3, 11, 13, 14, 30, 31, 47, 48, 49, 50, 51, 52, 53, 54, 55, 56, 57, 58, 60, 65, 66, 67, 68, 69, 75, 80, 81, 83, 86, 89, 91, 98, 101, 102, 105, 107, 108, 113, 114, 115, 118, 121, 125, 129, 130, 132, 133, 136, 142, 144
  processes, 79
  variables, 51

Ward, Michael, 10, 12, 31, 144